POSTHUMANISM IN ART AND SCIENCE

Posthumanism in Art and Science

A READER

Edited by Giovanni Aloi
and Susan McHugh

Columbia University Press
New York

Columbia University Press
Publishers Since 1893
New York   Chichester, West Sussex
cup.columbia.edu

Library of Congress Cataloging-in-Publication Data
Names: Aloi, Giovanni, editor. | McHugh, Susan, editor.
Title: Posthumanism in art and science : a reader / edited by
Giovanni Aloi and Susan McHugh.
Description: New York : Columbia University Press, [2021] | Includes index.
Identifiers: LCCN 2021003176 (print) | LCCN 2021003177 (ebook) |
ISBN 9780231196666 (hardback) | ISBN 9780231196673 (trade paperback) |
ISBN 9780231551762 (ebook)
Subjects: LCSH: Humanism. | Art and society. | Technology—Social aspects.
Classification: LCC B821 .P5925 2021 (print) | LCC B821 (ebook) | DDC 144—dc23
LC record available at https://lccn.loc.gov/2021003176
LC ebook record available at https://lccn.loc.gov/2021003177

Columbia University Press books are printed on permanent
and durable acid-free paper.
Printed in the United States of America

Cover image: Ken Rinaldo, 'Red Back Blond' from the
Seed Series—Virtual to Real Blooming: Dreams of Spring.
2014 copyright Ken Ronaldo.

CONTENTS

PART III: REGISTERING
INTERCONNECTEDNESS

PART IV: EMERGING ECOLOGIES

POSTHUMANISM IN ART AND SCIENCE

Envisioning Posthumanism

GIOVANNI ALOI AND SUSAN McHUGH

Posthumanism wrestles with emerging recognitions of the porousness of boundaries that mark the human condition. The posthuman is a creature of art, SF, literature, and philosophy as much as it is a form of response to the pressures and potentialities of technology, globalization, and extinction at the turn of the millennium. Although precise definitions remain subject to debate, there is general consensus that the term "posthuman" encompasses contemporary creative visioning of systems and networks toward a critical reevaluation of what it can mean to be human in an increasingly more-than-human world.

In his 1992 essay for the *Post Human* exhibition catalog, Jeffrey Deitch rightly predicted that artists' work would expand from defining art to include redefining life itself.[1] In its earliest articulations, posthumanist theory finally debunked the myths of classical humanism, applying systems and communications theory to critique the notion that the human ever could function as an autonomous individual, let alone the ideal of the artist whose genius transcends worldly trappings. Michel Foucault's groundbreaking argument in *The Order of Things* (1966), namely, that assertions of the universal status of "man" emerged historically as "the effect of a fundamental change in the arrangement of knowledge," has repositioned "man" as "an invention of recent date. And one perhaps nearing its end."[2]

For many, however, Foucault himself serves as a figurehead of the academic-institutional ascendency of theory, which, as literary scholar Barbara Christian observes, "surfaced, interestingly enough, just when the literature of people of color, of black women, of Latin Americans, of Africans, began to move to 'the "center'."[3] Among the many repercussions of Eurowestern colonialism, the political utility of weaponizing "man" as a standard of exclusion has made it so that decentering the human remains a politically fraught endeavor. Sylvia Wynter identifies that which "secur[es] our present ethnoclass (i.e., Western bourgeois) conception of the human" (or what Wynter distinguishes as "Man") as all too often that which "over-represents itself as if it were the human itself."[4] Although arguably they verge into anti- or counter-humanist discussions, these discursive moves highlight the axiological concerns motivating convergences of posthumanist theory and praxis.

Valuations of art as well as artists have become increasingly more important in redrawing the boundaries of the human. Responding directly to his most vehement critics, Foucault spelled out the implications of his theory of knowledge for writing as an artistic medium, asking whether "authorship" might best be understood not as a concept or status that precedes the work, but rather both together as functions of discursive and social practices anchored in it.[5] Such an approach allows us to see how authors and by extension all kinds of artists are subjects of and to the power structures in which all of our knowledges are entangled. The object deemed prestigious enough to be "art" gains interest in how it inevitably represents processes of exclusion and inclusion, becoming visible as such in a posthumanist frame.

Decades into the discussion, artists and authors today draw from an array of cross-disciplinary formations including bioinformatics, multispecies ethnography, and poststructuralist theory to craft new foundations for social thinking and action. Refusing the hierarchical dualisms through which people once separated and elevated themselves from "the other" in its many permutations, the posthuman unravels through heterogeneous assemblages that not only shift intellectual and political baselines but also transform the very terms of creative and ethical practice. This volume gathers together innovative and powerful contributions to the discussion in order to make the case that aesthetic production is a vital part of posthumanist thinking processes, which thereby grow ever more urgently relevant to social and ecological problem-solving.

Following the thirteenth edition of the quinquennial contemporary art exhibition dOCUMENTA in 2012, posthumanist approaches to environmental concerns set new compass points for artists engaged in the problems of how to work within more-than-human worlds. Carolyn Christov-Bakargiev's curatorial approach, in part, reflected this new philosophical turn. From including humanities and social sciences scholars like Donna Haraway in the exhibition's honorary advisory committee to featuring texts by Karen Barad and Jane Bennett in the catalog—dOCUMENTA (13) challenged the artworld by connecting innovative thinking across bio-aesthetics, dystopian juxtaposition, interspecies relations, and eco-futurism. This exhibition's rich program of talks and events has effectively propelled posthumanist questions to the forefront of contemporary artistic debates well beyond academia.

The permeability of theory and practice was heralded by Cary Wolfe's 2009 book *What is Posthumanism?* where the author traced a genealogy of posthumanist theory in part back to the Macy Conferences on cybernetics held in New York between 1946 and 1953. The new theoretical models for biological, mechanical, and communicational processes that emerged at the meetings deliberately decentralized humans' sovereign position in relation to meaning, information, and cognition.[6] A new, more enhanced, or transhumanist ideal of the human struck some as the inevitable outcome, but as N. Katherine Hayles was quick to note, the reversion to old utopian ideals is symptomatic of the difficulty of inhabiting a posthumanist perspective (as indeed can be said for critics of her theories of the digital or code manifestations of the posthuman condition as premised on separation from embodiment).[7] Bruce Clarke's recent questioning of such a "dialectical antithesis" points to the deep-seated provocations bodied forth by aesthetic moves to relinquish any "radical distinction between matter and information, substance and form."[8]

Literary and cultural theorists like Wolfe, Hayles, and Clarke are clearly empowered by Haraway, who self-identifies as a feminist historian of science but whose influence (like Foucault's) defies disciplinary boundaries. Her oft-cited 1985 essay 'A Cyborg Manifesto' reads today like a rallying cry for posthumanist theory. There she fashions the cyborg as an emblematic human-animal-machine hybrid figure that intermingles natural and artificial, physical and immaterial components, and otherwise outright targets Eurowestern ontology at its very roots in hierarchical dualisms.

An elusive foundational unit, her cyborg vision is indispensable to her argument: a phoenix rising from the ashes of humanist philosophical constructs, driven by a fervent desire to upturn, subvert, and reimagine. Crystallized in artist Lee Bul's *Cyborg* series (1997-2011), whose figures likewise question power relations, refuse narrative closure, and emerge from un/ natural (or in Haraway's terms naturecultural) histories, the creative gesture of speculative fabulation propels the cyborg into uncharted territory. Although some lament that Haraway's initial formulation falls short of capturing the vast potentials for blurring boundaries realized by everyday interactions with digital media—where most obviously, "what we make and what (we think) we co-evolve together," according to Hayles[9]—identity politics, species membership, otherness, and conceptions of nature have been relentlessly deconstructed and reconfigured through recourse to Haraway's cyborg as a model for posthumanist discourse.

While the posthuman revolution in the humanities and social sciences has gained momentum only during the last twenty years, the arts have spent the best part of the last century grappling with exactly the same epistemological and ontological preoccupations, notably through discourses of race and culture. An important turning point in the history of western representation came with the waves of Japonism that revolutionized Impressionist painting. The clashing of bright secondary colors and the rejection of drawing and perspective as the foundational principles of painting forever changed the very nature of the medium. Thereafter, the impetus of African art shattered the picture plane of cubist representations, opening the eyes of western artists to a range of untapped expressive potentials. The demise of optical perspective, the ultimate anthropocentric representational construct invented by the Italian Renaissance, enabled a rebirth of painting and a reinvention of art itself. No longer could artists act in faith that one truth, one way of seeing, existed. No longer could truth be perceived from one point of view alone. These moments in the history of early modernist art are critically fraught with accusations of cultural appropriation that remind us of the complexities involved in the reconfiguration of the human within the postcolonial context.[10]

In painting, notions of time shifted along with ideas of beauty. Albert Einstein's theory of relativity changed our conception of space and time, while cubism introduced an early form of flat ontology—all objects in the composition appeared equally unimportant and oblivious to the value systems that had made baroque still-life paintings speak of wealth, power, and worship. This is one of the most often unsung accomplishments of cubism. Picasso and Braque's ability to produce a vision of a world seen not just from an endless array of disinterested viewpoints anticipated Graham Harman's theorization of Object-Oriented Ontology by roughly a hundred years.

Thereafter, the revolutionary photomontages of Dada pioneer Hannah Höch directly tackled humanist divisions and categories on all fronts. Across the fragmentation of her photographic tableaux, Höch bravely explored gender fluidity, non-western ideas of beauty, and human-animal interconnectedness with an irreverent sense of playfulness and joy. Höch's subversive approach reverberates in today's Afrofuturist collages of Wangechi Mutu and the feminist sculptures and installation work of Lee Bul. It is not coincidental, therefore, that Haraway's cyborg theory should also foreground not only feminism but also antiracist, anticolonialist, anticapitalist, queer critique. Amid the arguments of Haraway and others that the human as a concept is created through exclusionary relationships, whether between play and abstraction,[11] or poetics and philosophy,[12] the history of art appears all the more purposefully to entertain productive alternatives that appear increasingly relevant today.

Marcel Duchamp's readymades further destabilized the inherent anthropocentrism that for millennia underpinned the very definition of the work of art, paving the way for live plants and animals to enter the exhibiting space. Edward Steichen's exhibition of live genetically-modified delphiniums, held at MoMA in 1936, invited viewers to consider anew established notions of authorship, materiality, permanency, and creativity, along with heralding the emergence of what artist Eduardo Kac by the end of the century would call Bio Art. At the same time, psychoanalysis brought artists to more carefully consider the importance of affect, agency, abjection, and the uncanny in art. Considering how current these concerns have become, it seems that the Surrealist movement may have been prematurely reduced to clichés by art historians far too concerned with oneiric symbolism. Until recently, this emphasis diminished the anti-anthropocentric slant in the brave and provocative explorations of nonbinary gender alternatives by transgender, Jewish artist Claude Cahun, or the abjection-ridden objects like Meret Oppenheim's cup and saucer covered in fur (1936), and even Man Ray's uncanny iron studded with nails (1921). But the point is not to determine who or what is posthuman—or to elide or untangle anti-humanisms and anti-anthropocentrisms in their many permutations—so much as to appreciate the power of art's growing challenges to any separation of Being from beings.

"What is art?" This question that seems to underline so much artistic production of the first half of the twentieth century. Amid a century of genocide and global conflict, characterized by an unprecedented existentialist sense of loss, asking what art is fed directly into the important questioning of what is the human. Alberto Giacometti's stylized figures of elongated men and women striding forward but going nowhere (1960) and Robert Rauschenberg's *Monogram* (1955-59) repurposing a taxidermy goat together with a trashed car tire are the perfect incarnations of the reckonings with traumas that characterized the second half of the last century. Amid the devastating loss of post-WWII hubristic certitude, humanity encounters in such figures a survivor-animal, a semi-domesticated, mostly mythological character and yet a very real reminder of how conflicted relationships are crystallized in the very concept of "non-human," and of representation as erroneously conceived to be a transparent world-making medium. The rise of performance art and the impact of movements like the Situationist International, Land Art, and Feminist Art marked the beginning of a new ethical awareness of what it means to be human among other non-human actants and to co-habit and negotiate ever more problematic conceptions of geopolitical space. Meanwhile, by the end of the 1960s, the experimental irreverence of the Gutai Group in Japan, Arte Povera in Italy, and the innovative approaches of artists like Yayoi Kusama, Joseph Beuys, Judy Chicago, Sun Ra, and Carolee Schneemann had drastically redefined the boundaries of what being an artist could entail.

Posthumanist thinking enters these conditions as an evolving instrument for artists whose practice aims to explore the possibility to rethink human/nonhuman relations in the context of modern imperial histories of settler colonialism and in the face of their irreparable environmental devastation. Among others, Ursula Biemann and Paulo Tavares's collaboration with philosopher Rosi Braidotti, titled *Forest Law* is a startling example of new multidisciplinary practices that focus on the social, cosmopolitical, and legal implications of climate change through the voices of Indigenous political leaders narrating the aftermath of colonial exploitation that they continue to live with. The repurposing of reindeer skulls in Máret Ánne Sara's installations like *Pile o'Sápmi* (2017) assert pan-Indigeous solidarity,

connecting Cree people's traditional "pile of bones" honoring bison materially and spiritually with her own Sámi heritage, and the ongoing struggles
of oppressed reindeer herders like her brother for cultural and ecological
justice. The reimagining of Indigenous cosmologies, whether through the
Machinima of Mowhawk artist Skawennati or the queer sf novels of Cherokee academic and writer Daniel Heath Justice, outline how imagining posthuman pasts and futures are at stake in Indigenous cultures.

Allora and Calzadilla's video installation, *The Great Silence* (2014), jux-
taposes images of the world's largest radio telescope, located in Esperanza,
Puerto Rico, with imagery of a critically endangered species of parrots,
Amazona vittata, that lives in the area. The artists collaborated with science
fiction author Ted Chiang, who wrote an original monolog for a parrot
pondering over the irreducible gaps between living and nonliving, human,
animal, technological, and cosmic actors. In its disarmingly straightforward
narrative, *The Great Silence* finds the power to challenge the very structures
that have supported scientific thinking over the past five hundred years. All
the pomp and hubris that have characterized our quest for knowledge are
made to crumble in a sixteen-minute video through which a parrot puts us
to shame as it simply reveals the paradoxes and contradictions that make
us human. Our language, which has been improperly used to separate and
elevate us from other animals is turned against us.

The emergence of the Anthropocene as a geological era accounting
for the indelible impact of human activities across the planet has prob-
lematized posthumanist discourses, even as it instills a renewed sense of
urgency in scholarly and artistic practices alike. In the shadow of a sixth
mass-extinction event and various associated diasporas, new aesthetic territories defined by the recent ontological turn have begun to take form.
From Ai Weiwei's focus on migrants that reminds us of the hard-to-con-
ceive struggles faced by ever-growing impoverished populations today, to
Rashid Johnson's plant-filled installations that invite us to be present in our
fast-changing environments and communities, new modes of critical and
political artistic engagement reveal simultaneously terrifying and beautiful
ecological fluidities. What emerges are *naturecultures*—a term that signifies refusal to separate (human) meaning and creativity from (nonhuman)
matter and decay. Recognizing that we inhabit naturecultures commits
us to the development of sufficiently complex ethical frameworks; seeing
how humans live only ever with others applies productive pressure to our

thinking through the heterogeneity of all of "us." It is within this framework that art, philosophy, and science become intersecting platforms upon which to trace the possibility for multiculturally diverse and biologically sustainable futures.

In the pages that follow, we outline the broader intellectual context of these developments. The book is divided into four sections to articulate what often appear to be disparate domains as instead an overlapping set of concerns: articulating post-identity politics; outlining life-shaping and other forces of materiality; registering connectedness as a baseline condition; and opening up the concept of (human) ontology to figure humans within emerging ecologies. In each section, contributions make the case on various fronts that the artistic arena has emerged as the most conducive epistemological space for conceptualizing as well as actualizing posthumanist projections that enmesh people in rhizomatic networks with animals, plants, machines, and microbes along with less easily identifiable social agents.

POST IDENTITY POLITICS

Far from signaling that identity politics are over, post-identity is a provocation to reconsider identity apart from humanist valuations.[13] To stay true to fast-shifting posthumanist developments, we start by noting the main points of contention regarding enhancement or transcendence of embodiment, along with key points of synthesis around the entanglements of non/human bodies and technologies. More than just adding to the taxonomies of identity, the posthuman identifies a growing sense of uneasiness with conventional categories that inform and connect the rise of otherwise diverse intellectual formations like critical race, decolonial, queer, disability, feminist, ecocritical, and animal studies. Our focus is on how these connections inform the choices and responsibilities of artists working today, and how they can guide public reception into more productive dialogues. Ultimately, we argue for maintaining the posthuman as an inclusive yet provocative conceptual and political framework for emergent ecologies and ontologies.

The first section of the book focusses on the artistic and philosophical currents that have relentlessly displaced human subjectivity from its historical position of sovereignty. At the core of the ontological turn proposed by posthumanist approaches to art lies a fervent desire to re-envision the modalities of epistemology. From tools and materials to perspectives and agencies, artists and scholars engaging with posthumanist ideas strive to devise new and compelling practices in order to conceive and discover what anthropocentric perspectives among other humanist legacies have obscured. It remains an ongoing struggle. After all, Manuela Rossini observes, academic posthumanism can prove "all too human(ist)" needing artistic inspirations along with provocations to change.

Partly, this situation stems from the fact that posthumanist theory is largely a product of scholars in Anglo-American studies, where institutional silos have encouraged, for instance, linguistic forms to remain underexamined as primary points of orientation in the otherwise thoroughgoing investigations of posthumanist theory at the leading edge of literary studies. From critical perspectives, they risk merely inverting elements of the human, missing the opportunity to consider the cross-disciplinary ramifications of the postwar turn from medical-clinical to computational-information science—as Jonathan Burt argues, a "deeply embedded science history that is far less easy to redirect, or dislocate, and in contact with which one cannot help but to inherit a lot of problematic cultural baggage."[14] More creative efforts to overcome logocentrism are glimpsed in deaf gay writer Raymond Luczak's publication of poetry in back-to-back American Sign Language gloss and English, and still more clearly Luczak's "spoken word"-style poetry performances in ASL. Posthuman subjects must approach life itself as creative practice, that is—to paraphrase disabled dancer, artist, and poet Neil Marcus—they must craft "an ingenious way to live."[15]

Visual forms of representation can intervene in these troubled contexts, identifying the quintessential epistemic space through which to reassemble the ruins of our humanist inheritance with an eye to the future. Artists working in the posthuman sphere have deliberately questioned more than they have answered. They have knowingly prodded and provoked more than they have dissected or resolved. And they can't help but become ethically entangled in politics. In so doing, they prise open the question of what is an artist as a particular way to "stay with the trouble," as Haraway says, of living and dying together on a troubled planet. Giving up our anthropocentric privileges—acknowledging that some humans have allowed themselves to be more equal than others—might constitute the first and most important step in rethinking the relational webs that surround us.

Avant-garde choreographer and filmographer Yvonne Rainer's "No Manifesto," included in chapter 14, is the most synthetic materialization of these ideas that emerged during the 1960s and '70s in the heyday of the poststructuralist theories of Jacques Derrida, Hélène Cixous, Michel Foucault, and Gilles Deleuze and Félix Guattari, but that only found their truest artistic incarnations in the artistic expressions of the new millennium. In response to the impact of these new philosophical waves sweeping the arts and humanities, in 2008 Rainer felt compelled to return to her manifesto to problematize its (no longer attainable) clean-cut radicality that heralded the essence of many postmodernist rules. Her calling attention to these revisions to the original manifesto appears symptomatic of changing tides, and of the new sensibilities that characterize the ontological turn elaborated below. And it also resonates deeply with performance artist Cassils who works through the paradoxes of trans identities, including their increasing visibility and vulnerability within the same period. Our interview with them—addressing among other things their third-person-singular *they*—clarifies further how artists can productively position themselves ahead of language, perhaps most obviously when insisting that we see their bodies as at once instruments and images.

The overshadowing of posthumanist art with literary representations also positions embodiment or "wetware" as a tangible, embodied, messy alternative to the abstract, detached, clean architectures of software. Clarke persuades that, although posthumanist perspectives commonly "relativize the human by coupling it to some other order of being," Hayles's scholarship led to a narrowing focus on "the coupling of human biology to digital machinery" in literary studies.[16] While some performance artists like Stelarc literalize such couplings in pursuit of transhumanist improvements, others like Kathy High, Kira O'Reilly, Špela Petrič, and Ken Rinaldo find more nuanced implications of posthumanism by working through the "animal turn" or cross-disciplinary development of animal studies.

At the end of the last millennium, Derrida's "The Animal that Therefore I Am" and John Berger's "Why Look at Animals?" flagged the philosophical and aesthetic cornerstones of innovative approaches to animals and animality.[17]

Largely now viewed as a subfield with a quite different agenda to something like vegan studies, posthumanist animal studies promoted an interest in representation as an agentially charged tool capable of unhinging philosophical certitude for the purpose of mapping new and exciting political territories. From this perspective, the kitsch elements characterizing the early video experiments of William Wegman with his dog become far less important than the questions raised by their apparent extension of aesthetic agency across species lines: is the artist absolved of responsibility, or establishing a new baseline for whose views matter to aesthetics, if not politics?

Long troubled by feminist critics, the power of the gaze proved central to both Derrida and Berger, and became important to the discourses of artists like Catts and Zurr, whose Bio Art experiments questioned and reconfigured the epistemic hegemony of rationalist scientific optics. Today their SymbioticA laboratory serves as a global hub for an ever-expanding cohort of diverse artists defying disciplinary boundaries. The gaze and the ability to return it, or lack thereof, has served as an essential delineator of human-animal relationships and other manifestations of power's asymmetries. It simultaneously exposed the ethical compromises marring the authenticity claims of natural history displays, as exemplified by the work of Hiroshi Sugimoto, Mark Dion, Snabjörnsdóttir/Wilson, and others, revealing limits to our ability to see past the ontological structures that we have inherited from classical art as well as from continental philosophy. As the more frequent encounters with the animal gaze brought human centrality further into question, a relentless and yet productive sense of instability also began to pervade creative thinking. At the forefront of interdisciplinary discourses of animal studies, race studies, and literary studies, Zakiyyah Iman Jackson shows how "racialized formations of gender and sexuality are actually central rather than subsidiary to the very human–animal binarism recent scholarship hopes to dislodge".[18]

In the midst of spiraling ecological degradation, Haraway's influential concept of the cyborg has gained more and more traction; identity constructs have begun to splinter and reconfigure as inextricable from machines and animals. No longer finite, no longer sovereign, the posthuman is a subject among subjects connected to everything in interrelated constellations of agential capacities and fragility. In this context, the virtual reality work of Skawennati recontextualized Indigenous heritage within a network of futuristic avatars as a form of political resistance.

It is from this uncertain but fertile ground that the latest assault to the remaining vestiges of anthropocentric thinking has been launched by the growing presence of plants in the gallery space. As Michael Marder illuminates, the ultimate alterity of the vegetal world reaches out from where animal studies for far too long comfortably lingered in the company of pets and farm animals, in turn posing urgent questions about the convergences of perceptual and ethical limits.

MATERIAL DIMENSIONS

The second section addresses the complementary conceptual changes regarding art objects that have followed from posthumanism's dismantling of anthropocentric frameworks. A startling array of materials make unprecedented migrations from tissue engineering laboratories, natural history museums, and agricultural experiments into art galleries (not to mention the rare ones who traverse inverse routes). Questions about who is responsible, and how, and for what, emerge from these new and evolving situations. Attending to the materiality of art is an important strategy for artists who resist the restrictions of identity politics, as Nandipha Mntambo explains in our interview with her, which helps to show further why the material remains of animal life are among the oldest but not the most readily acknowledged art-making materials.[19] Whether subtly incorporated, like the gelatin and other slaughterhouse products that Nicole Shukin shows to have been necessary to early film processing, or overtly manipulated in the form of Mntambo's modeled animal skins, the material remnants of animal life bring to the foreground art's long history of tracing the convergences of non/human lives and deaths.

Contemporary artists offer very different accounts of how sourcing, framing, and other decisions regarding bodily presences factor into perceptions of the value of an artwork. Especially fragments of mammalian bodies inspire broader debates of "how matter comes to matter," to borrow Karen Barad's resonant phrasing—that in turn speak to the social immediacy of posthumanist art's material dimensions. Barad's theory of agential realism anticipates artists' reconceptualizations of their materials. She connects different pasts, presents, and futures through quantum physics, where art's material dimensions presuppose that the formation of any given thing proceeds only ever through others because any discrete bit always (to paraphrase poet Walt Whitman) contains multitudes.

Likewise inspired by early actor-network theory, Harman's object-oriented ontology has successfully appropriated Heidegger's tool analysis to rethink our manipulations of the inanimate world as instead a situation in which humans emerge as objects amongst other objects, such that artists and artworks are not just inextricably enmeshed but ontologically leveled or flattened. Reframing Lynn Margulis's evolutionary-biological theory of symbiosis as a metaphor for humans' ongoing transformations of and through our relations with particular entities, Harman posits the conjunction of person and object as a basic aesthetic unit with distinct historical and ethical implications. That such relations are neither predictable nor fully controlled comes to the fore in the changing artistic and other representations of waste through which Myra Hird identifies a dynamic anti/Anthropocene aesthetic (and which suggest intriguing dimensions to Delvoye's 2002 bio-robotic feces-producing installation *Cloaca*). Rising to the challenge of traditional views of artists as mere manipulators of stuff, their contributions to the philosophies of object-oriented ontology along with speculative realism and new materialisms inspires an array of approaches to resourcing, archiving, even perceiving the vital aspects of artworks.

Artists engaging with the posthumanist implications of materiality also bring into focus how art always involves struggles with conceptual along with material constraints, locating artists' relations with their own bodily limitations along the front lines of these struggles. For instance, Orlan pushes those boundaries by using plastic surgery to approximate what she terms a "female-to-female transsexual" experience. But her work also underscores the complex dance of corporeal and psychic as well as mythic dimensions involved in all attempts at living in a gendered body, according to Jay Prosser, who cautions that narratives of transsexual life demonstrate how navigations of uneven power structures in the material world require still more complex thinking. Taking a different tack, Angela Last elaborates how playing with stereotypes about primitivism productively unsettles geographical and geological definitions of identity, most clearly by positing Afrofuturism in dialogue with Anthropocene concerns through the art of Ellen Gallagher.

Along with the spaces of the physical, materiality is governed by relations with time. Indeed, Timothy Morton's formulation as "hyperobjects" such different phenomena as plastics, plutonium, and global warming suggests that that which is so expansive in terms of space and time can exceed our very concept of the object. After all, posthumanist perspectives fundamentally reconceptualize our mental abilities to grasp art objects as timebound things. Morton's analysis of techno group Orbital's music video for

"The Box" identifies its attempt to visualize the process of seeing vastly different timescales—a capacity becoming increasingly apparently necessary in order to do justice to ecological awareness—and posits that the materiality of media's representation provides a route toward a radically non-anthropocentrically rethinking of how matter comes to matter.

Another pathway unfolds through Tim Ingold's identification of "inter-agentivity" in anthropological accounts of Indigenous metaphysics, a concept that assumes that non/human relations are never projected from us but rather continuously subsist between entities.

Materiality comes vividly to life when ways of being human are firmly rooted in assemblages of very precise relations to other animals, stones, bodies of water, and other features that otherwise die down when relegated to background or landscape features. Despite the difficulties, attending to these different dimensions and details of materiality reveals still more important and immediate distinctions, as James Elkins shows, between the speed with which academics analyze art and the "slowness of the studio" that artists require in their production processes.

REGISTERING INTERCONNECTEDNESS

The third section builds on the previous two by following the development of networked formations that exceed conventional concepts of organismal life. In this frame, Orlan's bringing together audiences across continents to witness her live-performance surgery *Omnipresence* are conceivably aligned in significant ways with Haraway's conception of the cyborg. Yet, as Lucien Gomoll clarifies, Haraway's insistence on feminism's strategic affinities provides a platform for challenging Eurowestern-colonial progress narratives implicit in Orlan's later work. More importantly, radically different "posthuman performances" of sexual, racial, national, and other boundaries are lofted by the artist Narcissister and the art collective La Pocha Nostra; in the case of Basia Irland's water-focused art practice, even the biological lines between species kingdoms and phyla are reconfigured as opportunities for strategic alignments. As scientific consensus grows around Margulis's theory of symbiogenesis, in which sub-cellular negotiations prove the key mechanisms of evolution, it becomes necessary to develop ways of articulating the human as inconceivable apart from other life forms.

That art fills a pressing need to imagine not simply newly perceivable life forms but more importantly seeing them as relevant to art practices becomes even more apparent through the Bio Art of Kathy High, which in various projects enlists transgenic rats, intestinal microbes, Tamagotchi, white blood cells, and always the artist herself to expand such investigations from technology and science to feminist sf and art.

Creating new ways of visualizing and articulating modes of entanglement also means opening spaces for working out the social implications of interconnected conditions of life, and in many ways collaborations among artists themselves serve as useful starting points. Cutting across oppositional nature/culture boundaries instead by positioning "life-web" as a starting point, the over-50-year partnership of Newton and Helen Mayer Harrison serves as a model for applying environmental science to stage productive, long-term interventions in local ecologies. The Harrisons reframe the human from the determining factor of the Anthropocene to instead a "force majeure"—by which they designate humans as important but by no means sole aesthetic and environmental forces contributing to the shape of things to come.

While these positionings enable artists to articulate a sense of responsiveness and responsibility to those who are being disproportionately affected by climate change and other perilous manifestations of the Anthropocene, they might also be seen as underestimating Bruno Latour's argument that "there is no acceptably recognizable 'we' to be burdened by the weight of such a responsibility." Latour finds an exception in James Lovelock's tricky concept of Gaia as the literal, local limiting factor of life as we know it, which adds a distinctly political node to triangulate the science-art nexus. Working as a collaborative art duo, Elizabeth Stephens and Annie Sprinkle expand this perspective through their "Ecosex Manifesto" as the basis of ongoing popup performances that sometimes stage as literal weddings the intimate connections of sex-positive education and ecological justice. On different grounds Kim TallBear and Angela Willey document, provoke, or imagine relations between humans, and between humans and nonhumans that go beyond and trouble normative categories of "nature," "sex," and "love." What this all indicates is that feminist materialism, post-materialist theory, postcolonial ecocriticism, queer ecology, and other intersectionalist approaches to mapping connectivity beyond human forms invite redefinitions of what constitutes art and—or as—activism.

EMERGING ECOLOGIES

Anthropology's "ontological turn" recasts our most basic assumptions about self, society, and ecology in a posthumanist frame: what if the difficulties of reconciling perspectives on the world stems from generating different, even incompatible realities? What if, as Philippe Descola suggests, we were to "take stock of the fact that worlds are differently composed," that is, to "endeavour to understand how they are composed without automatic recourse to our own mode of composition?"[20] Radically "anti-epistemological," according to Eduardo Viveiros de Castro, such an approach unleashes a "philosophical war machine" in social sciences that concedes no human community has special or privileged insight on how the living world is structured.[21]

Where this resonates most clearly in posthumanist art is in the further complicating of biological and social with representational notions of ecology through media forms. By expanding ideas about ecologies as at once material and political, as heterogeneous assemblages and evolving entities, posthuman thinking fundamentally challenges human capacities for perception. So the fourth section sketches some of the ways in which artists and authors de-nature ecologies and to what effect. Artists' engagements with mushrooms, plants, insects, and other stereotypically alien life forms provide several starting points for understanding posthumanist celebrations of bodies that are not like-us. But their legal and philosophical challenges also temper the promises of manipulating life beyond conventional forms, whether through transgenics or digital media.

Curator Betelhem Makonnen's interview with Black studies scholar Katherine McKittrick raises important questions about Canadian Black history and its erasures as an influence on what McKittrick terms "fugitive geographical thinking": "the complicated paradoxes that are revealed when black folks inhabit a nation that denies their histories, geographies, and experiences." McKittrick's multidisciplinary approach sets the tone for this chapter. Working with a scientist to assess and rearticulate human impact on the environment, artist Kelly Jazvac explains her interest in plastiglomerates, or plastic melted into lava rock recently discovered on Hawai'ian beaches, as more than an object of analysis: it becomes a provocation for visualizing and discomforting human presence in emerging ecological phenomena. She aligns her critical approach to artistic practice with

Duane Linklater's Indigenous re-appropriations of technology and urban space (plus animals in works like *Rez Dog*), Theaster Gates's reclaimed urban materialities, even Chris Jordan's iconic photos of the plastic-choked corpses of highly endangered albatrosses found also on Hawai'ian islands. Yet the productive element of uncertainty in Jazvac's collaborative practice also concerns responsibilities for and repercussions of destabilized boundaries.

A similar challenge is navigated by *Dear Climate*, a collaborative multimedia project headed up by Marina Zurkow and Una Chaudhuri to personify climate as a letter recipient. Taking it at its word, Louis Bury's series of missives playfully identifies and rehearses the fatalistic humor especially apparent in the project's 70-plus poster series to confront totalizing ecological discourse. The strength of the project is its ambivalent reliance on resistance and capitulation to anthropogenic climate change—in artist Patty Chang's words, modeling "art making as a grieving of living as opposed to fighting against it." Some might point to it as evidence that posthumanism, as Ian Bogost claims, "is not posthuman enough."[22] Yet, for Mel Chen, Bogost's own "alien phenomenology," or new-materialist attribution of subjective experience to all things equally, proves a red herring by raising rather than answering questions about who historically owns theories of matter.[23]

Chen's use of Gil Scott-Heron's song "Whitey on the Moon" to critique a broader "drive to go cosmic" as "a feature of capitalism and empire" itself suggests how different aesthetics of matter and ecology become articulated through music of the African diaspora, often in powerful conjunction with visual media. Explaining the sonic significance of Afrofuturism, Kodwo Eshun distinguishes the persistence of humanism in the "soulful" music of the likes of R. Kelly—"a perpetual fight for human status, a yearning for human status, a struggle for inclusion within the human species"—that becomes suspect when contrasted with the "postsoul" sound of Alice Coltrane, Sun Ra, Tricky and Martina, and others "characterized by an extreme indifference to the human," even an insistence that "the human is a pointless and treacherous category."[24]

Garry Steingo argues further that African-American Afrofuturism tends to envision the alien as an allegory for the slave, enabling a "crypto-humanism" that is pointedly rejected by African musicians, writers, and artists whose Afrofuturism centers on speculative practice. Through the music video for Xhosa singer Simphiwe Dana's "Ndiredi," he traces a trajectory toward the genuinely unknown and unanticipated, enabling the orchestration of a future with an altered past. Developing more somatic implications, Alexander Weheliye investigates the physicality of mobile phones as not just represented in but also altering experiences of R&B music and the television show *Metrosexuality*; as "mobile rhythms" become perceptible, practical uses of everyday technologies transform into aesthetic sensation that prove particularly important for black people. Throughout his analysis, a Deleuzian sensibility of communicative aesthetics emerges, which is concerned less with identifying an element of representation than with registering the variable physical forms in which it exists. The transformative potential further underscores postcolonial theorist Édouard Glissant's analysis of what gets neglected when the focus remains on the "metronymic beat of the inert" as a property of seemingly unchanging objects.

A more disturbing manifestation of changing material relations within posthumanist ecologies is made possible through practices involving hybridization. Whether in Patricia Piccinini's haunting sculptures that morph human and animal bodily traits into fanciful yet still plausible cross-species shapes, or the more literal combinations of human, animal, and robotic elements of Doo-Sung Yoo's *Organ-Machine Hybrid* series, posthumanist visioning concerns transformations at foundational levels. Thus, as Wolfe argues in our final selection, it never simply concerns representational content but the very methods of practice as shaping ways of looking that are compelled to evolve through posthumanist thinking.

Bringing a renewed urgency to posthumanist inquiries in the arts, the Anthropocene is well defined by the acknowledgment that, every year, human consumption is exceeding more than half the resources produced on the planet. In the Anthropocene, overconsumption is underpinned by a deep and general sense of disconnection with nature, which is compensated, albeit only representationally, by the emergence of sublime-catastrophic visions of rising sea levels and melting glaciers. Anthropogenic vantage points are currently reconfiguring our understanding of life on this planet, problematizing ecocritical and capitalist critiques of recent years. How art will continue to contribute to shape these processes remains to be seen.

Our aim is to provide a representative range of cautionary responses to current posthumanist theories and art practices, philosophy, and literature from around the globe. We want you as readers to gain greater appreciation for the problematics that representation presents to the overcoming of anthropocentrist and humanist legacies, and the mitigation of their impacts on our relationship to nonhuman beings, ecologies, and the environment. By gathering together examples that address these problematics through posthumanist writing across philosophy, art history, literary criticism, architecture, media studies, and even natural and physical sciences, our over-arching goal is to create a new perspective through which to grow our understanding of a fundamental and irreversible change in art's methods and worldviews.

No one artist, artwork, or analysis of them could capture the momentousness of such a change. In the chapters that follow, you will find key extracts of landmark theoretical statements by academic thinkers alongside statements from artists demonstrating parallel or intersecting engagements with the topic in their work and its impacts. Their continuities are as instructive as their juxtapositions for envisioning posthumanism. Our organization of the book in four sections is only meant to provide a structure to navigate the wealth of perspectives and voices we have gathered here—by no means could it be possible to do justice to the subject's necessarily ever-growing complexity.

The introduction of this book has been written during one of the most difficult years the world has witnessed. The unprecedented impact of a once-in-a-century world pandemic has brought to light the sheer scale of social injustice as well as the inherent global vulnerability that hides beneath capitalist veneers. From the rise of social justice movements, the collapse of economic structures, and the dwindling power of cultural institutions, 2020 will certainly be remembered as a threshold: a moment in which posthuman thinking and practice will begin to focus on new and previously unthinkable challenges. The idea for this edited collection emerged from the critical conviction that climate change and the sixth mass extinction had already applied substantial productive pressure to posthumanist discourses and that the time was right to ask ourselves, "What is posthumanism now?" In the light of recent developments we also feel that this volume will stand as a companion to pre-COVID-19 discussions, issues, and perspectives on posthumanism thus providing a foundational introduction to a subject that is only going to become more important in the near future.

Due to the fast-paced developments of posthumanist discourse, much of it scattered and difficult to access, a related goal of this volume is to serve as a handbook that will bring to the surface essential insights into significant discussions in art, culture, and contemporary thinking. While we hope for artists and academics to find the book a useful reader on posthumanism and the arts for research and teaching, our aim is to also appeal to a wide audience of art lovers who are curious about what lies behind the most significant contemporary artistic trends. For art in the twenty-first century to realize its world-making potentials, these discussions must move beyond both the ivory towers of academia and the white cubes of the art gallery.

NOTES

1. Jeffrey Deitch, *POST HUMAN, 1992/93*, FAE Musée d'Art Contemporain, Lausanne; Castello di Rivoli, Turin; Deichtorhallen, Hamburg; Deste Foundation, Athens; Israel Museum, Jerusalem.
2. Michel Foucault, *The Order of Things: An Archaeology of the Human Sciences* (London: Routledge, 1970), p. 387.
3. Barbara Christian, "The Race for Theory" in *Within the Circle: An Anthology of African American Literary Criticism from the Harlem Renaissance through the Present*, ed. Angelyn Mitchell (Durham: Duke University Press, 1994), p. 352.
4. Sylvia Wynter, "Unsettling the Coloniality of Being/Power/Truth/Freedom: Towards the Human, After Man, Its Overrepresentation—An Argument," *CR: The New Centennial Review* 3.3 (2003): pp. 257–337, at 317.
5. Michel Foucault, "What Is an Author?" in James D. Faubion (ed.) (1998) *Aesthetics, Method, and Epistemology* (New York: The New Press, 1969), pp. 205–222.
6. Cary Wolfe, *What is Posthumanism?* (Minneapolis: University of Minnesota Press, 2010), p. xii.
7. Ibid, p. xv.
8. Bruce Clarke, *Posthuman Metamorphosis: Narrative and System* (New York: Fordham University Press, 2008), p. 5.
9. N. Katherine Hayles, "Unfinished Work: From Cyborg to Cognisphere," *Theory, Culture, and Society* 23.7–8 (2006): p. 159.
10. Michael Onyebuchi Eze, "Cultural Appropriation and the Limits of Identity: A Case for Multiple Humanity (ies) 1," *Chiedza, Journal of Arrupe Jesuit University*, Vol 20, No. 1 May 2018.
11. Donna Haraway, *When Species Meet* (Minneapolis: University of Minnesota Press, 2008), p. 22.
12. Jacques Derrida, *The Animal That Therefore I Am*, ed. Marie-Louise Mallet, trans. David Wills (New York: Fordham University Press, 2008), p. 7.
13. Janani Subramanyan, Editor's Introduction to *Post-Identity*, *Spectator* 30.2 (2010): 5.
14. Jonathan Burt, "Invisible Histories: Primate Bodies and the Rise of Posthumanism in the Twentieth Century," in *Animal Encounters: Human-Animal Studies*, ed. Manuela Rossini and Tom Tyler (Leiden: Koninklijke Brill, 2009), p. 161.
15. Neil Marcus quoted in Sunaura Taylor, *Beasts of Burden: Animal and Disability Liberation* (New York: New Press, 2017), 136.

16. Bruce Clarke, "Mediating *The Fly*: Posthuman Metamorphosis in the 1950s," *Configurations* 10.1 (2002): pp. 171–172.

17. John Berger, "Why look at animals?" in *About Looking* (New York: Vintage, 1980), pp. 3–30.

18. Zakiyyah Iman Jackson, *Becoming Human: Matter and Meaning in an Antiblack World*, Sexual Cultures (New York: New York University Press, 2020), p. 14.

19. Giovanni Aloi (2015), "Animal Studies and Art: Elephants in the Room," *Antennae Special Editorial, online*: http://www.antennae.org.uk/back-issues-2015/4589877799.

20. Philippe Descola, "Modes of being and forms of predication," *Journal of Ethnographic Theory* 4.1 (2014): p. 279.

21. Ananya Chakravarti, "Viveiros de Castro, Eduardo. 2015. Metafísicas Canibais. São Paulo: Cosac Naify. 280 p.," *Vibrant: Virtual Brazilian Anthropology* 12.2 (2015).

22. Ian Bogost, *Alien Phenomenology, or What It's Like to Be a Thing* (Minneapolis: University of Minnesota Press, 2012), p. 8.

23. Mel Chen in David Joselit, Carrie Lambert-Beatty, and Hal Foster, "A Questionnaire on Materialsims" *October* 155 (2016): 23.

24. Kodwo Eshun, *More Brilliant than the Sun: Adventures in Sonic Fiction* (London: Quartet Books, 1998), p. 5.

PART I

Post-Identity Politics

Chapter One

INTERVIEW WITH CASSILS

Becoming an Image

GIOVANNI ALOI AND SUSAN McHUGH

GIOVANNI ALOI AND SUSAN MCHUGH: In 2001 with Enkelarts, Clever Riri, and Juliet Steinmetz, you co-founded The Toxic Titties, a performance collective that was active for nearly a decade. Together the artists created a process-oriented and event-based practice focused on conceptual performance. Could you tell us about why identity politics were central to the works? And, in your views, what are the main shifts that have characterized transgender identity politics in art over the recent years?

CASSILS: First, I would say Toxic Titties was not involved in making transgender work at all. It was a different time really. In terms of years, it wasn't that long ago, but so much happened so quickly, in terms of representation and just the speed of consumption or relationship to online culture and all of that.

At the time, we met doing our thesis collectively at CalArts, and our process was very much a reaction to this kind of professionalization that we were finding in the master's program in art school. We showed up wanting to have a discourse, experimentation, and what we found was students turning the studio spaces into tiny galleries and having closed-door meetings or locking their thesis show because they were afraid someone would steal their idea. We formed this collective Toxic Titties. We were a biker gang, but we had no motorcycles, and we would show up at openings with helmets under our arms regardless and we would glue wigs into them and we would take the helmet off and the wig would come with us.

FIGURE 1.1. Cassils, *Advertisement: Homage to Benglis*, 2011. c-print, 40 x 30 inches, edition of 3. Photo: Cassils with Robin Black. Courtesy the artist and Ronald Feldman Gallery, New York.

It was just this absurdist sort of defiance to this sort of very masculinist, very commercialized art world that we saw being fostered and that we wanted to reject. It was this coming together of being like three queer artists. At that point I was definitely masculine or perhaps butch. But there wasn't even the sort of language that we had access to the idea of identifying as "trans masculine" or anything like that.

But as it has been pointed out, for example, in the essay collection *Trap Door*, as there is more rising visibility around this kind of trans tipping point, with Laverne Cox on the cover of *Time* magazine etcetera, there is also a significant rise in violence against trans people. This is kind of the conundrum that we're in right now. There is more visibility and yet more and more of our civil rights are being eroded daily. It's an interesting and tricky time I think for trans representation.

GIOVANNI ALOI AND SUSAN MCHUGH: Yes absolutely. Part of this book is about visibility and how the human body has been changing through different concepts, ideas, but also technology and the desire to transcend the binaries of gender itself. Is there something specific about the visibility of the Internet, like you mentioned, that you think might play in specific ways? It feels like social media and the Internet more generally are platforms for under-represented voices, and at the same time there seems to be a darker side to that possibility, too.

CASSILS: To give an example, I just had my second solo show at Ronald Feldman Fine Arts in New York last fall. There I created *PISSED*, a brand new piece that was in relationship to Trump's rescinding of the Obama-era executive order that allowed transgender students to piss in their bathrooms of choice. It was a collection of every drop of urine that my body produced from the date of the rollback up until the night of the opening, a minimalist cube that was filled with 200 gallons of urine. That show got some press, but what I couldn't have anticipated was that the work was picked up by alt-right publications, in articles that were shared about the work over 17,000 times. I started to become the recipient of death threats and a lot of social media attacks.

It is double-edged. I was live talking to someone who contacted me on the Facebook Messenger app, and they said, "Your work really resonated, thank you so much." I wrote back saying, "Well, thanks for letting me know, I'm glad it did something for you," and then the response was, "JK I wish I had my hand around your neck."

In terms of my relationship to visibility, my earlier work was dealing a lot with my own body and the mutability of my body. As you probably know I have a background as an athlete. I've run a personal training business for 20 years. I'm really thinking of the body as both an instrument and an image, not just in relationship to trans identity. Working off my body, the risk was that it fetishized muscular physique in this white body, this particular sub-jectivity. On some level, it is very valid: it is my body; it is a vulnerable body; it is my honest place of expression.

GIOVANNI ALOI AND SUSAN MCHUGH: When and why did you start adopting the pronoun *they*? Do you think pronoun attribution should be primarily a matter of personal choice, or is your request in pursuit of a larger political vision to move away from gendered pronouns, and thereby to enlist language and art in the work of envisioning non-gender-binary life for everyone?

CASSILS: Good question. I feel like visual artists are ahead of language in many ways. We're able to imagine possibilities that we don't yet have words for. In terms of just pronoun requests, because I'm not on a lot of testosterone and I haven't had surgery, I don't have those markings of masculinity. People who don't know me often will read me as a lesbian, as a woman, and that's not how I identify. For me, this pronoun choice creates an indication for people to realize actually, no, I don't identify as a woman. I look forward to there being better choices, more nuanced choices.

GIOVANNI ALOI AND SUSAN MCHUGH: *Cuts: A Traditional Sculpture* is a com-plex work that began with a six-month durational performance and gener-ated video installations, photographs, watercolors, and a magazine. As part of this project, you gained 23 pounds of muscle over 23 weeks, transforming your physique into a traditionally masculine muscular form. What is the value of durational experimentalism in your practice?

CASSILS: Working with others' bodies professionally on a day-to-day basis—people who are recovering from open heart surgery, or have a new hip replacement and can't walk—there is a sort of analogue process to the body that I think is actually more and more beneficial to embrace as we become more and more interdependent and interlaced with technology. Because there is a slow, focused patience that yields a great sort of learning and understanding and connection to something much vaster than this instant gratification that we get from technology.

GIOVANNI ALOI AND SUSAN MCHUGH: What started your interest in body-building as a personal commitment, and how did it become part of your aesthetic practice?

CASSILS: I started training for many reasons. When I was a very young person, I had undiagnosed gallbladder disease, and was quite sick. It's something that you usually find in alcoholic 70-year-old men. No one would really take me seriously, and it got to the point where my bile duct ruptured, the whites in my eyes turned green and my skin turned green. I had to have multiple surgeries. I was literary disintegrating on the inside, my internal organs were rotting, and I almost died when I was 13, bleeding out from ulcers. I was tiny, I was weak, and I had this strong experience of being called hysterical, dismissed.

I realized at a young age that the agency of my body and my person was up to me. When I recovered, I became interested in becoming strong and being really grounded in my own body, so that I could have agency and articulate when something was wrong. Then, of course, the other thing was puberty and not identifying with being a woman, again not having words for it, but using the training as a way to control my expression of gender, although I don't think I would have ever been able to articulate as such at that age.

Then as a young artist, making my way in the world, it just so happened that training was an excellent job for me to do whilst being an artist because of it's totally flexible hours. You're your own boss. You make decent money, and it's separate from the art world. It's not like when you're teaching art and then you go home and find you're drained for your own art. I'm able to compartmentalize in a way.

GIOVANNI ALOI AND SUSAN MCHUGH: How does fitness factor in the strong responses to your more recent works in *Becoming an Image*?

CASSILS: *Becoming an Image* is about hitting 2,000 pounds of clay for as long as you can, as hard as you can. That's about cardiorespiratory strength. That's about the conditioning of your tendons, having ballistic power to jump and leap, and also the performance is done in the dark, with just photographers' flashes making it visible.

I have to train for disorientation because, when the flash of light goes off and you see an afterburn, the same thing happens to me. I'll be hitting a sculpture in front of me, but I have to learn to not trust my eye actually. It's an entirely different physiological re-patterning of the body that has nothing to do with bodybuilding. The body that you see in relationship to that performance is more about being informed by the work informing me, as opposed to me forming the work. Meaning the clay creates me. In fact, clay has such a particular pressure that, when you exert force upon clay, it exerts the exact same force back upon you. It's a really much more reciprocal act.

The sculpture and the performance was made initially for this idea of an archive where I was asked to speak to the missing trans-representation in the archives. It's not just about the act of beating the clay, but it's really about the absence of what you can see in that moment: making people cognizant as audience members about what truths and histories are making it into their visual representation to their eyes. Like, what are they actually seeing versus what has happened around them, and how much, in fact, they are not seeing?

GIOVANNI ALOI AND SUSAN MCHUGH: As you said about *Becoming an Image*, the performance is only illuminated by a photographer's flash, which leaves an afterimage on the viewers' retina, raising questions of witnessing documentation, memory and evidence. Can you explain why this aspect of the work was specifically woven into the performance?

CASSILS: Initially, this work was commissioned for the largest LGBTQI archive in North America. I was given this task of speaking to the missing trans-representation, but not given very much time to make this project. It's like, how am I supposed to go through this entire archive and probably find the one or two subjectivities there? Because, like many archives, this is filled with the work of dead, white, and in this case gay men. The piece asks, where are the missing representations, and also the physical violence that occurs along with the violence in exclusion? The retinal burn was playing with this idea that a lot of my work does, which is questioning the notion of the documentary and truth factor of images.

The retinal burn was very much about thinking of hijacking the viewers at the meat of their body. Making them experience the performance as almost live archivists because, with the flash, you don't see a photograph per se. It's not like the documentation. It's not a faithful document at all in fact, but you do have this almost a holograph or a hovering trace, a ghost image. The piece is always done with a white male photographer, shooting blind, and it's about the white male photographer never being able to capture me, about inverting the power relationship in relation to this idea of representation.

GIOVANNI ALOI AND SUSAN MCHUGH: Can we say that there's a positive productive violence embedded into the presence of these flashes?

CASSILS: I think so because it is a violent experience for the viewers to be so accosted, if you will. It's unpleasant. I was just speaking to someone the other day who told me that they found the performance exhausting to watch, which is funny because it's much less exhausting than it is to perform it.

Even when you're standing in place as a viewer it's an incredibly disorienting performance. Not only that, but there's also a set up involving the ushers who place you as an audience member in the round. There's no sitting.

You have to stand and you're pressed very closely to the person next to you, uncomfortably close to them. You're aware of everybody's body and it creates a very strong energy in the room. You're feeling the people next to you. We're not used to touching people that we don't know. It's about really pressing upon people, pushing their boundaries in many, many ways, and feeling in many ways the discomfort of maybe a fraction of what some trans people feel on a day-to-day experience all the time.

It's about bringing an awareness to the corporeal. That's something that you can't ignore.

GIOVANNI ALOI AND SUSAN MCHUGH: How do you see your very early work with feminist performance artist Martha Wilson at the Franklin Furnace as influential in the development of your practice, and particularly the return to archives? What is it that the engagement with archives uniquely contributes to making art?

CASSILS: It's interesting, no one's asked that question. Martha Wilson was a Canadian like me who had gone to Nova Scotia College of Art and Design, and then she went to New York and started this impressive organization. I applied to work as an intern there and received a very precious informal education and a job, at the same time.

The Franklin Furnace had just been busted for exceeding the amount of bodies they could have in a performance space. Slapped with a massive fine, the physical organization had to shut down, and Martha decided to go virtual and to start doing streamed live performances. This was in the very early days of the Internet. My job was to digitize and edit this important footage from the 70's that probably no one had access to, then put it online. I think that, definitely, just seeing the range of approaches taken by other artists, and getting to work with and be trusted with that material in order to make work that no one would otherwise see accessible—all of that very much formed my practice. And just having Martha as just this very wacky, eccentric, and original woman as an example of what was possible was also really inspiring, and continues to be inspiring to me. Returning to the archive for something like *Becoming an Image*, I think there's probably a connection in there.

GIOVANNI ALOI AND SUSAN MCHUGH: A lot of people bring the three—aesthetics, politics, and embodiment—together to critique negative view of bodily transformation, whether Roxanne Gaye's bestselling memoir *Hunger* or Eleanor Antin's *Carving: A Traditional Sculpture*, the latter of which you reference directly in your own *Cuts: A Traditional Sculpture*. But we think

FIGURE 1.2. Cassils, *Becoming an Image Performance Still No. 3* (Pennsylvania Academy of Fine Arts, Historic Casting Hall), 2016 color photographs, plexi mounted with aluminum backing, series of 6 images, 20 x 30 in., Ed. 1/6. *Source*: Photo by Cassils with Zachary Hartzell. Courtesy the artist and Ronald Feldman Gallery, New York.

your work inspires hope for livability and endurance outside normative ideals of how bodies are valued, legislated and otherwise regulated. Maybe the two extremes are more intricately related from your perspective?

CASSILS: Of course, aesthetics, politics and embodiment are interwoven not only in my art, but it's something that you experience when you walk out the door in the morning, really. It can be exhausting because when people don't have something, for example, a hard binary to hold onto, there is this constant assertion that you have to do to reinscribe and that can be tiring.

It's also an exhaustion of being constantly read as always a trans artist. Of course, I am a trans artist because I'm an artist and I'm trans. Certainly, my works take on the mantle of politics in discussing the civil rights issues that we're living through right now. At the same time, I guess for me and I don't know if this is really an answer to the question, but I think the parts that are troubling to me are the fact that you get a sort of umbrella thrown around you. Many of the nuances and many of the other ideas that you're really working hard at in your work are overlooked and subdued by identity sometimes, and that could be frustrating.

There is a very particular way in which people want to read the aesthetics of politics, the embodiment to fit neatly into this agenda that they may have, but those are large categories, aesthetics, politics, embodiment. They don't just fit into a very particular niche definition; they're quite broad and they can interweave in more than one cord. They can make an infinite number of possibilities and probabilities out there. I think I'm interested more in the latter than I am just in one unified vision of how those things can intersect. I am interested in all the ways that it can intersect and be generative.

Chapter Two

FROM SF

Speculative Fabulation and String Figures[1]

DONNA HARAWAY

Consider a fictional multiple integral equation that is a flawed trope and a serious joke in an effort to picture what an intersectional—or intra-actional—theory might look like in Terrapolis.[2] Think of this formalism as the mathematics of sf. Sf is that potent material semiotic sign for the riches of speculative fabulation, speculative feminism, science fiction, science fact, science fantasy—and, I suggest, string figures. In looping threads and relays of patterning, this sf practice is a model for worlding. Sf must also mean "so far," opening up what is yet-to-come in protean time's pasts, presents, and futures.

$$\Omega$$
$$\int \text{Terra}\,[X]_n = \iiiint \ldots \iint \text{Terra}(X_1, X_2, X_3, X_4, \ldots, X_n, t)\,dX_1\,dX_2\,dX_3$$
$$dX_4 \ldots dX_n\,dt = \text{Terrapolis}$$
$$\alpha$$

$$X_1 = \text{stuff/physis},\ X_2 = \text{capacity},\ X_3 = \text{sociality},\ X_4 = \text{materiality},\ X_n = \text{??}$$

α (alpha) = not zoë, but EcoEvoDevo's multispecies epigenesis
Ω (omega) = not bios, but recuperating terra's pluriverse
t = multi-scalar times, entangled times of past/present/yet-to-come, worlding times, not container time[3]

Terrapolis is a fictional integral equation, a speculative fabulation.[4]
Terrapolis is an n-dimensional hyper volume; in ecological theory, a niche space.[5]

Terrapolis is a niche space for multispecies becoming-with.[6]

Terrapolis is a n-dimensional volume in naturecultures.

Terrapolis is the semiotic material worlding of EcoEvoDevo in multi-scalar times and places.[7]

Terrapolis is the cat's cradling set of string figures tied in intra-action and intra-patience.

Terrapolis is networked re-enactments for flourishing in mortal terran living and dying.

Terrapolis is multispecies storytelling, multispecies worlding in sf modes.

Terrapolis is open, not poor in world, full of connections and networked re-enactments.[8]

Terrapolis is a chimera of materials, languages, histories; a mongrel of Greek and Latin.

Terrapolis is playing cat's cradle with Isabelle Stengers' cosmopolitics, tugging at the threads of coherence in the interests of co-habitation.[9]

Terrapolis is the home of transdisciplinarities that are at risk of becoming-with.

Terrapolis is at risk of dropping threads and missing dimensions in the action and passion of caring.

Terrapolis is full of companion species—not "post-human" but "com-post."

Terrapolis is of and for humus, the stuff of *guman*, an old earthy Indo-European word for workers of the soil, not the stuff of *homo*, that figure of the bright and airy sacred image of the same.

Terrapolis is not a system, not even a hopeful 3rd-order or nth-order cybernetic system; but its values are determinable, locatable, accountable, and open to change.

Terrapolis is abstract and concrete.

Terrapolis is sf.

A WORD ON THE CALCULUS OF INTEGRAL EQUATIONS

Visualizing in one dimension is said to be easy for members of the species *Homo sapiens*; lines abound, and lots of people think they know what a line is. Visualizing in two-dimensional areas is said to be equally easy, and three-dimensional volumes are thought to be quite readily imagined in the mind's eye (such an odd organ, the mind's eye), as well as rotated on the computer screen in really pretty colors. Integrating areas under a curve defined by a function, from one variable to another, for three dimensions would give us a volume, irregular and intra-active, to be sure, if the values for one variable are mutated by the functional happenings with another variable, but still quite manageable, even able to be held in ordinary hands if they are agile enough. This volume might be quite bubbly and dynamic, not just irregular, but still, not a shock to the epistemological, visual, manual, or digestive systems. It's with areas and volumes in four and more dimensions that things start seeming unwieldy for bi-ocular bipeds. After all, areas are *defined* by two dimensions, and volumes by three dimensions. Geometry says so . . . That's when more colors and more databases and more computer softwares are called into play to persuade us visually that a non-visualizable world is not really so scary.

What is an n-dimensional niche space; how do Terrapolis' multiple integral equations give us a hint of worlds not dreamt of in Horatio's philosophy,[10] but nonetheless worlds more real by far in all their indefinite intra-active and ongoing connectivity? Worlds where place is palpated and inhabited, not just lost in the misplaced concreteness and void of space? An equation is a model; that model here is an sf proposition about unimaginable, bubbly, hyper-real, bumptious placings and shapings. These are the sorts of n-dimensional doings that make fleshy mortal worlds in loop after loop held together with n attachment sites. Go play; go figure.

NOTES

1. In the Navajo language, cat's cradle figures or string games are called *Na'atl'o'*. [. . .]

Naabeehó Bináhásdzo (the Navajo Nation, the legal geographically defined territory for the semi-autonomous nation), or Diné Bikéyha (the people's name for Navajoland), is located in the Four Corners area of the southwestern United States, surrounded by Colorado, Arizona, Utah, and New Mexico. For Navajo scholarship on their history, written in the web of Diné creation stories and the discipline of academic history, see Jennifer Nez Dinetdale, *Reclaiming Diné History* (Tucson: University of Arizona Press, 2007).

There are several sources for Navajo string games and string figures, with varied stories and names. For example, see: http://dine.sanjuan.k12.ut.us/string_games /games/opening_a/coyotes_opposite.html and the large Library of Navajo string games at: http://dine.sanjuan.k12.ut.us/string_games/games/index.html, © 2003 San Juan School District, Tucson. For an extraordinary video of an elder Navajo woman, Margaret Ray Bochinclonny (called Grandma Margaret in this short clip), playing string games, see www.youtube.com/watch?v=5qdcG7Ztn3c. Margaret Ray's grandson, Terry Teller, explains Navajo string figure star constellations at: www.angelfire .com/rock3/countryboy79/navajo_astronomy.html. Navajo string games are played mainly in winter, Spider Woman's storytelling season. These string figures are

thinking as well as making practices, pedagogical practices, and cosmological performances. Some Navajo thinkers describe string figures as one kind of patterning for restoring *hózhó*, a term imperfectly translated into English as "harmony,"
"beauty," and "right relations of the world," including right relations of humans and
nonhumans.

In the late nineteenth and early twentieth centuries, American and European
ethnologists collected string figure games from all over the world; these discipline-
making travelers were surprised that when they showed their hosts the string figure
games that they had learned as children at home, their hosts already knew such
games in greater variety. String figure games came late to Europe, probably from
Asian trade routes. All of the epistemological desires and fables of this period of the
history of comparative anthropology were ignited by the similarities and differences,
with their undecidably independent inventions or cultural diffusions, tied together
by the threads of hand and brain, making and thinking, in the relays of patterning
in the "Native" and "Western" string figure games. See Caroline Furness Jayne, *String
Figures and How to Make Them: A Study of Cat's Cradle in Many Lands* (New York:
Charles Scribner & Sons, 1906).

Situated in histories and zones of contact, conflict, conquest, and contending
sovereignties of place and ways of knowing, in this notebook entry for dOCU-
MENTA (13) I am non-innocently proposing a string figure looped on many hands
with the threads of a fabulated equation for Terrapolis and the continuous weaving
of *Ma'ii Ats'áá' Yilwoi*, Coyotes Running Opposite Ways. In *Swept under the Rug: A
Hidden History of Navajo Weaving* (Albuquerque: University of New Mexico Press,
2002), Kathy M'Closkey gave me a way of approaching cosmological performance
and continuous weaving in Navajo thinking and aesthetics in their sheep, wool, and
weaving practices—including, with only a little stretch of the threads, *na'atl'o'*.

2. Karen Barad, *Meeting the Universe Halfway: Physics and the Entanglement of Matter
and Meaning* (Durham, N. Car.: Duke University Press, 2007), gives us both agential realism and "intra-action," her neologism to emphasize the fact that actors do
not precede the acting, that relations are primary, that we are of the world, not in
the world, that partners are the determinate consequences of intra-action, not pre-
existing entities entering into inter-action. She asks what it would mean to think
about thinking as part of what *the world* does. This is also a core question posed in
sf, in the string figure games of speculative fabulation.

Developed especially by black feminist theorists, intersectional theory has been
an immensely fruitful analytic tool for anti-racist analysis and action and for critical
theory and legal theory broadly. See Kimberlé Crenshaw, "Mapping the Margins:
Intersectionality, Identity Politics, and Violence against Women of Color," *Stanford
Law Review* 43, no. 6 (1991), pp. 1241–99. It would be a mistake to literalize and then
oppose the prefixes "intra-" and "inter-" in reading both of these theories in relation
to each other.

3. For this kind of time, see Astrid Schrader, "Responding to *Pfiesteria piscicida* (the
Fish Killer): Phantomatic Ontologies, Indeterminacy and Responsibility in Toxic
Microbiology," *Social Studies of Science* 40, no. 2 (2010), pp. 275–306.

4. Marleen Barr taught me about *Feminist Fabulation: Space/Postmodern Fiction* (Iowa
City: University of Iowa Press, 1992). Helen Merrick knotted together wonderful
string figures in *The Secret Feminist Cabal: A Cultural History of Science Fiction*

Feminisms (Seattle: Aqueduct Press, 2010). Joshua LaBare taught me about sf as a theory and practice of history in *Farfetchings: On and in the SF Mode*, PhD dissertation, Santa Cruz: University of California, History of Consciousness Department, 2010. He figures the sf mode as a practice of "paying attention to the great omniversal collective that is our home." Natalie Loveless taught me about the "making of thinkers and thinking of makers" in her postdoctoral proposal, "Practice in the Flesh of Theory," 2010.

Orion, a constellation, is also Sha and Natalie's baby son. This star child gestated in the flesh of theory in the sf mode. The word for "constellations" in Navajo is *So' Dinéé* or "Star People." At www.angelfire.com/rock3/countryboy79/navajo_astronomy.html, I learn that *Átse Ats'oosi* (First Slender One) is the "figure synonymous with the [European] constellation 'Orion' in its location in the sky. *Átse Ats'oosi* represents protection, as it is depicted in the sky as it moves ahead of the children that make up the constellation *Dilyéhé*, protecting them. . . . *Dilyéhé* (The Planters) is synonymous with the constellation 'Pleiades' in its location in the sky. It is said that when some of the Holy People were coming to this world by a rainbow, these were children that were too busy playing and got left in the sky. These children represent youth. When this constellation appears over the morning horizon, it indicates it is time to plant. This constellation is also a figure in the string-game." Cat's cradle and string figures tangle provocatively in the conflict and contact zones of Navajo-Anglo histories. [. . .]

There are more stories about how these stars got into the sky, put there by Black God/Fire God. "The fine and tiny structure of the Pleiades [*Dilyéhé*] contrasts with the vast expanse of sky, making the Pleiades a microcosmic symbol of the orderly universe—the universe that is the mask of Black God." In this story, the Trickster Coyote, in a fit of disorderly temper, throws many other star crystals into the sky randomly, in world-making friction with the orderly acts of the Fire God. Seven Stars/Sparkling Particles is a time-keeper and a marker of seasons. Crystal Fire, these sparks clock the night. See Teresa M. Schulz, "Mask of the Black God: The Pleiades in Navajo Cosmology," Science Department, Lansing Community College. Schultz's teaching module on the Pleiades/Mask of Black God was supported by a U.S. National Science Foundation Grant for a Case Studies in Science workshop in 2004. Http://sciencecases.lib.buffalo.edu/cs/files/pleiades_notes.pdf.

5. For a formal definition of "niche space," a kind of mathematical model of activity ranges along every imaginable dimension of an ecology or world, see George Evelyn Hutchinson, "Concluding Remarks," *Cold Spring Harbor Symposium for Quantitative Biology* 22 (1957), pp. 415–27. Hutchinson was my PhD dissertation adviser in a lab as likely to read Kurt Gödel, Simone Weil, or Karen Stephens, sister of Virginia Woolf, in its journal club meetings, as to peruse the latest in molecular biology or theoretical ecology. These writings were all part of the relays of cat's cradle or string figures, definitely coyotes running opposite ways, as tricksters will do. Remember that those coyotes running apart in the string figure at the head of this little notebook entry are tied together in intra-action. A talented mathematician, limnologist, and theoretical ecologist, as well as a student of thirteenth-century Italian illuminated manuscripts, Hutchinson nourished "worlding," an sf discipline if ever there was one. Poor in world, Heidegger's worlding is barely distant kin. Hutchinson is my inspiration for playing equations as speculative fabulation. On the importance of fabulation and

historically situated genres of fables in both science studies and science practice, see Martha Kenney, "Cultivating Wilds Facts: Fables in Technoscientific Worlds," PhD dissertation proposal, Santa Cruz: University of California, History of Consciousness Department, April 2011.

6. For multispecies becoming-with, see Donna Haraway, *When Species Meet* (Minneapolis: University of Minnesota Press, 2008). "Becoming" to my ear is a very annoying abbreviation, or depletion and impoverishment, of "becoming-with."

7. EcoEvoDevo is "ecological evolutionary developmental biology," a major synthesis in recent sciences of terran naturalcultural worldings. See Scott F. Gilbert and David Epel, *Ecological Developmental Biology: Integrating Epigenetics, Medicine, and Evolution* (Sunderland, Mass.: Sinauer, 2008); Scott F. Gilbert, Emily McDonald, Nicole Boyle, Nicholas Buttino, Lin Gyi, Mark Mai, Neelakantan Prakash, and James Robinson, "Symbiosis as a Source of Selectable Epigenetic Variation: Taking the Heat for the Big Guy," *Phil. Trans. R. Soc. B* 365 (2010), pp. 671–78; Margaret McFall-Ngai, "The Development of Cooperative Associations between Animals and Bacteria: Establishing Détente among Domains," *American Zoologist* 38, no. 4 (1998), pp. 593–608; McFall-Ngai, "Unseen Forces: The Influence of Bacteria on Animal Development," *Developmental Biology* 242 (2002), pp. 1–14.

8. Katie King, *Networked Reenactments* (Durham, N. Car.: Duke University Press, forthcoming 2012). King writes: "Working out in a multiverse of articulating disciplines, interdisciplines, and multidisciplinarities, such transdisciplinary inspection actually *enjoys* the many flavors of details, offerings, passions, languages, things, even while also demonstrating that its own forms of validity are not entailed only within those elegant but divergent parsimonies of explanation. Instead, one index for the evaluation of transdisciplinary work is in how well it learns and models *how to be affected* or moved, how well it *opens up* unexpected elements of one's own embodiments in lively and re-sensitizing worlds." King notes here her debts to and ties with Eva Hayward, "Fingery-Eyes: Impressions of Cup Corals," *Cultural Anthropology* 25, no. 4 (2010), pp. 577–99. My own thinking is also indebted to and entwined with the trans-sensualities and trans-thinking of Hayward's "fingeryeyes," of her understanding of the transversality of optic-haptic touch. I am affected, moved, caught in the relay of this cat's cradle game.

9. Isabelle Stengers, *Cosmopolitics I* and *Cosmopolitics II*, trans. Robert Bononno (Minneapolis: University of Minnesota Press, 2010 and 2011 [orig. 1997]). Stengers picked up loops from my doing science studies and feminist theory as a cat's cradle game to give me back a relay from Félix Guattari that taught me about staying still in intrapatience in order to receive, so as to propose another pattern in intra-action. See Isabelle Stengers, "Relaying a War Machine?," manuscript, 2010.

10. Horatio is the bewildered empiricist, or rationalist, portrayed in Shakespeare's *Hamlet*, act 1, scene 5. When he sees the ghost with his own eyes, Hamlet admonishes him: "And therefore as a stranger give it welcome. There are more things in heaven and earth, Horatio, than are dreamt of in your philosophy." Hamlet, of course, is not to be trusted with ghosts.

Chapter Three

FROM NOMADIC THEORY

ROSI BRAIDOTTI

Politically, nomadic thought is the expression of a nonunitary vision of the subject, defined by motion in a complex manner that is densely material. It invites us to rethink the structures and boundaries of the self by tackling the deeper conceptual roots of issues of identity. It is particularly important not to confuse the process of nomadic subjectivity with individualism or particularity. Whereas identity is a bounded, ego-indexed habit of fixing and capitalizing on one's selfhood, subjectivity is a socially mediated process of relations and negotiations with multiple others and with multilayered social structures.

Consequently, the emergence of social subjects is always a collective enterprise, "external" to the self, while it also mobilizes the self's in-depth structures. Issues of subjectivity raise questions of entitlement, in terms of power as restrictive (*potestas*) but also as empowering or affirmative (*potentia*). Power relations act simultaneously as the most "external," collective, social phenomenon and also as the most intimate or "internal" one. Or, rather, power is the process that flows incessantly in between the most "internal" and the most "external" forces. As [Michel] Foucault taught us, power is a situation or a process, not an object or an essence. Subjectivity is the effect of these constant flows of in-between power connections. [. . .]

Poststructuralist philosophies have produced an array of alternative concepts and practices of nonunitary political subjectivity. From the "split subject" of psychoanalysis to the subject-in-process of Foucault, the "sexed subject which is not one" of [Luce] Irigaray and the rhizomatic complex of Gilles Deleuze and [Félix] Guattari, multiplicity and complexity have been widely debated in Continental philosophy. After the decline of postmodernism—reductively associated with cognitive and moral relativism—those experimental approaches to the question of the subject raise some skeptical eyebrows. What exactly is the advantage of these alternative notions and practices of the subject? What are the values—ethical and political—they can offer? What good are they to anybody? And how much fun are they? This volume is an attempt to answer these crucial questions by producing an adequate cartography of our historical situation as well as to expose the logic of the new power relations operative today.

Nomadic thought takes a very different route—by positing the primacy of intelligent, sexed, and self-organizing matter, it approaches the process of subject formation in a distributive, dispersed, and multiple manner. Modulations or processes of differing within a common matter rely on a definition of power as both productive and restrictive and strike an affirmative route between empowerment and entrapment. As a consequence, nomadic thought rejects melancholia in favor of the politics of affirmation and mutual specification of self and other in sets of relations or assemblages.

Central to the nomadic subject is the emphasis on the intimate connection between critique and creation. Critique is consequently not only a sterile opposition but also an active engagement of the conceptual imagination in the task of producing sustainable alternatives [. . .].

Nomadic theory grows from these fundamental assumptions. It critiques the self-interest, the repressive tolerance, and the deeply seated conservatism of the institutions that are officially in charge of knowledge production, especially the university but also the media and the law. Foucault (1975) explicitly singles out for criticism the pretension of classical philosophy to be a master discipline that supervises and organizes other discourses and opposes to this abstract and universalistic mission the idea that philosophy is just a toolbox.

What this means is that the aim of philosophy as nomadic critical theory is the production of pragmatic and localized tools of analysis for the power relations at work in society at large and more specifically within its own practice. The philosopher becomes no more than a provider of analytic services: a technician of knowledge. In the same spirit, Deleuze (1953, 1962) redefines philosophy in the "problematic" mode as the constant questioning of the dominant "image of thought" at work in most of our ideas with the purpose of destabilizing them in the "nomadic" mode. In my own work on nomadic thought I adopt a creative redefinition of thinking that links philosophy to the creation of new forms of subjectivity and collective experiments with ways of actualizing them.

This results in a critique of representational regimes that focus especially on the dominant image of thought as the expression of a white, masculine, adult, heterosexual, urban-dwelling, property-owning subject. Deleuze and Guattari label this dominant subject as the Majority, or the Molar formation; Irigaray calls it the Logic of the Same. For nomadic thought, this replication of sameness is counteracted by creative efforts aimed at activating the positivity of differences as affirmative praxis [. . .]. Replacing the metaphysics of being with a process ontology bent on becoming, that is to say, subversive moves of detachment from the dominant system of representation. Nomadic theory combines potentially contradictory elements: it is materialist and vitalist, fluid and accountable and it remains resolutely pragmatic throughout. The central tenet of nomadic thought is to reassert the dynamic nature of thinking and the need to reinstate movement at the heart of thought by actualizing a nonunitary vision of the thinking subject.

In these times of accelerating changes, many traditional points of reference and age-old habits are being recomposed, albeit in contradictory ways. At such a time more conceptual creativity is necessary—a theoretical effort is needed to bring about the conceptual leap across the contemporary social landscape. Nomadic thought is a response to this challenge. This includes the schizoid affective economy of inertia, nostalgia, paranoia, and other forms of critical *stasis*, on the one hand, and overzealous excitement, on the other, that is induced by the contradictory conditions of advanced capitalism. In such a context, we need to learn to think differently about ourselves and the ongoing processes of deep-seated transformation.

A major concern [. . .] is consequently the deficit in the scale of representation that accompanies the structural transformations of subjectivity in the social, cultural, and political spheres of late postindustrial culture. Accounting adequately for changes is a challenge that shakes up long-established habits of thought. In order to produce grounded accounts and more subtle differentiation in the kind of different nomadic flows at work in our world, we need more conceptual creativity. More ethical courage is also needed and deeper theoretical efforts to sustain the qualitative shift of perspective that may help us confront the complexities of our era.

Chapter Four

TOWARDS A NEW CLASS OF BEING

The Extended Body

ORON CATTS AND IONAT ZURR

A rough estimate would put the biomass of living cells and tissues, which are disassociated from the original bodies that once hosted them, in the millions of tons. In addition, there are tons of fragments of bodies (cells, tissues, organs) that are maintained in suspended animation in cryogenic conditions. All of this biomass requires an intensive technological intervention to prevent transformation to a non-living state. This type of being (or semi-being/semi-living) does not fall under current biological or even cultural classifications. The notion of the Extended Body can be seen as a way to define this category of life, maintaining the need for classification, while at the same time attempting to destabilize some of the rooted perceptions of classification of living beings. Much of this living biological matter can, in theory, be co-cultured and fused (cell fusion), or share its sterile environment (to varying degrees of success). Age, gender, race, species, and location do not play the same roles in the Extended Body as in other living bodies. Research on co-culturing animal and plant cells is currently being conducted.[1] This means that, in theory, every tissue in every living being has the potential to become part of this collection of living fragments. The Extended Body can be seen as an amalgamation of the human extended phenotype and tissue life; the fragmented body that can only survive by technological means: a unified body for disembodied living fragments, and an ontological device, set to draw attention to the need for re-examining

FIGURE 4.1. The Tissue Culture & Art Project, *Victimless Leather*—a Prototype of Stitch-less Jacket grown in a Technoscientific "Body" 2004. *Source*: The Tissue Culture & Art Project (Oron Catts and Ionat Zurr). Hosted at SymbioticA—the Centre of Excellence in Biological Arts, School of Anatomy, Physiology and Human Biology, the University of Western Australia. Copyright the Tissue Culture & Art Project.

current taxonomies and hierarchical perceptions of life. The Extended Body is by no means a fixed, scientifically binding order; it rather is a soft, artistic, and conceptual view of the subject of technologically mediated and augmented life. [. . .]

The flexibility and versatility (vulnerability) of the Extended Body "opens up" a niche for new semi-living semi-beings. It is our intent to take their—the Extended Body—"point of view" in order to examine new taxonomies and our new relations with the living and semi-living world around us from a fresh perspective.

Honor Fell (1900–1986), one of the pioneers in the field of tissue culture, encouraged her scientists to adopt what she referred to as "the tissue culture point of view"[2] as a way to better understand the processes and needs of cells in vitro. In TC&A, we are trying to expand this non-anthropocentric aspiration to a somewhat more complex "entity," which is not human and not nonhuman, but rather a semi-living being. This way we hope to open up a fresh perspective from which to discuss humans' relations to other beings.

Our position may be somewhat reductionist, however not as reductionist as taking the DNA or the code point of view (the non-living/information-based point of view). We are taking a position that is reductionist with regard to the complexity of the living being; however, this reduction to a more visceral point of view enables, at least from a symbolic perspective, the engagement with different complexities, which are defining notions of living, non-living, species, race, gender, the individual, as well as the I (Am I a discrete being? Am I an accumulation of all my cells?). [. . .]

However, everything is not all-engulfing and harmonious in the Extended Body metaphor (or in the Extended Body community, in which scarce resources can lead to a struggle for life and death, and the chance of contamination and death is almost inevitable).

One more complication arising from the Extended Body as a manifestation of the techno-scientific project is that it may create an illusion of a victimless existence. There is a shift from "the red" in the teeth and claws of nature to a mediated nature. The victims are pushed farther away; they still exist, but are much more implicit.

Parts of the living are fragmented and taken away from the context of the host body (and this act of fragmentation is a violent act) and are introduced to a technological mediation that further "abstracts" their liveliness.

By creating a new class of semi-being, which is dependent on us for survival, we are also creating a new class for exploitation.

NOTES

1. Research on two artistic projects involving the cultivation of plant and animal cells in the same environment currently is underway in Symbiotic A; cell fusion between carrot and frog cells has been achieved in 1970 by Harris.
2. Cited in S. Squier, "Life and Death at Strangways" in P. Brodwin (ed.), Biotechnology and Culture: Bodies, Anxieties, Ethics (Indiana University Press: Bloomington, IN, 2000).

Chapter Five

A FEMINIST GENEALOGY OF POSTHUMAN
AESTHETICS IN THE VISUAL ARTS

FRANCESCA FERRANDO

In the posthuman[1] era, the decision to strictly focus on works produced by (self-identified) female artists could be criticized as essentialist, for it suggests the possibility of pursuing an analysis based on a set of bio-cultural characteristics. I shall thus clarify that such a move is currently needed for strategic reasons, to reestablish an inclusive genealogy of the posthuman itself. Posthumanism is becoming a highly fashionable trend. By going mainstream, the hierarchical schemata that (Critical, Cultural and Philosophical) Posthumanism (Wolfe, 2010; Braidotti, 2013) wishes to deconstruct are reappearing, affected by what may be defined as hegemonic essentialism—that is, the historiographical tendency and methodological habit of quoting "thinkers, artists or theorists who belong to the cultural hegemony" (Ferrando, 2012: 13) who often are, in the current episteme, white and male. In line with a posthumanist methodology, this genealogy wishes to maintain a comprehensive and inclusive way of recognizing the large variety of artists who have contributed to the development of Post-human Studies. Given such premises, I will adopt a strategic essentialist standpoint (Spivak, 1987) to emphasize the centrality of female artists in the development of posthuman aesthetics. And still, it is important to remark that there is no specific type of woman who can symbolically represent every woman ever born, but there are women (in the plural form) with different social and individual characteristics. The postmodern feminist shift offered controversial interpretations of the concept of "woman" itself, presenting it as a cultural construct (Butler, 1990) to the extent of what has been criticized as a "Feminism without women".[2] In the following, I should mention that I will only address artists who were born after the first wave of Feminism, although not all of them defined themselves as feminist. From a queer perspective, it shall be noted that a considerable number of them shared an open view on sexuality, which did not fit into heterosexual normativity.

Another important aspect to highlight is that this genealogy will focus only on the visual arts, not including artists who have expressed posthuman intentions in other forms, such as science fiction (that is, Octavia Butler, Marge Piercy and Kathy Acker), electronic music (such as Pauline Oliveros, Laurie Anderson and Pamela Z) or dance (Pina Bausch, Anna Halprin and Tai Lihua, among others). There are different reasons why I have chosen this type of analysis. Visual culture has played an increasing role in the development of Western civilization, becoming central in the elaboration of Modernity, as Foucault (1975) pointed out in his articulation of Panopticism; it has replaced logocentrism, turning into a distinctive feature of Postmodernism, to the extent that Baudrillard (1994) saw the simulacrum not as a copy of the real, but as a reality of its own, the hyperreal. Cybernetics has only augmented the power of representation. Programmers have developed codes that mostly relate to one sense, the sight, leaving other senses such as taste, smell and, to a lesser extent, touch, in a marginal position. In the words of Judith Halberstam and Ira Livingston: "The posthuman body is a technology, a screen, a projected image" (Halberstam and Livingston, 1995: 3). Our posthuman present is visual, interactive and linkable; the power of representation in knowledge production is becoming less and less innocent, if it has ever been.[3] [. . .]

Futurism. To reassemble a map of posthuman grandmotherhood, I will focus on the three main avant-garde movements that arose in Europe at the beginning of the XX century: Futurism, Dadaism and Surrealism. Let us begin with Futurism—the term was coined by Filippo Tommaso Marinetti in "The Futurist Manifesto" (1909/2006), and shall not be confused by the contemporary use of the word to refer to scientists and social theorists engaged in the attempt of predicting the future of humankind and life in general. There are many reasons why Futurism should be listed in this genealogy, including the fact that it has been regarded as one of its sources by Transhumanism, especially in Europe and, particularly, in Italy.[4] First of all, I would like to emphasize its drive towards the future, which was not perceived as something to come in a chronological way, but it was welcomed in a "here and now" mode, and it relied in accepting the new possibilities offered by the present. Futurism was about dynamism; its artistic research was not aimed to express objects in movement, but movement itself, creating an aesthetic of simultaneity. To generate a space for dynamic imagination, Futurism wished to pose a symbolic break from the past. This is one of the crucial differences with Posthumanism, which, to fully embrace the future, does not disregard the past. On the contrary, Posthumanism draws on many different sources, histories and herstories,[5] in an academic attempt of inclusiveness that opens to other species and hypothetical life forms: from non-human animals to artificial intelligence, from aliens to the possibilities related to the physic notion of a multiverse. As I have stated in a previous article: "Posthumanism offers a theoretical invitation to think inclusively, in a genealogical relocation of humanity within universality ('Posthumanism' as a criticism of humanism, anthropocentrism and universe-centrism), and alterity within the self ('Posthumanism' as a recognition of those aspects which are constitutively human, and still, beyond human comprehension)" (Ferrando, 2014b: 220).

Another important difference between Futurism and Posthumanism regards life. In its attempt to decentre the human from the centre of the discourse, Posthumanism opens to environmentalism and animal rights; if it embraces technology as essentially human (Gehlen, 1957; Stiegler, 1998), it still warns about its destructive side, already experienced through many catastrophes, such as the drop of the atomic bomb or the ecological impact of industrialization. By contrast, the futurist exaltation of contemporary challenges included the fascination with war, defined by Marinetti as "the only world's hygiene" (Marinetti, 2006: 14), and with machines, as we can read in his "Technical Manifesto of Futurist Literature" (1912/2006): "we are preparing for the creation of mechanical man, one who will have parts that can be changed" (*Ibid.*: 113–114). Even though the term "cyborg" was articulated much later by Clynes and Kline (1960), we can trace in Futurism the fatherhood of such conceptualization. Marinetti also foresaw its militaristic developments; in "Extended Man and the Kingdom of the Machine",[6] he wrote: "This non-human, mechanical species, built for constant speed, will quite naturally be cruel, omniscient and war-like" (*Ibid.*: 87).

The fascination with speed, machinery and war was shared within the movement by men and women alike, as remarked in the "Manifesto of Futurist Woman" (1912/2001).[7] Despite the chauvinist and contradictory value of the futurist discourse,[8] a high number of female artists joined the movement, as an act of challenge and criticism towards the female stereotypes of self-denial and sacrifice theorized hitherto for women. There are many futurist painters we can recall, such as Rougena Zátková (1885–1923), Benedetta Cappa Marinetti (1897–1977), Marisa Mori (1900–1985), Olga Rozanova (1886–1918) and Alexandra Exter (1882–1949), but I will focus in particular on two specific artists for different reasons: the Russian painter Natalia Goncharova (1881–1962), and the Italian painter Olga Biglieri Scurto (1916–2002). Natalia Goncharova[9] was not only one of the main contributors to Russian Futurism, but also one of the founders of Rayonism, a style of abstract art that she developed in 1911 with her companion, painter Mikhail Larionov (1881–1964), after hearing a series of lectures about Futurism by Marinetti. Rayonism focussed on representing the rays of light reflected from objects, rather than objects themselves, in a pre-intuition of the central role of light in virtual reality and the consequent electrical infrastructure of cyberspace. Our other posthuman futurist grandmother is Olga Biglieri Scurto, Barbara,[10] who I will present not only for her futuristic paintings and attitude (she became a patented pilot at only 18 years of age, before she even encountered Futurism), but also for the fascinating twist in her own poetics. Her life crosses the XX century, starting with her adhesion to Futurism, passing through World War II and the death of her husband; she then encountered Feminism and the philosophy of Luce Irigaray, which she elaborated in her "noetic paintings"; she finally became a strong supporter of the peace movement and donated her piece "L'Albero della Pace" (1986) to the Hiroshima Peace Memorial Museum.

Dada. If Futurism sustained the war and the Fascist drive to colonization, Dada arose at the outbreak of War World I as a cultural movement of protest against such expansionist policies. Henry Ball, author of the first Dada Manifesto (1916), stated: "For us, art is not an end in itself (. . .) but it is an opportunity for the true perception and criticism of the times we live in" (Ball, 1974: 58).[11] Before presenting our dada grandmothers, I would like to mention the prosthetic work of US artist Anna Coleman Ladd (1878–1939), who produced masks of thin copper for soldiers who were disfigured in World War I; such masks were sculpted and painted to resemble the portraits of the soldiers before their disfigurement. The connection between war mutilations and dada aesthetics has been widely remarked. As Stanton B. Garner has stated: "To place (. . .) the body-object hybrids of Dada collage and photomontage next to war-time prosthetic devices, (. . .) is to glimpse the wider cultural field where the modern body was fragmented, altered, and re-imagined" (Garner, 2007: 507). Anti-bourgeois and anarchistic in nature, Dadaism strongly repudiated the war, as we can read in Ball's words: "The war is based on a crass error. Men have been mistaken for machines. Machines, not men, should be decimated" (Ball, 1974: 22). More than ludditism, what characterized Dadaism was a cynical approach towards ideas of progress and control. Dada artists did not reject the machine, they actually embedded the mechanic in their aesthetics. Some of them, such as Marcel Duchamp (1887–1968) and Francis Picabia (1879–1953), went so far as to develop a dada machine art, but the specificity of such machines can be found in their futility and nonsense, in an interpretation of the new that radically differed from Futurism: the advances of technology were recognized by Dadaism as part of a larger reality, chaotic and existentially unstable, anticipating the uncanny feelings often associated with cyborgism.[12]

Even if there are many dada artists whose artworks have contributed to create a posthuman canon, such as Sophie Tauber-Arp (1889–1943), Sonia Delaunay (1885–1979) and Beatrice Wood (1893–1998), in this visual genealogy I will focus on German artist Hannah Höch (1889–1978), following Matthew Biro's suggestion, who places the motherhood of the cyborg in the Dada movement,[13, 14] and, specifically, in her collages. Extending the origins of the cyborg to Dadaism offers not only the possibility of an alternative genealogy to the functional definition articulated by Clynes and Kline of cyborgs as "self-regulating man-machine systems" (Clynes and Kline, 1960: 31) conceived "to meet the requirements of extraterrestrial environments" (*Ibid.*: 29), but also to the militaristic one foreseen by Marinetti. Such re-rooting, as Biro has stated, "expands the concept beyond its traditional definition (. . .) including the cyborg as representing hybrid identity in a broad sense" (Biro, 2009: 1). [. . .]

This genealogy elaborates on the richness and variety of the artists presented, emphasizing the contribution of female radical imagination to the present and to the forthcoming times. Starting with the main avant-garde movement of the first half of the twentieth century, [. . .] this genealogy passes through the sixties and seventies, with the feminist exploration of the body opened by performance art. It lastly takes into account the nineties and its radical re-elaboration of the self: from Cyberfeminism and its revisitation of technology, to the insights of bioart; from critical techno-orientalist readings of the future, to its political and social articulations, pointed out by Afrofuturism and Chicanafuturism. The great variety of works, inputs and perspectives presented, demonstrates the need to maintain a comprehensive methodological approach of the posthuman, avoiding cultural appropriations and discriminatory erasures [. . .] of [. . .] visionary artists, whose works have radically contributed to the configuration of posthuman aesthetics and, more in general, to the manifestation of the posthuman turn.

NOTES

1. The posthuman is an umbrella term for different types of movements, including Posthumanism, Transhumanism, New Materialism, Antihumanism and Meta-humanism. On the differences and relations between all these movements, see Ferrando (2014a). On the specific differences between Posthumanism and Transhumanism, see Ranisch and Sorgner (2014).

2. Such criticism is emphasized in the title of Tania Modleski's homonymous essay, 1991.

3. In Rosi Braidotti's words: "to see is the primary act of knowledge and the gaze the basis of all epistemic awareness" (Braidotti, 1994: 80).

4. Roberto Campa, the President of the Italian Transhumanist Association, has stated: "siamo gli eredi del futurismo italiano e russo, siamo neofuturisti, anche se il prefisso 'neo' non dovrebbe nemmeno essere necessario. Il futurismo è per definizione un movimento di idee e d'azione che rinnova perennemente se stesso, guardando sempre avanti" (Guerra, 2009).

5. In the late sixties, the neologism "herstory" was coined as a revisitation of "*history*", which, even though it originally derives from ancient Greek ἵστωρ (witness) and so it did not embed the masculine form in its signifier, perfectly suited its signified, in a sort of semiotic freudian slip. In their work "Words & Women", Casey Miller and Kate Swift wrote: "When women in the movement use *herstory*, their purpose is to emphasize that women's lives, deeds, and participation in human affairs have been neglected or undervalued in standard histories" (Miller *et al.*, 1991: 146). In this passage, I am using the term "herstory" to refer specifically to the historical experience of women, which was mostly left unrecorded, but has been traced using alternative means, such as oral history, private diaries and handcrafts.

6. Written in 1910, it was first published in "Guerra sola igiene del mondo" (1915/2006, b) (*Ibid.*: 85–88).

7. Written in 1912 by Valentine de Saint-Point as a response to Marinetti's Futurist Manifesto (1909/2006), it states: "Women are Furies, Amazons, Semiramis, Joans

of Arc, Jeanne Hachettes, Judith and Charlotte Cordays, Cleopatras, and Messali-nas: combative women who fight more ferociously than males, lovers who arouse, destroyers who break down the weakest and help select through pride or despair" (de Saint-Point, 1912/2001: 214).

8. In "The Foundation and Manifesto of Futurism", Marinetti (2006: 14) wrote: "We wish to glorify war—the sole cleanser of the world—militarism, patriotism, the destructive act of the libertarian, beautiful ideas worth dying for, and scorn for women".

9. In 2007 she became the world's most expensive female painter: her painting "Picking Apples" (1909) was sold for £4.9 million.

10. I have discovered Barbara and her interest for Luce Irigaray, thanks to Prof. Franc-esca Brezzi, author of the exhaustive essay: "Quando il futurismo è donna. Barbara dei colori" (2009).

11. It is interesting to note that, in the view of German philosopher Peter Sloterdijk: "Dada is basically neither an art movement nor an anti-art movement, but a radical 'philosophical action'. It practices the art of a militant irony" (1987: 391).

12. For an articulated presentation of the cyborg and the uncanny, see Grenville (2001).

13. Such roots were already pointed out by Jennifer González in the article "Envisioning Cyborg Bodies: Notes from Current Research" (1995).

14. "The cyborg was, paradoxically, also a creature on which many Weimar artists and other cultural producers could project their utopian hopes and fantasies" (Biro, 2009: 1).

REFERENCES

Ball H (ed) (1916) *Dada Manifesto*. In: Ball H *Flight Out of Time: A Dada Diary*. Viking Press: New York, pp 219–221.

Ball H (1974) *Flight Out of Time: A Dada Diary*. Viking Press: New York.

Ballard JG (1973) *Crash*. Jonathan Cape: London.

Baudrillard J ([1981] (1994)) *Simulacra and Simulation*. The University of Michigan Press: Ann Arbor, MI.

Biro S (2009) *The Dada Cyborg: Visions of the New Human in Weimar Berlin*. The University of Minnesota: Minneapolis, MN.

Braidotti R (1994) *Nomadic Subjects: Embodiment and Sexual Difference in Contemporary Feminist Theory*. Columbia University Press: Cambridge, UK.

Braidotti R (2013) *The Posthuman*. Polity: Cambridge, UK.

Brezzi F (2009) *Quando il Futurismo è Donna: Barbara dei Colori*. Mimesis: Milano, Italy.

Butler J ([1990] (1999)) *Gender Trouble: Feminism and the Subversion of Identity*. Routledge: New York.

Clynes ME and Kline NS (1960) Cyborgs and space. *Astronautics*; 5 (9): 26–27, 74–76. Reprinted. In: Hables Gray, C and Figueroa-Sarriera, HJ (eds) (1995), 29–34.

De Saint-Point V (1912/2001) Manifesto of futurist woman. In: Caws MA (ed) *Manifesto: A Century of Isms*. University of Nebraska Press: Lincoln, NE, pp 213–216.

Ferrando F (2012) Towards a posthumanist methodology: A statement. *Frame Journal for Literary Studies*; **25** (1): 9–18.

Ferrando F (2014a) Posthumanism, transhumanism, antihumanism, metahumanism, and new materialisms: Differences and relations. *Existenz*; **8** (2): 26–32.

Ferrando F (2014b) The body. In: Ranisch R and Sorgner SL (eds) *Post- and Transhumanism: An Introduction*. Peter Lang Publisher: New York, pp 213–226.

Foucault M ([1975] (1995)) *Discipline and Punishment: The Birth of the Prison*. Vintage Books: New York.

Garner SB (2007) The gas heart: Disfigurement and the dada body. *Modern Drama*; 4 (50): 500–516.

Gehlen A ([1957] (1980)) *Man in the Age of Technology (European Perspectives)*. Columbia University Press: New York.

González J (1995) Envisioning cyborg bodies: Notes from current research. In: Hables Gray C and Figueroa-Sarriera HJ (eds) *The Cyborg Handbook*. Routledge: New York, pp 267–279.

Grenville B (ed) (2001) *The Uncanny: Experiments in Cyborg Culture*. Arsenal Pulp Press: Vancouver, BC.

Guerra R (2009) Tutto il Potere ai Cyborg! Intervista a Riccardo Campa. *Associazione Italiana Transumanisti*; online publication 26 January 2012: Transumanisti.it.

Halberstam J and Livingston I (eds) (1995) *Posthuman Bodies*. Indiana University Press: Bloomington, IN.

Marinetti FT (1909/2006) The futurist manifesto. In: Berghaus G (ed) *Critical Writings: F. T. Marinetti*. Farrar, Straus & Giroux: New York, pp 13–16.

Marinetti FT (1912/2006) Technical manifesto of futurist literature. In: Berghaus G (ed) *Critical Writings: F. T. Marinetti*. Farrar, Straus & Giroux: New York, pp 107–119.

Miller C and Swift K ([1976] (1991)) *Words & Women: New Language in New Times*. HarperCollins Publishers: New York.

Ranisch R and Sorgner SL (eds) (2014) *Post- and Transhumanism: An Introduction*. Peter Lang Publisher: New York.

Sloterdijk P ([1983] (1987)) *Critique of Cynical Reason*. University of Minnesota Press: Minneapolis, MN.

Spivak G (1987) *In Other Worlds: Essays in Cultural Politics*. Routledge: London.

Stiegler B (1998) *Technics and Time, 1: The Fault of Epimetheus*. Stanford University Press: Stanford, CA.

Wolfe C (2010) *What is Posthumanism? Posthumanities Series*. University of Minnesota Press: Minneapolis, MN.

Chapter Six

ANIMALITY AND BLACKNESS

ZAKIYYAH IMAN JACKSON

While many scholars have critiqued the conflation of black humans with animals found in Enlightenment discourses, many have also fundamentally misrecognized the logic behind the confluence of animality and racialization. Enlightenment thought should not simply be considered from the perspective of black 'exclusion' or 'denied humanity' but rather as the violent imposition and appropriation—inclusion and recognition—of black(ened) humanity in the interest of plasticizing that very humanity, whereby 'the animal' is one but not the only form blackness is thought to encompass. Plasticity is a mode of transmogrification whereby the fleshy being of blackness is experimented with as if it were infinitely malleable lexical and biological matter, such that blackness is produced as sub/super/human at once, a form where form shall not hold: potentially 'everything and nothing' at the register of ontology. It is perhaps prior scholarship's interpretation of this tradition as 'denied humanity' that has facilitated a call for greater inclusion, as a corrective to what it deems is a historical exclusion of blackness. One consequence of this orientation is that many scholars have essentially ignored alternative conceptions of being and the nonhuman that have been produced by blackened people.

I pose three arguments to fundamentally reframe the animalization of blackness. First, I argue that philosophers' and historians' emphasis on antiblack formulations of African reason and history have overlooked the centrality of gender, sexuality, and maternity in the animalization of blackness. Liberal humanism's basic unit of analysis, 'Man', produces an untenable dichotomy—'the human' versus 'the animal,' whereby the black(ened) female is posited as the abyss dividing organic life into 'human' or 'animal' based on wholly unsound metaphysical premises. I argue that black female flesh persistently functions as the limit case of 'the human'. This is largely explained by the fact that, historically, the delineation between species has fundamentally hinged on the question of reproduction; in other words, the limit of the human has been determined by how the means and scene of birth are interpreted.

Second, Eurocentric humanism needs blackness as a prop in order to erect whiteness: to define its own limits and to designate humanity as an achievement as well as to give form to the category of 'the animal'. Current scholarship in posthumanism, animal studies, new materialism, and theories of biopolitics has begun a broad inquiry into the repercussions of defining 'the human' in opposition to 'the animal'. *Becoming Human* clarifies the terms of the relationship between what Cary Wolfe calls the "discourse of species" and racial discourse by demonstrating that racialized gender and sexuality serve as an essential horizon of possibility for the production of "the animal" as a preoccupation of Modern discourse.[3] At times antiblackness colors nonhuman animal abjection. Anxieties about conquest, slavery, and colonial expansionism provided the historical context for both the emergence of a developmental model of 'universal humanity' and a newly consolidated generic 'animal' that would be defined in nonhuman *and* human terms. In this context, discourses on 'the animal' and 'the black' as well as those on 'race' and 'species' were conjoined and are now mutually reinforcing narratives in the traveling racializations of the globalizing West. Both science's and philosophy's foundational authority articulate black female abjection as a prerequisite of 'the human', and this abjection helps give credence to the linear taxonomical or ontological thinking present scholarship is trying to displace. Thus, racialized formations of gender and sexuality are actually central rather than subsidiary to the very human–animal binarism recent scholarship hopes to dislodge.

My third argument is for a decisive break with a commonly held position in the study of race. I do not propose the extension of human recognition as a solution to the bestialization of blackness. Recognition of personhood and humanity does not annul the animalization of blackness. Rather, it reconfigures discourses that have historically bestialized blackness. Forms of human recognition—inclusion in biological conceptions of the human species and the transition from native to universal human subject in law and society—are not at odds with animalization. Thus, animalization is not incompatible with humanization: what is commonly deemed dehumanization is, in the main, more accurately interpreted as the violence of humanization or the burden of inclusion into a racially hierarchized universal humanity. I look beyond recognition as human as the solution to the bestialization of blackness, by drawing out the dissident ontological and materialist thinking in black expressive culture, lingering on modes of being/knowing/feeling that gesture toward the overturning of Man.

Within the structure of much thought on race there is an implicit assumption that the recognition of one as a human being will protect one from (or acts as an insurance policy against) ontologizing violence. Departing from a melancholic attachment to such an ideal, I argue that the violence and terror scholars describe is endemic to the recognition of humanity itself—when that humanity is cast as black. A recognition of black humanity, demonstrated across these pages, is not denied or excluded but weaponized by a conception of 'the human' foundationally organized by the idea of a racial telos. For Wynter, the Negro is not so much excluded from the category Man and its overrepresentation of humanity but foundational to it as its antipodal figure, as the nadir of Man. I argue that the recognition of humanity and its suspension act as alibis for each other's terror, such that the pursuit of human recognition or a compact with 'the human' would only plunge one headlong into further terror and domination. Is the black a human being? The answer is hegemonically yes. However, this, in actuality, may be the wrong question as an affirmative offers no assurances. A better question may be: If being recognized as human offers no reprieve from ontologizing dominance and violence, then what might we gain from the rupture of 'the human'?

As long as 'the animal' remains an intrinsic but abject feature of 'the human', black freedom will remain elusive and black lives in peril, as 'the animal' and 'the black' are not only interdependent representations but also entangled concepts. While there are particular Euroanthropocentric discourses about specific animals, just as there are particular forms of antiblack racialization based on ethnicity, gender, sexuality, and national origin, for instance, these particularizing discourses are in relation to the organizing abstraction of 'the animal' as 'the black'. To disaggregate 'humanity' from the production of 'black humanity', the one imposed on black(ened) people, assumes one could neutralize blackness and maintain the human's coherence. But the neutralization of blackness requires the dissolution of discourses on 'the animal' and vice versa, but that is, to say the least, unlikely because 'the animal' is a mode of being for which Man is at war. What is more plausible is that attempts to neutralize blackness and 'the animal' will continue to be in practice, if not word, a means of discipline and eradication.

NOTES

1. *Sylvia Wynter: On Being Human as Praxis*, ed. by Katherine McKittrick (Durham: Duke University Press, 2015), p. 23.
2. Zakiyyah Iman Jackson, *Becoming Human: Matter and Meaning in an Antiblack World*, Sexual Cultures (New York: New York University Press, 2020), p. 14.
3. Cary Wolfe, *Animal Rites: American Culture, the Discourse of Species, and Posthumanist Theory* (Chicago: University of Chicago Press, 2003), p. 2.

Chapter Seven

ASSERTING ABORIGINAL TERRITORIES IN CYBERSPACE

Interview with the artist Skawennati

AMY GE

FIGURE 7.1 *Becoming Sky Woman* from *'She Falls For Ages'* (2016). Courtesy: Skawennati.

Skawennati is a Mohawk multimedia artist who currently resides in Montreal, QC. She is a Co-Director of Aboriginal Territories in Cyberspace (AbTeC), a research network of artists, academics and technologists investigating, creating, and critiquing Indigenous virtual environments and also co-directs their Skins workshops in Aboriginal Storytelling and Digital Media. Recently, she served as the 2019 Indigenous Knowledge Holder at McGill University. We met Skawennati at this year's *WOW Dinner*, an event celebrating inclusion in the tech industry. In a report conducted by Tech for All, statistics show that less than 1% of all tech roles in Toronto were occupied by indigenous folks. That is why we at Feminuity were particularly fascinated by Skawennati's art and sat down with her to learn more about the need for more indigenous perspectives in tech.

AMY GE: Could you tell us about your art and particularly the medium called Machinima?

SKAWENNATI: Well, Machinima itself is simply making movies in virtual environments. Virtual environments are like video games, where you have an avatar and can operate that avatar to move around and do things that you want it to do. I use a game, or massively multiplayer online world called Second Life. So, it's a lot like making a movie. Instead of casting people, I customize avatars. I write a script. I get the avatars' wardrobe and hairstyling. And I find voice talent to record the voices of the dialogue.

AMY GE: You've mentioned that the machinima, *She Falls For Ages*, is a retelling of the creation story in a futuristic setting. This is really interesting because there is a mainstream portrayal of indigenous folks as always being stuck in the past. You've consciously placed their stories into the future. Could you talk a little bit about that?

SKAWENNATI: One of the things I wanted to do was provide the world with images of indigenous people in the future. I love to think about what we'll be doing, how will we look, who we will be in a relationship with in the future. I also love to think about some of the incredible concepts and cultural artifacts and policies and thoughts that our ancestors had that made them think they were so great that they wanted to survive. How can those translate into the future? How can we re-adapt them or revitalize them or basically bring them with us into the future?

AMY GE: Your art seems to be driven by this theme of 'time', whether it's about the past or the future or just the act of change and transformation itself. What drew you to that idea?

SKAWENNATI: I have always been a fan of science fiction, because I loved thinking about the future. But at one point I realized that Native people are rarely shown in the future. In literature, movies and video games, we are used to represent the past.

It made me think that the tragic statistics associated with Native people, such as the highest dropout rate, highest incarceration rate, and a very high suicide rate in the country, could be linked to the fact that we couldn't see ourselves in the future. There's a real political urgency to it. I felt that we needed to have some different images to work from.

AMY GE: I view your work as a piece of resistance because a lot of the narratives about indigenous folks in Canada have been rewritten by those in power to mitigate the atrocities that happened—which is a reprehensible way of retelling stories. But you're rewriting these narratives in a positive light, because you're thrusting them into the future and showing indigenous people that they do have a place there and that they do survive.

SKAWENNATI: That's what I hope. And I think it's also important not to just show us as just surviving, but also thriving. For example, in *TimeTraveller*™, [one of my machinimas], we start off with a young man who lives in the future, but he's not doing so great. He can't find a job and has to work as a hired gun. He lives alone, he's lonely, he doesn't fully know who he is. He knows he's Mohawk, but he doesn't have a good connection to his community. He lives in a storage locker because he can't afford anything better.

And so, the whole story is about him getting to know who he is and then having success: learning to love himself and another person, becoming rich and famous. It's not that I think money and fame equal success, but they are a way of showing success in this society. It's a kind of success that Native people are not often shown having. I made this because I thought it was important to show a rich, famous happy, loving, and loved Native person. That is thriving.

AMY GE: What do you think is the effect of you showing this counter-narrative through tech rather than a live action movie?

SKAWENNATI: That's a great question. No one's ever asked me it like that before. I think I'm using the medium that fits the message. The medium of machinima—especially when using Second Life, where your avatar can fly, your avatar can teleport, your avatar can instantaneously communicate with other avatars—It seems so futuristic to me. And of course, you can build sets that look futuristic. It seemed like it was a great way to convey the future.

AMY GE: Are you working on any new projects right now?

SKAWENNATI: I am and thank you for asking. My team and I recently completed a project called Calico & Camouflage. It began as a virtual fashion collection of "resistance wear" and is based on two patterns and two items of clothing that a lot of Native people relate to. The first pattern, calico, which is a flowery print, is usually found on the ribbon shirt, an element of Haudenosaunee regalia. People wear them to ceremony. People wear them to the UN when they're representing their nation. People wear them to graduation. Some people get married in them. The second is camouflage. During a lot of our significant moments of resistance, such as Wounded Knee, the Oka Crisis, or the Dakota Access Pipeline protests, you can see Native people wearing army clothes.

I thought it would be interesting to put those two things together and make ribbon shirts in camouflage print, and army pants in calico print. With the help of my team at AbTeC, I designed a new calico and also a new camouflage pattern, choosing colours that represent the different landscapes of our time: rural, urban and cyber. The clothing was all created for avatars and then I took their portraits as they held virtual protest signs. I then got the opportunity to show the collection in a real-life runway show, at Indigenous Fashion Week Toronto, so I made all the outfits in real-life as well, custom-printing the fabric and modifying commercial patterns. They are currently in an exhibition at ELLEPHANT called *Calico & Camouflage: Demonstrate. Demonstrate.*

Chapter Eight

FROM *POSTHUMANISM AND THE GRAPHIC NOVEL IN LATIN AMERICA*

EDWARD KING AND JOANNA PAGE

The multiple and often conflicting modes of posthumanism, in their many disciplinary and discursive iterations from philosophy to mass culture, are united in their interrogation of what it means to be human. Noel Castree and Catherine Nash, in their lucid survey of 'post-human geographies', argue that the term posthumanism is 'used to describe a historical condition and to signal a theoretical perspective'. In the first of these, it constructs a narrative concerning ways in which scientific and technological developments—from advances in biotechnology to the increasingly pervasive use of smart devices in everyday objects like fridges and thermostats—are displacing the figure of the human as 'separate and liberated from nature and fully in command of self and non-human others'. This is the posthumanism that is often embraced by mass culture, including the 'humanoids' of DC comics and the 'superhumans' of Marvel satirized in *Watchmen*. It has also been fuelled by decades of speculation in cybernetics concerning the relationship between human intelligence and artificial intelligence and the possibility that the latter may equal or even surpass the former. This is partly why such narratives tend towards a dystopian—and ultimately, thoroughly humanist—vision, registering a nostalgia for a human uniqueness that is under threat and destined to disappear.

Posthumanism as a critical perspective, on the other hand, draws on a history of human-technological-animal entanglements to interrogate the ways in which agency and the production of knowledge have always been the emergent product of a distributed network of human and non-human agents. Critical posthumanisms explore ways in which the construction of the category of the human as separate from and superior to nature is intricately bound up with the assertion of hierarchical differences among humans, both racial and sexual. These perspectives therefore distance themselves from more nostalgic or reactionary narratives of the demise of the human in a technological world, which are often, of course, decidedly humanist in their 'othering' of non-humans—cast as terrifying aliens or robots running amok—and in their desire to replace humans at the centre of history. However, critical posthumanisms also oppose the celebratory modes of posthumanism that triumphantly announce the human transcendence of the prison house of the flesh through technological progress. This fantasy is taken to an extreme in the transhumanist dream of downloading human consciousness into computer systems. In her highly influential work, N. Katherine Hayles argues that these conceptions of posthumanism are actually extensions of the humanist Cartesian privileging of dematerialized consciousness over the body. In order to 'keep disembodiment from being rewritten, once again, into prevailing concepts of subjectivity', she uncovers the erasures of materiality carried out by the dominant discourses of information theory and asserts instead an understanding of the posthuman as grounded in matter and the body.

It is this critical posthumanist framework that we have found most useful for exploring the entanglements between the human and the non-human in Latin America. As Tania Gentic and Matthew Bush have observed, few scholars have worked on posthumanism in the Latin American context. They cite just one, Mabel Moraña, whose book *Inscripciones críticas: Ensayos sobre la cultura latinoamericana* explores the potential in posthumanist thought to challenge the tenets of European humanism to decolonizing effect, thereby 'provincializing Europe' in the manner envisaged by Dipesh Chakrabarty. Moraña's argument would certainly receive support from the graphic novels discussed in this book, whose critiques of European humanism and the ideology of progress contest the dominance of these discourses in historical and contemporary accounts of modernity and, more specifically, in the modernizing principles that governed the founding of the nation in Latin America. [. . .]

The turn to posthumanism [. . .] is intricately bound up with a focus on materiality in studies of media, both old and new. For Pieter Vermeulen, the term indicates not just a framework for thinking about the subjectivities of the digital age but also a 'transition' in the humanities, and in particular literary studies, 'from the excessively textualist and literary focus on deconstruction to a more affirmative engagement with the world outside the text—with bodies, animals, affects, technologies and materialities of different kinds'. The concept of the literary text as dematerialized and independent from its material media supports, and of reading as a practice of forming mental images, may be understood as the counterpart to a Cartesian humanistic conception of subjectivity that divides mind from body. A critical post-humanist perspective should therefore focus on the materiality and embodiment belied by this discourse. This becomes a central purpose in the work of Hayles, which explores posthumanist thought from the basis of a conviction that materiality is a central component in the production of meaning in cultural texts. In *Writing Machines* and *My Mother WAS a Computer*, Hayles constructs methodologies for a posthumanist textualist scholarship that contest the humanistic conception of print literature as 'not having a body, only a speaking mind'. For critical posthumanists, she argues, it is imperative to 'think about what kinds of textuality a dispersed, fragmented, and heterogeneous view of the subject might imply'. Although she does not address comic books or graphic novels, Hayles' focus on artists' books and literary works that reflect on and engage with their own materiality at both a thematic and a formal level provides a useful point of entry for the analysis of the posthumanist graphic fictions emerging from Latin America. The posthuman elements embedded in these texts' narratives are expanded by their emphasis on a materiality that is central to the medium as it continues to morph and mutate in response to the growth of digital culture.

Indeed, the graphic novel as a medium is impossible to analyse as an autonomous, 'unified' and dematerialized entity in the humanist manner decried by Hayles. It is a medium that foregrounds both its unique properties and the weakness of the boundaries that distinguish it from comic book publication practices. As a form, it emphasizes its connections to multiple, sometimes conflicting, visual and literary cultures, as well as its intersections with both popular and elite narrative traditions. [. . .]

Our interest lies in the particular affordances of this medium: what kinds of thought, perception, action or embodiment it makes possible, and how we may understand the specific modes of reading it demands, the materiality of the book, or the book as a transmedial encounter, within the context of a critique of humanism and an exploration of the posthuman. [. . .]

This approach is the one most clearly suggested by the posthumanist graphic fictions that have recently emerged in Latin America, given the very strong relationship in these texts between a thematic focus on posthumanist questions of embodied perception and formal qualities that elicit a bodily engagement on the part of the reader. An understanding of the reading experience as an embodied performance will be developed throughout our analyses. In her account of 'embodied knowledge'—how cultural systems are 'incorporated' through bodily memory and habit—Hayles argues that changes in these 'deeply sedimented' incorporating practices 'are often linked with new technologies that affect how people use their bodies and experience space and time'. The posthumanist graphic novel, we argue, not only narrates modes of dehierarchized incorporation but also actively produces them through the readerly performances demanded by their form. [. . . G]raphic novels intervene in the ongoing process of technological incorporation to question and unsettle the prevailing social hierarchies encoded in humanist conceptions of the body and subjectivity.[. . .] Posthumanist graphic novels typically foreground their position within a complex, constantly morphing media ecology. [. . .]

[T]he characteristic reflexivity and transmediality of graphic novels in Latin America are often used to construct a genealogy for the medium that ties contemporary practice both to ancient forms of visual culture and to futuristic virtual reality technologies. In the hands of Latin American scriptwriters and illustrators, graphic novels become a particularly acute mode of reflection on—and critique of—the new media and technology assemblages that bring humans into intimate relationships with the nonhuman. They represent a unique point of connection between the popular and the elite, the local and the global, the material and the virtual[, . . . and] reveal something of the enormous potential in graphic fiction to embark on a sophisticated exploration of posthuman subjectivity, agency and ethics and to engage in powerful critiques of the hubris of Western humanism and its exploitative, exclusionary modernity.

Chapter Nine

WITNESSING ANIMALS

Paintings and the Politics of Seeing

SUNAURA TAYLOR

What has always moved me to paint is the act of seeing itself. In many ways I am someone who is obsessed with seeing. And by this, I mean very literally looking. As a painter, I have spent countless hours of my life staring at canvasses, at colors, at pictures, at blank walls, at photographs of exploited animals. Like so many other artists, I have been deeply influenced by philosopher Paul Valery's much referenced words: "To see is to forget the name of the thing that one sees."[1]

My earlier work had mostly been portraits of individuals who were close to me, as well as self-portraits that dealt with the complex relationship I had as a disabled person to my own body. It is easy to make the leap from my body to my seeing. From my wheelchair I learned how to see, how to watch the world. Since my tactile skills are weak, my body made up for this by constantly exercising my eyes. I watched the things that others touched. I watched as I waited, as I moved. I do everything with my mouth—I cook, clean, kiss, sing, carry, and paint through my teeth, jaw, tongue and lips . . . and my mouth is very close to my eyes. I see so many things most people don't get the opportunity to really see. When something is carried between one's teeth, it means it must have at one point been staring them in the eye. Every shadow, every color change, every shape and piece of grime is there. This is how I learned to see detail, to pay attention to my visual world; to in effect, fall in love with the act of seeing. My mouth taught me.

But this is too easy; only partly true. As a disabled person, it is too simple to bring everything back to my body. I very likely would have loved seeing if I were able-bodied. In fact, perhaps I notice the things that are close to my eyes in my daily life because of a love of seeing that I would have had regardless of disability. Perhaps I love to see because seeing is political. Who and what we choose to see, when we choose to see—these are political choices we are constantly making.

Animals, and especially animals in factory farms, are an unfortunate example of the ways in which what we choose not to see profoundly affects the lives of others. The private suffering these animals go through is an extremely important place to explore the act of paying attention. In modern day CAFOs (Concentrated Animal Feeding Operations), animals are subjected to terrible violence and are never recognized as living beings. During their brief lives, these animals are seen only as units of production in the ever increasingly efficient machine that is the meat industry.

I often paint from photographs, my own and those taken by others, including imagery that comes from various animal advocacy organizations. Photographs of animal cruelty are usually taken by activists from various organizations who go undercover to expose the atrocities that exist behind the slaughterhouse and factory walls. However, these images are often never seen by the public, or if they are seen, they are largely dismissed as manipulative animal rights propaganda.

I am incredibly grateful that images of this sort are taken, as they are vastly important documents of violence and wrongdoing that have led to various successes in punishing specific instances of cruelty, as well as raising awareness about animal exploitation more generally. Various "ag-gag" bills, which criminalizes shooting this sort of footage, are so scary precisely because of how important this imagery is in the campaign to end animal cruelty. Nonetheless, despite how valuable these images are, there is also something that has always troubled me about how these images are used in campaign literature. Perhaps the trouble comes from the accompanying text with the persistent bold words pleading "Go Veg!," which seems to simply turn these dying or dead animals into slogans. Or perhaps the bad flavor of many of PETA's media antics has rubbed off on these images. Or perhaps the problem of these images is best expressed in a question many artists have asked—what are one's responsibilities when representing exploitation and death?

I have tried to answer the concerns these images raise for me, by transforming this imagery into paint. What happens to images when they transform from something that took an instant to be captured by a camera, into something completely inefficient, something that can take months of individual labor and time spent looking to create? (The dilemma of course is that here, as they appear in this article, the images are once again photos—photos placed beside words and thoughts.) By painting these photographs I hope to transform these images into memorials. They are works of portraiture. Through looking, through paying attention, I mourn these individual animals. The process of seeing is at once political and profoundly personal. It is personal, as trying to see without "names," as Valery describes, is deeply subjective. It's political in its slowness, in its individuality, and its absurd inefficiency. There is something powerful to me about the slowness of painting. It took me more than a year and a half to paint the 102 chickens that make up chicken truck—longer than the actual chickens were alive.

Painting is an utterly inefficient way of creating a representational image in the twenty-first century. But that is why I love it. It's inefficiency. That is one of the most remarkable things about disability too—how fantastically inefficient it is! Of course I am partly joking here, but also serious. Efficiency oppresses both nonhuman animals and human animals: the exhausted and disabled dairy cow is made into meat when she no longer efficiently gives milk; the slaughterhouse worker is laid off when he begins to show signs of disability from the repetitive stress of the job. I like that my body does not follow the laws of efficiency. I will never be the most efficient employee or efficient consumer. I'll take my time—use my mouth or feet instead of my arms—spend a year on a painting that many will say looks like a photo, instead of taking a photo.

Where agricultural animals are rarely seen as anything other than products, disability is rarely viewed beyond stereotype and metaphor.

Hackneyed and problematic representations of disability are consistent and pervasive around us. The politics of seeing (in other words, of representation) is profoundly important in regard to disability.

Disability is a social justice issue, but it's a social justice issue that Americans, and even very progressive Americans, often don't really understand. The way most people view disability betrays a deep misunderstanding of what it means to be disabled. Being disabled is seen as an individual tragedy. The problem is seen solely as a medical one, versus a social, political and economic one.

Disabled people confront stereotypes, stigmas and major civil rights infringements daily due to disability. We are some of the world's poorest peoples, some of the least educated, some of the most likely to be abused, and on top of these things, it is legal to keep us from participating in many social spaces due to physical and attitudinal barriers, to segregate us into institutions and "special" programs, and it is seen as acceptable to talk for us instead of to us (or in the case of those who are nonverbal and profoundly intellectually disabled, to those who know them best and have their best interests at heart).

Historically, and throughout the world, people with physical and mental differences have been marginalized in one way or another—whether through extreme and violent measures such as sterilization, infanticide, eugenics, and institutionalization or through more systematic inequality like impoverishment, institutionalization, imprisonment, and lack of access to housing, work and education. Given all this, our actual physical or cognitive impairments are often the least of our worries.

According to the Convention on the Rights of Persons With Disabilities, "10 percent of the world's population, or 650 million people, live with a disability." Disabled people are actually the world's largest minority.[2] However, most people are still unaware that disability is more complex than a personal narrative.

FIGURE 9.1 (c) SunauraTaylor *Animals With Arthrogryposis*, oil on canvas, 2009, 6' x 9'(72" x 108").

Disability scholars realize how ableist stories reinforce how we are treated socially and politically everyday, but we also realize the same is true of other kinds of representations, images, and cultural perceptions. There are countless ways from pity mongering charity drives to sappy "super-crip" characters in movies to representations in political discourse of disabled people as scroungers, fakers or economic burdens, in which the lived lives of real disabled people are replaced with metaphors and stereotypes. As an artist, I am fascinated by visual discourses of disability: the talented and agile sideshow freak, who uses her mouth or feet to play the guitar or light a cigarette. The invalid in a wheelchair who is surrounded by doctors touching and prodding. The smiling child under a rainbow, who is about to drop the crutches he holds because he believes in a cure.

My other visual work explores these narratives, especially sideshow imagery and medical photography, which are some of the most persistent and enduring discourses of disability. These representations construct disability as exotic, freakish, and horrifying, as well as pitiable, tragic and in need of cure. By altering this imagery with paint, I hope to disrupt these narratives and present disability as something else—a political issue.

With this imagery, it is not the time spent looking that is important to me (these images are actually paint on top of digital prints of photographs), but rather the immediacy of visual intervention. Through painting directly onto the images I alter their meaning, transforming the way disability is seen.

In some of my images my subversive mission is clear—the freaks are "pissing on pity" or flicking the gazers off, but in others my marks are less obvious, asking my audience to critically reflect upon their own assumptions and projections as viewers. I often try to bring attention to the thing that isn't exposed in the image, but that is most desired, most curiously considered and yet left covered: Did a half man have a penis? How hairy was the hairy woman? In my sideshow work, the marks I make often already exist within the fantasy of the gaze and its conflations with the image.

While I expose the freak, I often (but not always) cover up the individuals in the medical photographs. The medicalization of disability forms the ways in which disabled bodies are understood. Doctors probe, measure and stare, but as the joke often goes "at least the Freaks got paid." The medical gaze is calculated, measuring, labeling and dissecting. The patient becomes a body to be cropped, numbered and labeled—not unlike a butcher's diagram. I often erase or white-out the individuals in the medical images in a gesture towards returning privacy to these individuals, but also as a way of removing disability from the gaze of medicine and pathology.

Animals and animality are central themes in this work. By bringing animals or the suggestion of animals directly into this imagery I hope to raise questions about our relationship to their bodies as well. What does it means to be compared to an animal? How and where do the oppressions of animals and the oppressions of disabled people intersect? As a freak, as a patient, I do not deny that I'm like an animal. Instead I want to be aware of the mistreatment that those labeled animal (human and non) experience. I am an animal.

NOTES

1. Weschler, Lawrence, "Seeing is Forgetting the Name of the Thing That One Sees", p. 203
2. http://www.un.org/disabilities/convention/facts.shtml accessed Feb 22nd 2011

Chapter Ten

VIDEO DOG STAR

William Wegman, Aesthetic Agency, and the Animal in Experimental Video Art

SUSAN McHUGH

I'm trying to sell you a new or used car from our downtown lot and trying to talk you into buying one and I hope that if perhaps I have this dog on my lap you'll come to see me as a kind person, because a mean person . . . if I was a mean person and a shark so to speak, this dog wouldn't let me touch him and paw him so; he'd uh, he wouldn't have such faith in me. And so too, just as this dog trusts me, I would like you out there to trust me and come down to our new and used car lot and buy some of our quality cars.

—WILLIAM WEGMAN IN *NEW AND USED CAR SALESMAN* (1978)

William Wegman, the artist whose videos and photographs of his own Weimaraner dogs claim unique cultural prominence as both the subject of a 1990 retrospective at the Whitney Museum of American Art and a recurring feature in daily episodes of the children's public television program *Sesame Street*, used to try to tell people what his dog was thinking. Especially when staged in video format, these attempts to convey cross-species communication gained widespread interest not only because they struck viewers as "funny" or "true" but also because Wegman used to play directly to the video camera, usually in situations contrived to undermine the truth-value of his claims. In these texts, a crucial component of Wegman's challenge to human authority is the presence of his then companion animal, the Weimaraner [breed] dog Man Ray, who, whether read as falling for or openly resisting Wegman's prompts, was a key player in these pieces, undermining the all-too-human power of the artist's statements.

For instance, in *New and Used Car Salesman* (1978), Wegman momentarily drops the monotone sales-pitch monologue he directs, television-advertisement-style, to the camera to turn his attention to his dog. More precisely, he has to stop talking in order to struggle with the dog, who

FIGURE 10.1. William Wegman, Still from *New and Used Car Salesman*, video (black and white, sound), 1973–1974. *Source*: Copyright 2019 William Wegman. Courtesy Electronic Arts Intermix (EAI), New York.

tries to get off of his lap just at the moment when Wegman, speaking as a "new and used car salesman," points to the dog's presence on his lap as evidence of his own trustworthiness. The flash of resistance on the dog's part fades immediately; having redistributed his weight, he settles down again without actually getting off Wegman's lap, and the artist, having paused to wrangle the dog, resumes his droning sales pitch as if it never stopped.

This moment of bodily interaction, formulated as human speech containing a dog's expression of thought, in one sense outlines what Garber (1996) terms an "erotics of dominance," the canine-human resignation to a relationship characterized by power imbalance that is predicated by dogs' inability to speak human languages (p. 125). Yet the interaction also materializes the shifting field of "trust" on which human speech—here conceived as a tired sales pitch—hinges. The synergy of man and dog provides not simply a competing narrative in which the dog turns on the man's speech, quietly taking over the role of the video's star. In this short piece, the cross-species interaction signals the development of a dialectical form in which canine-human interaction and artistic self-reflexivity intersect.[1]

Wegman relies heavily on the dog's spontaneous interaction with prompts, primarily speech, to develop a video aesthetic that both establishes the material conditions of artistic production and challenges conventional conceptualizations of them, particularly the notion of singular artistic agency. The early work with Man Ray, through which Wegman develops this aesthetic, stands in pointed contrast to Wegman's current work, which positions his relationship with his dogs as the very instrument of his own alienation, the trap of a signature-style into which the successful artist is lured and caught by the commercial structures of the fine art industry. But, as *New and Used Car Salesman* suggests, cross-species interaction offers different ways of mediating the relationships among humans, animals, and the institutions of art, a range of aesthetic possibilities that Wegman's work, taken as a whole, explores. Staking out the poles of this spectrum, the selfsame human-canine interaction that once enabled Wegman to disrupt his own self-sales pitch—his supplication to an individualistic and static system of art—now works to confirm it.

These experimental video pieces, weaving together questions of influence with questions of misprision, trouble readings that insist on the absolute identification of artist and dog. They betray, in the broadest sense, Wegman's later "anxiety of influence" (Bloom, 1973) concerning the dog, Man Ray. Although the pieces suggest that Wegman began working with the dog to interrogate the problem of artistic authority, his critics' identification of "the" artist with "his" dog works in tandem with the artist's own retroactive adoption of these terms to exacerbate this very problem by subordinating the contributions of the dog to the promotion of the artist's career. I read the images against these responses, however, to suggest that the success of the early pieces depends on dog and artist's joint ability to erode the one-to-one correspondence framed by their critics' anthropocentric aesthetics.

Confounding this approach to the artwork as the property of a singular author and the dog as therefore a human substitute or object, the Wegman/Man Ray art opens up questions about how such art involves a collective process, an alternate approach that I term "pack aesthetics."[2] To foster this alternate approach, the interspecific context of these pieces is wielded in such a way that it triangulates the process of art making, opening out from a dynamic between human artist and dog model and incorporating multiple artists, assistants, and models in ways that unsettle species boundaries. Without wholly promoting or critiquing a single set of artistic values, the early Wegman/Man Ray images in this way cultivate pack aesthetics, provoking conceptualizations of history, aesthetics, and communication that situate the human within the context of other animal cultures. [. . .]

The crucial point here is that the images trouble the separation between nonhuman cognition and aesthetic systematization, between individual thoughts and their consolidation into cultural forms. What is striking about the Wegman/Man Ray images is that, when these images incorporate the dog's thought processes, they hold the potential not only to resist reduction to simply human terms but also to validate canine culture and, by extension, pack aesthetics. In this respect, the grounds of animal-rights philosopher [Tom] Regan's objection to Wegman's current cross-species-dressing images are illuminating. Regan notes that the images are "offensive," not because they demonstrate cruelty to the dogs but because they erode species boundaries in a way that compromises the dog's difference from the human. The images offer, in Regan's terms, "a way of denying their dogness, so to speak."[3] [. . . Yet] the Wegman/Man Ray videos that incorporate others [such as the 1977 video *Two Dogs*, sometimes known as *Dog Duet*] throw species difference into stark relief, encouraging and inscribing contemplation of their object as well as of these thought processes themselves. Particularly when the texts incorporate other dogs, they not only challenge the exceptional status of the video dog star but also demonstrate how pack aesthetics can inscribe multiple aesthetics across species lines.

NOTES

1. My conception of this video piece in terms of dialectical form derives from Jameson's (1971) idea that "dialectical thought is in its very structure self-consciousness and may be described as the attempt to think about a given object on one level and, at the same time, to observe our own thought processes as we do so: or to use a more scientific figure, to reckon the position of the observer into the experiment itself" (p. 340). As I will argue, Wegman's experimental work engages dialectical thinking by fostering a sense of sociality that includes dogs and, as Jameson argues in his reading of Sartre, in turn emphasizes dynamic and "collective[,] rather than individualistic" and static, systems (p. 244).

2. This concept proceeds from Deleuze and Guattari's (1987) claim that the same individuated animals can function as metaphors for humans as well as metonyms of

heterogeneous "packs" (pp. 240–241). Elsewhere, I relate this dynamic to the emergence of the dog breeding narrative in the twentieth century by developing the related concept of "pack sexualities" (McHugh, 2000, p. 23).

3. Regan initially addressed these concerns at a public lecture and later was contacted by Wegman, who, as Regan recalls, "was surprised that I would take exception to his work" and, after a brief discussion, "relieved to learn that I was not accusing him of cruelty" (personal communication, January 17, 2001). This exchange is striking as well because it is a rare instance of the worlds of art and of animal rights coming into contact.

REFERENCES

Bloom, H. (1973). *The anxiety of influence: A theory of poetry.* New York: Oxford University Press.

Deleuze, G., & Guattari, F. (1987). *A thousand plateaus: Capitalism and schizophrenia* (B. Massumi, Trans.). Minneapolis: University of Minnesota Press.

Garber, M. (1996). *Dog love.* New York: Simon and Schuster.

Jameson, F. (1971). *Marxism and form: Twentieth-century dialectical theories of literature.* NJ: Princeton University Press.

McHugh, S. (2000). Marrying my bitch: J. R. Ackerley's pack sexualities. *Critical Inquiry, 27* (1), 21–41.

Wegman, W. (Director). (1978). New and used car salesman: Reel 4. On *Best of William Wegman, 1970–78* [videocassette]. New York: Electronic Arts Intermix.

Chapter Eleven

INTERVIEW WITH GARRY MARVIN

In It Together

SUSAN McHUGH

SUSAN MCHUGH: So often (so urban?) popular opinions are disconnected from what is involved in animal killing that it must have been especially tricky for you to take on bullfighting as a research subject. I imagine your research subjects were instantly on the defensive, making anthropological analysis tricky.

GARRY MARVIN: What has made bullfighting and hunting difficult research subjects is not the difficulty of analysis or interpretation but the difficulties of access as a researcher because of how those involved in the events have been concerned about the interests and agendas of outsiders. Clearly, bullfighting was an event that had at its heart a set of relationships between men and bulls. But I thought about my fieldwork with matadors, aficionados, and bull breeders not as something *new* but rather as generating a standard, although hopefully interesting, piece of anthropological ethnographic work that attempted to reveal the complexities of the relationships in the event. This I hoped would make a contribution to anthropological studies of Spain, and perhaps to the literature on ritual, rather than contribute to understanding human-animal relations *per se*. My work on bullfighting, in a rather convoluted way, led to my work on English foxhunting and it was then, in the late 1990s, that I began to be aware of the first literature of what was to become human-animal studies (HAS) and it was exciting to discover scholars who thought of human-animal relations in terms of very different concerns. What intrigued me was what drew them to animals. Were they simply in search of new research subjects (a tricky topic that—animals as subjects of research)? Or was this new interest in animals generated because of, in response to, something in the intellectual air at the time that allowed animals to become significant?

SUSAN MCHUGH: As a researcher focused on narrative form, I can't help but note how your story echoes those of Vicki Hearne, Donna Haraway, and others in implicitly rejecting an obvious answer, that is, the notion that HAS ridden in on the coattails of the animal rights movement. And with good reason. The more I think about it, it's for activists that Peter Singer's *Animal Liberation* works as a watershed moment precisely because it extends a tradition of analytical philosophy that remains deeply invested in a notion of rights grounded in individual (read: human) subjects, and that comes to a crisis by the end of the twentieth century. For academics, however, much of the research responsible for changing institutional and intellectual climates today pursues the wildly different potentials opened up by poststructuralist theory, which posits a far more significant liberation of all from the foundational units of humanist thought. Posthuman, nonhuman, counterlinguistic—call it what you like—a major significance of this turn is that it enables discussions of animals as agents, [. . . which] challenges humanist conventions. Reframing the terms from human- to bio-politics, theorists are uncovering alternate traditions—whether in philosophy or biology, through the work of Jakob von Uexküll, Henri Bergson, and so many others—to claim legitimacy for HAS research on these new terms. At least, that's the view from where I embarked in 1997 on my thesis that sought to theorize how animals come to have stories in literary and cultural studies, where and when very few people were venturing, although that has changed abruptly in the last decade. But your much deeper grounding in your discipline makes me pause. Was that what drew you to interdisciplinary work as well?

GARRY MARVIN: In the late 1990s I had been to anthropology conferences in which there were panels on animals and human-animal relationships but our discussions were about ethnographic issues, the intricacies of local cultures and the nature of interpretations. In short: anthropological concerns. I then saw details of Erica Fudge's 1999 *Animals in History and Culture* conference in Bath—this I think was the first HAS conference—and I realized that there was an entirely new field of scholarship. I was unable to attend that conference, but I was able to attend Nigel Rothfels's and Andrew Isenberg's *Representing Animals* conference in Milwaukee in 2000 and it was there that

I really began to see new issues and concerns across a range of disciplines. There I met so many fine scholars and wonderful people . . . that's when it really took off for me.

SUSAN MCHUGH: My sense is that the field emerged through such events. I attended Jo-Ann Shelton's wonderfully interdisciplinary animal studies conference in Santa Barbara earlier in the spring of 2000, but perhaps because of its much larger scale *Representing Animals* proved the decisive event for me, too. From there, it seems easy to trace the history of HAS— through Nigel Rothfels's subsequent edited collection *Representing Animals*, Steve Baker's *Society & Animals* special issue *The Representation of Animals*, Jonathan Burt's *Animal* book series, Erica Fudge's *British Animal Studies Network*, Robert McKay's Sheffield Animal Research Centre (ShARC), to name a few examples that also show how you and I have been in it together ever since—but not really coherently before.

GARRY MARVIN: I use the term HAS and we used it for the Handbook—other people use other terms. How do you understand or define HAS?

SUSAN MCHUGH: HAS emerged as a community of scholars who aren't just positing the same sort of questions from a whole bunch of different directions, but also working hard to respond to each other directly and responsibly, in a way that works to continue the conversations that ultimately build the field. It is not always or equally working that way, and I can't claim to have seen it coming, though in retrospect the project that I was working on at the time—and that eventually became *Animal Stories*—really needed it to happen. Thinking back to 2000, I was a new Ph.D., midway through a harrowing search for a tenure-stream job in literary studies deferred by the line that affect theorist Lauren Berlant captures so brilliantly: "I love your work, but I hate your archive." Small wonder that with HAS folks I felt like a runaway from an abusive home who miraculously finds shelter with fellow travelers. Maybe my experiences reflect how much slower the humanities have been to embrace HAS? Or, to return to the question of formative moments, we could say that they might be better understood as indications of a broader struggle at the center of HAS to move toward studying animals in a new way? And one that is certainly not defined by method or even by subject-matter . . .

GARRY MARVIN: Animals have been unquestionably worthy of academic study in sciences such as biology, ecology, ethology, veterinary medicine, and zoology, but thinking about animals in human lives seems to me to be what is new about HAS. Can we say more, though? Is there some way of thinking about the time being right for this interest? What might that be in intellectual terms? What were the trickles that came together to form streams and then to create a river? Did this require new ways of thinking?

SUSAN MCHUGH: For me, studying verbal and visual representations of the most celebrated and prolific cross-species relations like those of people and dogs has fueled an enormous appreciation for academic as well as creative people who challenge audiences to join them in taking the trivial seriously. Doing so requires developing new languages and forms that respond to the demands of lives shared across species lines, but also conditioned by others' condescension or hostility toward the recognition that the human can never be the sole agent, let alone lay sole claim to the category of agency, in power relations. Again I wonder how different this looks to someone trained as a social scientist as opposed to a humanist, for whom animals conventionally are seen (as psychoanalysts used to say) as bad object-choices.

GARRY MARVIN: For my part, I have always tried to think hard about what sorts of studies we are pursuing and presenting. And I have real difficulties with the idea that we are studying animals, or, rather, how we in the humanities and social sciences can study animals in any significant ways. This is why I have no sympathy with the use of the term "animal studies" for our field or any term that does not have "human" closely attached. Although I am with Haraway when she said that she sought to understand dogs. [. . .] Maybe it is a lack of imagination, but I fail to understand how it is to be an animal can ever be revealed in other than human ways in the most human of enterprises, literature. How does one avoid anthropocentrism when the only languages available to write about animals are human languages? I cannot understand how an animal's subjectivity—its thoughts, emotions, etc.—can be rendered by us in any ways that escape human language and representation. For example, I cannot think how I could have access to how it is to be an elk confronting a pack of wolves and then represent that in elkish terms rather than human terms. Even to say "the wolf howled" traps me in human language, binds me, into an anthropocentricity. But maybe I am being naïve.

SUSAN MCHUGH: I don't think you're being naïve so much as honest about the ways in which HAS shakes our faith in subjectivity as the foundational unit of humanist discourse. The contradictions of voice in writing, embodiment in representation, strike me as other dimensions of the distancing problem, and ones that apply to literary subjectivity as much as to all attempts to capture or, rather, create the illusion of an individual in any media form, whether visual, verbal or both. This is where ethologists' separation of anthropomorphism from anthropocentrism proves especially helpful because it frees recognitions of similarities and differences from teleology.

GARRY MARVIN: I know that you are deeply concerned with ethical issues, but in your work there does not seem to be overt advocacy. Could you say something about this aspect of your research, and also give some thoughts about advocacy and HAS?

SUSAN MCHUGH: I don't know what people mean by scholarship in the service of advocacy unless it involves working as a scholar to advocate for underrepresented fields of study like HAS. Research requires a commitment to empiricism, which in turn presupposes the kind of openness to being surprised at the answers to your initial questions that all too often advocates cannot afford. While I sympathize with efforts to ban cruel practices, I also feel obliged to question what that means in any given situation and to think through the larger process whereby even well-meaning practices become harmful. So that makes me the skunk at the picnic who answers "Are you vegan?" with counter-questions about when and how eating refrigerated meat substitutes sourced in monocropped, genetically modified soy and packaged in non-recyclable or even re-usable petroleum-based plastic constitutes an ethical alternative to consuming animal products. My ethics are not smart in the sexy sense of having sharp, fast answers; instead, all I can do is painfully, plainly, earnestly try to move toward what Marxist literary critic Raymond Williams once termed "the long and difficult revolution of the mind" to rethink the structures of power and everyday life.

GARRY MARVIN: Where does this lead you?

SUSAN MCHUGH: Scary and sad places. Seriously, my current work gravitates towards stories of at-risk or gone human-animal relations, often incredible traditional cross-species achievements erased through extinctions and genocides. It has made me highly aware of something that you touched on earlier, namely, how the most vulnerable populations of humans and animals, who have the most to teach us researchers, yet are often also are those who have the most to lose by engaging with us. But I guess I should back up and ask, what is your position on advocacy in HAS?

GARRY MARVIN: Of course this is immensely complex and I cannot do justice to the literature of the field. So, rather crudely—and there might be other ways of dividing it up—I can think of two broad streams of advocacy-driven research. One might be that which focuses on welfare issues that can be studied "scientifically," for example, a researcher being concerned whether animals in zoos suffer physically, mentally, emotionally in such conditions. In that kind of research, animals could be examined in terms of bodily damage, stress levels, and behavior, and all this could be recorded numerically. Academic papers presenting all these issues could then be used to help zoo authorities to improve conditions in their zoos, or, more generally, as part of a political campaign to improve the welfare of animals or to show that certain animals should never be exhibited in zoos. All this seems fine and commendable. In this sort of research, the focus is on the animals concerned and certain things can be demonstrated here.

SUSAN MCHUGH: So there's quantitative scholarship that informs advocacy. And the other kind?

GARRY MARVIN: Another form of advocacy-driven research also has concerns about animals within the research, but here the focus is a much more critical one of the ways humans are involved with the animals. It is this which clashes with my anthropological approach because it often involves meaning being imposed from outside rather than understanding being drawn from within. It is this which causes me concerns because it is often so speculative, and yet insistent, and so quick to fill in the blanks of broad statements like "Meat eaters are X," "Hunters are Y," or "Zoo visitors are Z", without making the effort to understand what is going on. I totally understand why many people find bullfighting abhorrent, but I do not believe that starting with abhorrence leads to understanding in the context of a research project. I am sure that too much of the advocate-researcher's self would be there and make them less open to the complexities of the relationships before them.

SUSAN MCHUGH: It's a danger to all HAS research that investigators taking the second approach might be tempted to force their findings to support their initial hypothesis, however ethically motivated or politically correct it may be. And, while I see your point about outsiders being easily led astray, I've actually struggled most with this problem while attempting to write as an insider. Researching stories of girls and women with horses, it was incredibly satisfying to try to write back against what all of my experiences confirmed as straightforward stupidity, particularly when others' symbolic readings were also so clearly agenda-driven. But I decided that I had to strike lines like "horses are not substitutes for penises" because they detracted from the more compelling questions of why and how sexualized violence has crept into girl-horse stories in the past half-century. In that instance, archival research helped to leverage the necessary critical distance from agendas, including my own, but I know your approach has to be different.

GARRY MARVIN: The anthropology I practice requires what one anthropologist termed "deep hanging out,"—one has to find ways of immersing oneself, over a long period (ethnographic research is slow research), in the culture, the world, of the people one hopes to understand. It is "hanging out" because I seek to join with them, I do not study them, I study with them, I come to any understanding I have only because of my relationships with them. [. . .] Animals have always been significant and necessary (although perhaps unnoticed to those outside them) in many human cultures and societies, and HAS has brought this into the open to a wider audience. Of course, they will have always been noticed by those who live with them or whose lives depend on them. One of my concerns looking at HAS now is that I think, although I might be being unfair here, that the studies have an urban and perhaps 'western' bias or focus.

SUSAN MCHUGH: That's what I'm trying to unpack in my current research, which moves away from examining representations of human-animal relations specific to modern-industrial cultures and deeper into those that get disrupted, even obliterated in the processes of making modern worlds—including, not coincidentally, those that are specific to traditional hunting and farming communities. Some do this by negotiating different communities within ecosystems, but the really interesting ones seem to be calling forth notions of cross-species community on the brink of destruction. These kinds of representations make me wonder: have whole cultures and species died because they are simply unprofitable from a capitalist standpoint? Or more complexly unwanted by the ways in which first-world, urban-industrial-enculturated folks want to force life to be in the twenty-first century?

GARRY MARVIN: For me, such questions are immensely important in thinking about what I would like to see more of in HAS and, personally, where I see my work going. I am certainly not suggesting anything like an agenda; we all develop what we are interested in and for our own good academic reasons. As we already agreed, we both believe that HAS has come of age, and in the last twenty years there has been fabulous work that has brought humans and their animals (and I suppose I should say animals and their humans, although I am less sure of that) to center stage of scholarly interest and concern. However, that stage is still, I believe, a rather regional one.

SUSAN MCHUGH: Yes, there is a live threat that HAS can work to replicate the white, western, patriarchal, heteronormative, ableist, and other dominating notions that warp otherwise well-intended scholarship in other areas as well as activism.

GARRY MARVIN: I am certainly interested in seeing more studies from beyond North America, Western Europe, and Australasia. I hope for a lot more from Africa, the Middle East, South America, Asia, Eastern Europe, the Arctic, the Balkans . . . so many intriguing and complex cultures in which human and animal lives are intertwined, cultures and regions alike that are rich in animals. Of course, as an anthropologist, I would say that—more ethnographies, please!

SUSAN MCHUGH: Yes, although I fear I agree automatically because, as a literary scholar, I learned to dance to the tune of multiculturalism. But, to paraphrase Orwell, doesn't the risk of some animals being more equal than other animals cut both ways?

GARRY MARVIN: I take your point about cultures and species dying out because of unprofitability or, I might add because they are undervalued or unvalued in terms other than economic. I also take your point about human-cultures being complexly unwanted, marked for prohibition and, I would add, unrecognized, not understood or unacknowledged by those outside the immediacy of these concerns; we need to know so much more about human-animal cultures and socialities and those who seek to, need to, maintain them. Here again, I can see a research task of bringing them center stage. So—more multicultures and multispecies in HAS.

SUSAN MCHGUH: Yes, and multiple naturecultures leading to more multi-naturecultural understandings.

GARRY MARVIN: What I am also hoping for is more 'multi' in our HAS community, a bringing together of our particular research and intellectual cultures to produce more interdisciplinarity, although I know that is so hard to achieve. I think Haraway has written about a new zoographic—a new way of researching and writing about animals. In terms of my own research, I am excited about projects I share with biological anthropologists/primatologists, with zoöarcheologists, and with conservation scientists—researchers from different disciplines working jointly on projects. This, I am sure, is a way of tackling the complexities of human-animal relations. HAS has not simply arrived and done good work, it has a future and it is going somewhere. I look forward to sticking with it.

SUSAN MCHUGH: Or, in Haraway's terms, staying with the trouble. That's an exciting prospect, one that will involve leveraging some big culture shifts in the funding and other structures of academics. But the growing pains will be all worthwhile if only because it helps us to continue to be in it together.

Chapter Twelve

FROM *PLANT-THINKING*

A Philosophy of Vegetal Life

MICHAEL MARDER

The productive ambiguity haunting the title of this volume further emphasizes the ineluctable paradoxes of vegetal ontology. "Plant-thinking" refers,
in the same breath, to (1) the non-cognitive, non-ideational, and non-imag-
istic mode of thinking *proper to* plants (what I later call "thinking without
the head"); (2) the human thinking *about* plants; (3) how human thinking
is, to some extent, de-humanized and rendered plant-like, altered by its
encounter with the vegetal world; and finally, (4) the ongoing symbiotic
relation between this transfigured thinking and the existence of plants. A
sound philosophy of vegetal life must rely on the combination of these four
senses of "plant-thinking," so as not to dominate (and in dominating, dis-
tort) the target of its investigations. The chances of aggravating the abuse
of plants by theorizing their existence can be minimized, if the theorists
themselves expose their cogitation to the logic of vegetal life and learn from
it, to the point where their thinking is ready to melt into this logic, with
which admittedly it will never be identical.

No genuine encounter happens without our eventful exposure, unwilled
and unplanned, to that which, or the one who, is thus encountered. "Plant-
thinking" is in the first place the promise and the name of an encounter,
and therefore it may be read as an invitation to abandon the familiar terrain
of human and humanist thought and to meet vegetal life, if not in the place
where it is, then at least halfway. Part I, "Vegetal Anti-Metaphysics," clears

the philosophical ground for this event by putting in question the meta-physical constructions of the plant and of what constitutes "the ground," by showing how in its very being the plant accomplishes a lived destruction of metaphysics, and by carrying out a transvaluation of metaphysical values as they pertain to vegetation. The outcomes of the critique of metaphysics are not entirely negative, given that the contours of plant life come into view as a result of the hermeneutical multiplication of its meanings released from the reductive tendencies of metaphysics that, from Aristotle to Nietzsche, ascribed to it but a single function. Indeed, these contours get redrawn as soon as we turn back to the classical notion of "plant-soul"—a notion that, despite its metaphysical heritage, exceeds the limits of metaphysics from within, to the point of overflowing them—with its countless potentialities, valid, in distinct ways, for plants, animals, and humans.

In discussing plant-soul, it would be unforgivable obdurately to insist on the traditional metaphysical separation between the "soul" and the "body" of the plant, which is only one of the many dichotomies—self and other, depth and surface, life and death, the one and the many, and so forth—practically deconstructed in vegetal existence. The positive dimension of plant-being, as the outcome of the critique of metaphysics, will spell out an inversion of traditional valuations, valorizing the other over the self, sur-face over depth, and so on. More crucially still, it will incorporate the core existential attributes philosophers have tended to reserve for human beings alone. I call the elements of this budding ontology, discussed in part II, "vegetal existentiality."

The intimation that it is high time to approach the existence of plants existentially is surely scandalous within the confines of Heidegger's thought and of post-Heideggerian existentialism, let alone the humanist and anthropocentric traditions of philosophy. In technical terms, its cardi-nal sin is that it transgresses the boundaries, firmly set in *Being and Time*, between the categorial and the existential analytics, between the categories of readiness-to-hand and presence-at-hand and the *existentiales*, such as the moods or anxiety. The initial shock the transgression may provoke will have been absorbed already in the analysis of the vegetal soul in the pre-ceding part of the study, and it should gradually wear off once I formulate and flesh out the central concern of "Vegetal Existentiality": What are the modes of being-in-the-world appropriate to plants? Among such modes, I concentrate on temporality, freedom, and wisdom.

Just as the soul of the plant is hardly distinguishable from its body, so its time is barely dissociable from space: its outward growth and augmentation, devoid of any final accomplishment, constitutes the "bad infinity" of vegetal temporality. To be more precise, the spatio-temporal movement of plants, nonsynchronous with human time, is directed toward and by the other (light, the changing seasons, etc.) and therefore, unfolding as a hetero-temporality, is governed by the time of the other. Seasonal variation, for its part, imposes cyclical and iterable existence on perennial plants and spells out the finitude of the annual ones.

The indissoluble connection of the plant to the time of the other mirrors its spatial rootedness in the soil, a feature responsible for its coding as the figure of unfreedom. Tragically, occidental thought conflates the most plastic form of existence with the most rigid; not only does this view disregard the ontic exuberance and uncontrollable efflorescence of vegetal life, but it also ignores this life's ontological potentialities, still working themselves out in various guises in animals and human beings—the variations that free it to be otherwise than it is. On the one hand, both colloquial and philosophical discourses associate the rooted mode of being with immobility and captivity, but, on the other, the perceived indifference of plants interlaces their freedom with human liberty in the domains of ethics, aesthetics, and religion. Despite their undeniable embeddedness in the environment, plants embody the kind of detachment human beings dream of in their own transcendent aspiration to the other, Beauty, or divinity.

The living tending of plants toward their other, the tending expressed in growth, the acquisition of nutrients, and procreation, amounts to the non-conscious intentionality of vegetal life, the cornerstone of its "sagacity." In keeping with vegetal ontology, plant-thinking practices an embodied, finite, and material expression; is wholly oriented to the other without establishing either an identity or a self-identity achievable by means of its return to itself; and stands for the impersonal, non-individuated *it thinks* underlying and subverting the ever-present synthesis of *I think*, the accompaniment of all conscious representations. The uninterrupted connection between plant-thinking and human thought finally becomes apparent when we circle back to the figure of the vegetal soul—from which the animal and human psyches emanate and which is sublimated (and, to a significant extent, dematerialized) in them—and discover the rudiments of a living intelligence in this figure.

An encounter with plants awaits us. Far from a head-on confrontation, it will verge on what, in Portuguese, is called *desencontro*—an untranslatable word, which roughly refers either to a narrowly missed meeting, a crossing of paths that was about to happen but ended up not taking place, or to an encounter that is too improbable and was never meant to happen, or, again, to a divergence of two or more (usually human) beings, each of them existing on her or his own wavelength. To meet the plants themselves, the plants as such, is not the goal of this study, if only because, in the absence of identity, they are never "themselves" and because, resistant to idealization, they do not fit within the strict philosophical confines of the "as such." All we can hope for is to brush upon the edges of their being, which is altogether outer and exposed, and in so doing to grow past the fictitious shells of *our* identity and *our* existential ontology. Are we ready to take the initial, timid steps in the anamnesis of the vegetal heritage proper to human beings, the very forgetting of which we have all but forgotten? Whether or not we will be capable of recognizing plants, and especially ourselves, in the wake of the anamnestic encounter-*desencontro* is yet to be seen.

Chapter Thirteen

A PROGRAM FOR PLANTS

GIOVANNI ALOI, LINDA TEGG, JOSHI RADIN, AND BRIAN M. JOHN

JOSHI RADIN: Why don't we start with plants?

GIOVANNI ALOI: What came first? Did it all begin because Linda was working with plants? Brian isn't your project about empathy in a way? Playing for plants? Do you see that as empathy?

BRIAN M. JOHN: Absolutely, yes. This started as an idea for something we could do within the show *Mercury*, which Linda and I were collaborating on. We were thinking about the circumstances we'd set up, and then thinking what can we do with that.

How can we activate it in different ways? We knew the plants were going to be in a gallery exhibition context. We asked, "what can we do for them or with them to activate the exhibition differently," is that fair to say?

LINDA TEGG: Yes. We were considering the gallery as a site of cultural production. We had already decided to cultivate plants in the gallery, from within this process we wanted to see where else our thinking might lead, what possibilities would open up. It wasn't a large leap to begin thinking about the Video Data Bank, an archive of video art works that are maintained at the school, as a source of nourishment for the plants. So, I think there is confluence there as well.

BRIAN M. JOHN: It was a generous enough gesture towards both, the archive and the plants, that it didn't feel like a subversion, it was more additive than that. I was thinking about how absurd but also how wonderful it would be

FIGURE 13.1. Linda Tegg and Brian M. John, *One World Rice Pilaf and the Vital Light, Mercury* installation view, 2015. *Source*: copyright Linda Tegg.

to take whatever database they had and add this column for every video in their archive, this extra piece of information because of our intervention, that said how good it is for plants. It's this strange metric that no one would bring to their own archive, but again that's additive, it's producing new content, new information. So it didn't feel like a subversion at first, until we actually started dealing with the thing and got this push back. And they were fine with us doing it, but they weren't willing to come towards us at all.

GIOVANNI ALOI: In a way what it reveals is how those systems of knowledge work—what is relevant to the Video Data Bank is of course what we think, it's very anthropocentric so, the duration of the film, the data you need to locate material historically and culturally. Who cares about a plant's perception of it? Right? And I guess that's part of the strength of what you've done. Inserting that column is a disturbance of some degree of that anthropocentric stability whereby we categorize these videos this way. But what about using this metric? That's hefty, in a way. I like that it's productive, and then the subversion is generated as something productive. I wonder if we can think of this idea of productivity more carefully, and in what other senses you think it was productive in an additional, expansive way?

JOSHI RADIN: I was interested in issues of empathy and creating meaning in communities that were outside the art institution, and that was the position I came from. I took an interest in nature—Linda's work was very interesting to me, and I was wondering how to evolve those two conversations together. One of the things that's productive in the context of *Mercury* is holding that recentering for an audience that wouldn't normally seek it out; you disrupt normal ways of viewing these elements just by having them in the same space. It's productive in the sense of disrupting perceived ideas. If it were for plants in a garden or greenhouse or space where you'd normally expect to find plants, it wouldn't have the same cultural connection that they're engineering by the site-specificity of that work.

GIOVANNI ALOI: One of the interesting aspects of this project lay in the choice of plants. You did not play with plants with an individualized identity, there were no rose bushes. The plants that were chosen already exist as a pack. Deleuze and Guattari wrote about the pack, as a deterritorializing element, and I'm thinking about the productivity involved as plants are so difficult to relate to as individuals in most cases anyway. They always come off as replaceable multiples. This was particularly visible at the beginning of the project as all seedlings sort of looked like blades of grass for some time.

LINDA TEGG: With Grasslands, in particular, I'm continually challenged with how they're perceived by the human eye. We have to shift our perspective in order to see the complexity in it. In terms of landscape, and of plant communities, it seems as if there is nothing we're more geared to look over and across. Grasslands are historically seen for human use, as either backdrop, or a site of human prospering for agriculture and expansion. I encounter it all the time, the difficulty of shifting human perception to recognize the variance of species in that setting.

GIOVANNI ALOI: Kenneth Shapiro wrote an interesting essay on animals and ontological vulnerability. There he weaves a complex argument about the pack attitude toward certain animals, farm animals especially. A multitude of mass-farmed pigs lose their individuality and therefore that loss enables a base-level of objectification that allows us to, in Shapiro's words, "mow them like blades of grass." The mowing metaphor is important here as it highlights a generalised and indiscriminate approach. But I think the machine-design, and the way it operates, suggests our relationship to the materiality of animals and plants. We're not interested in preserving individual blades of grass, and the machine reflects that. It acts like an equalizer.

BRIAN M. JOHN: That was definitely one of the challenges presented by *Mercury*. You can't anthropomorphize a bunch of small shoots in a large field.[. . .] It seems obvious once you start thinking about plants in this way, but it isn't for an audience that isn't following along this chain of inquiry, so when you present them with a field of plants it's hard to communicate that shift. In *A Program for Plants*, when we were projecting the videos, everybody wanted the plants to be a screen, which was fine because we wanted to give the light to the plants directly. But that was a point of tension—how to present the video work to the plants, and how to maintain the plant audience as the audience.

JOSHI RADIN: How not to create a spectacle for a human audience that involves plants.

BRIAN M. JOHN: Yes, how to not instrumentalize them.

GIOVANNI ALOI: That is a big question in aesthetics right now. Are you performing for a human audience or are you really trying to create a connection with this non-human being that you're claiming you're engaging in the work? There's a lot of controversy about whether you're still performing for an audience of humans rather than doing anything that engages that non-human being.

BRIAN M. JOHN: I found one empirical study that looked at frequency ranges and how they affected growth of some corn sprouts. It measured the amount the root tendril of the sprout would grow towards the source of the sound through a water medium. It found consistent results for a certain frequency range. There were different results for the sound I curated–not all of the artists were necessarily working with the idea of this frequency range. I made two different pieces that responded directly to that study, but the range is 200–300 hertz, so it's on the low side but well within the range of human hearing. It's not even in that spectrum that you lose as you get older. So everything we hear, to whatever extent this study applies to other plants, these plants hear. So all of my stuff was designed around these frequencies, in both cases modulating music that was originally designed for a human audience–changing it, adapting it to try and create a bridge or a medium between human cultural content and a vision of what cultural content for plants could be.

JOSHI RADIN: I feel a lot of the performance work hinged on intention. We spoke a lot about intention with Linda K. Johnson and she brought up the example of experiments on water crystals, which I used to be very dismissive of. I found that when I considered performing for a plant audience as opposed to a human audience, it changed how I felt about it. Linda and I were walking back to the studios, and I was telling her about it, "there I go, anthropomorphizing plants, again, imagining that they're going to somehow be a more generous and receptive audience than humans." When the truth is I just don't know, I have no idea. Perhaps the plants just think I'm full of it, and that I'm a bad dancer. It's the kind of thing where I found myself peeling off layer after layer of constructed meaning that I was imposing. So getting at the truth of what a phytocentric perspective could be in that context felt very elusive.

BRIAN M. JOHN: For me actually learning and performing this fragment of *Trio A* was operating on a totally different register than the original video screenings for plants or the music that we made for plants where it was not as much about trying to have a literal material impact on the plants—to actually project culture across this species divide, but that it was more about learning through this work. The process of learning the work was more about opening up our own perceptions. By engaging in this strange process you're opening up all these questions and you're peeling back all these layers of construction. So for me it was more about that process, revealing these layers of projected meaning that are maybe arbitrary or externally imposed so they're not very meaningful. So for me it became about boiling down the self and stripping away layers of preconceived notions about these two bodies—the body of the plant and the body of the human. I found it really productive in terms of thinking about ourselves as bodies, and the plants as bodies, and there's a parity in a way. You strip away until you find parity—we're basically living human beings.

GIOVANNI ALOI: Living beings acknowledging each other. [...]

LINDA TEGG: One aspect about our collaboration that I found interesting is how we edit documents in real time, seemingly endlessly, together. So we have this shared headspace which is quite unique. I think within a collaborative group there is that loosening of the boundary and destabilization, that challenges me.

GIOVANNI ALOI: I like this idea of a collaboration that has a 'shared headspace'.

BRIAN M. JOHN: It's very cybernetic.

GIOVANNI ALOI: Yeah. But there is something fascinating in this idea of flat ontology if you can allow ... what you've done is basically allow the plants to have some agency . . . and I don't mean "allowed" as a patronizing gesture. I am not saying: "oh let's allow these plants to have agency". But you've sort of taken a step back, deliberately, lots of times, by saying: "let's let the plants decide which is the video we like?" And you've set up this system through which you could enable that choice to emerge and become visible. And I think that's interesting, because if you think about the history of capitalism and humankind in relation to nature, this is never the case. It's never the case of allowing nature to make a decision, it's always a case of diverting the river. I mean, we live in a city that has actually reversed the flow of the river, which sounds incredible, but it has been done.

The idea of cyborgs that has already come up in this project is something that could be different from a project that could've been similar in the 1960s, right?

JOSHI RADIN: I see this a lot. I see the themes recurring, as I've been revisiting this hippie commune, and the plethora of communes that emerged in that time period, after 1968, because of the social crises that were occurring, and that fleeing urban centers to go to the less populated areas as a response to levels of unprecedented violence and social crises. There's a lot of impetus to reorient towards nature now, to reorient towards sustainability and personal responsibility and locality. MIT's Media Lab has a farming group now, which has these ties to that time period, but it's done in this totally . . . When the Media Lab farms, how do they do it? It's in this cyborgian, techno-heavy way. So, I see these repeating responses but of course they're going to be different now. And they should be.

GIOVANNI ALOI: And thinking about agency once more, and plants . . . Did you situate agency that you can call agency, and to what degree this agency was detectable, in relation to the presence of the plants in the gallery space? You worked around them, and through them, and with them, right?

JOSHI RADIN: They got themselves a gallery show. That's pretty crafty.

Chapter Fourteen

NO MANIFESTO

YVONNE RAINER

1965

No to spectacle.

No to virtuosity.

No to transformations and magic
and make-believe.

No to the glamour and transcendency
of the star image.

No to the heroic.

No to the anti-heroic.

No to trash imagery.

No to involvement of performer or spectator.

No to style.

No to camp.

No to seduction of spectator by the wiles
of the performer.

No to eccentricity.

that's the name of the game.

No to moving or being moved.

2008

Avoid if at all possible.

Acceptable in limited quantity.

Magic is out; the other two
are sometimes tolerable.

Acceptable only as quotation.

Dancers are ipso facto heroic.

Don't agree with that one.

Don't understand that one.

Stay in your seats.

Style is unavoidable.

A little goes a long way.

Unavoidable.

If you mean "unpredictable,"

Unavoidable.

(Yvonne Rainer revisited her 1965 "No Manifesto" in 2008 for Manifesto *Marathon* at Serpentine Gallery.)

PART II
Material Dimensions

Chapter Fifteen

INTERVIEW WITH NANDIPHA MNTAMBO

Materiality and Vulnerability

GIOVANNI ALOI AND SUSAN McHUGH

GIOVANNI ALOI AND SUSAN MCHUGH: Your iconic, modeled cow-skins have attracted much attention in recent years. Their ghostly presence seems to allude to the transhistorical, metaphorical, and economic overlap between feminine and animal bodies through notions of exploitation and domestication. Critics see in your work the representation of identity-politics that can uniquely emerge from a black woman artist originally from South Africa.

However, in more than one interview, you have rejected these interpretative perspectives, appealing to your own right as an artist not to be pigeon-holed in what the art market or to what a western conception of diversity would like to see. In what sense is your work "not feminist or antiracist", and why is it important to you that your work should not be seen as such?

NANDIPHA MNTAMBO: First off, let's say that even within South Africa, and not just on an international level, people feel the urge to stereotype me because I happen to be black and because I happen to be female.

South Africa's artistic language is very limited and was even more so when I was younger. This makes the process of classification easier—people expect you to fit either here or there. Of course, the imagery that I produce is about the female form because I chose to use myself as the model. But my work alludes to more than just a feminist story or a story about being a woman.

FIGURE 15.1. Nadipha Mntambo, *Mother and Child*, 2017. Cowhide, resin, and polyester mesh. 195 x 208 x 45cm. *Source*: Copyright Nandipha Mntambo. Courtesy of Stevenson, Cape Town and Johannesburg. Photography: Nina Lieska.

When I was younger it was easier to reject the idea of having a feminist element in my work. Back then, much of my practice involved the research of an artistic language that I could feel comfortable with. It was a genuine search—a true journey through which I wasn't 100 percent sure where I was going. This gave others the opportunity to pigeonhole my work into categories that were fashionable and culturally respectable. I never really was drawn to making comments on gender or race as much as others would have it. The material was leading the way, taking me into unexplored directions.

GIOVANNI ALOI AND SUSAN MCHUGH: So, how do you feel about the gender/race charged readings that critics have teased out of your work?

NANDIPHA MNTAMBO: Today, I am much more aware of the implications and of what others see in my work. But what remains more important to me is the destabilizing power the cowhides embody. How the hides bring everything into question in an open way, like for example the idea of gender and its relation to a work of art. They question our expectations of what materials should be better suited to men or women artists. Working with cowhides is traditionally a male job, of course.

I am interested in gender fluidity and what defines gender beyond the markers of traditional representation, beyond visibility, and beneath the skin-surface of who other people think we are. I think these concerns somewhat extend beyond the remit of feminism, for instance. Maybe, mine is more of a humanist existential question that revolves more specifically around things that are not necessarily visible.

But of course, at the other end of the spectrum of creative freedom is the reality of the art markets and art historians who need to write your work into the philosophically and commercially important categories of today. Right now, the western art market is receptive towards work about Africa, which is great. But much of this interest is a side-effect of the postcolonial wave. This interest for African histories is a double edge sword: on one hand, it gives African artists exposure; but, on the other, it still perpetrates colonialist perspectives as the individual histories of African artists are over-simplified to fulfil expectations.

GIOVANNI ALOI: I appreciate your honesty! This is a conversation that I can only truly have with artists who are involved enough in the market and in its cultural dimension and who can appreciate how complicated the game really is. Once professional success arrives new limitations come to define one's own practice. As you know, an artist's success depends on many variables. Certain cultural and institutional aspects need to perfectly align in order to enable artistic exposure and subsequent professional longevity.

In this respect, the art world is very similar to the fashion world. There is a theme in the air, a new philosophical wave; one's work might have been ignored for years, but when it gets swept up by the right wave, things suddenly begin to happen. The phone starts to ring, and things can become disorienting. But waves come and go, and today, possibly because of social media, they seem to shift faster than ever before.

Like in many other industries, it is hard to fly high while remaining true to one's own artistic journey.

NANDIPHA MNTAMBO: Yes, it is a constant challenge.

SUSAN MCHUGH: It is our impression that one of the most noticeable accomplishments of your work lies in the possibility it provides to envision new and alternative modes of looking at both the animal and the female body. What do we learn about female existence through the skin of a cow, and what can we learn about the existence of a cow through the morphology of a woman's body? And how does it connect to more recent artworks in which you cross traditional species as well as gender lines by envisioning yourself as a minotaur and as a *torera* (female bullfighter)?

NANDIPHA MNTAMBO: The main thought process around the cow and the female body isn't necessarily connected to the fact that both are feminine, because not every cowhide that I use is necessarily from a female animal. I can't know the sex of the animal whose skin I am using. I think my interest is more in the fact that cows are very special animals in that they connect almost every person in the world. The materiality of their bodies is disseminated across the planet in so many different forms: whether you eat the animal's flesh, drink its milk, use it for transportation, or wear its skin. Almost every civilization has a current and a historical connection to cows.

This is of paramount importance to me in my work because my interest has always been in what connects us rather than what separates us, makes us different people, or defines us as members of a particular tribe.

The story of the minotaur emerged in my work because of my interest in the relationships between us and animals as something that occurs across cultures.

From African rock paintings to the imagery on the walls of the Lascaux caves, or mythology, human beings understand their place in the world through their interchange with animals. In this context, I wanted to create an image that transcended time, place, species, and gender at once. I spent time talking to bullfighters and bull breeders in order to better understand their relationship with the animals and the space that separates them, in order to find a space in which human and animal can come together.

On another level, the work is also about categories and belonging—this has to do with my upbringing. I ended up in situations where, because of how my parents decided to lead their lives, I was in schools where sometimes I'd be the only black child. Initially, I went to a Jewish school and we're not Jews by any means. Being accepted on some level, but not really close enough to be the genuine thing . . . that's the story of my life.

GIOVANNI ALOI AND SUSAN MCHUGH: Ah, that explains a lot. What is special about the materiality of cow hides? What is it like to manipulate it?

NANDIPHA MNTAMBO: The materiality of the animal skins I work with helps me to negotiate the space between life and death. In one sense, the material is dead, but it keeps opposing resistance—you engage in a representational and well as material dialogue with it. Tanning is not a simple process. The chemicals are toxic, the room gets hot as you work. If you get things wrong, the hide can rot, or become vulnerable to pests. The material constantly reminds you that you are not fully in charge. It's not quite like carving wood or molding clay, if you see what I mean.

GIOVANNI ALOI AND SUSAN MCHUGH: Your skins are always headless. Is there a specific meaning linked to this seemingly important erasure of both animal and female heads? With what do you associate headless bodies?

NANDIPHA MNTAMBO: I think it's both. On one hand, a head would make the representation too specific—it would invite a different kind of relation, one of reciprocity. My interest has never really been about individualization.

GIOVANNI ALOI AND SUSAN MCHUGH: Could you envision yourself using the skins of other animal species?

NANDIPHA MNTAMBO: No—I chose the cow because of its transcultural value. I would not be interested in the meaning that other animal skins might carry into the space I have explored.

Chapter Sixteen

LOCATING ME IN ORDER TO SEE YOU

NANDIPHA MNTAMBO

I have produced a series of sculpted cast figures in the medium of cowhide as part of my Masters degree. This document [. . .] serves as an explication of the practical component.

Initially I examine the broad context in which my sculpture has been produced, and that in which it will be presented and likely to be received. In attempting to position myself within Contemporary Art discourse, I have specifically considered how Contemporary Art from Africa is often read and comprehended by both those producing work on the continent and the Diaspora, and those interpreting, critiquing, collecting and marketing it, mainly in the West.[1]

The basic premise for this is a discussion of the inescapable labels of Black Artist and Black Art and what they imply within the context of Contemporary Art discourse with reference to Africa and more specifically, South Africa. As an emerging Contemporary African Artist I am faced with confronting some of the stereotypes and assumptions associated with art and artists of the continent and/or the legacy of the Apartheid regime.

My experiences as a woman existing between two cultural spaces, Western and Nguni[2], and the artwork I have created and how it may be read as a result is significant in this regard. Through exploring the art created by a variety of Black South Africans and other African artists, particularly women artists in South Africa, it is clear that modes of creating

FIGURE 16.1. Nandipha Mntambo, *Emabutfo*, 2009. Cowhide, resin, polyester mesh, waxed cord; 24 figures, each approx. 120 x 60 x 20 cm; installation dimensions approx. 120 x 230 x 440 cm.
Source: Courtesy of the Artist and Stevenson, Cape Town and Johannesburg. Copyright Nandipha Mntambo. Photography: Nina Lieska.

art have shifted and that the reading and interpretation of art created by these women, including myself can and should be reconsidered without being conditioned by existing assumptions. In this study I have sought to uncover some of the reasons that may account for the limited shifting in interpretations, and to identify how engagement with my own work could be directed and expanded.

I choose to create work in cowhide, this material is one that has histori-cal associations and is linked to my cultural background in various ways but for this body of research, exists and is considered within a context that is also removed from these aspects. Subjective views of the significance of this material, drawn from the past but with reference to the present, impact on both understanding and engagement with the work I create. It has been suggested, within the context of my research that the way in which I work as well as the material I use could be compared, for example, to the work and materials used within Inuit[3] cultural practices.[4] My use of cowhide, although linked to various cultural experiences, is not intended to directly reference historical indigenous cultural practices. My intention is to engage with the physical and tactile properties of hide and aspects of control that allow or prevent me from manipulating this material in the context of the female body and Contemporary Art. I have used cowhide as a means to subvert expected associations with corporeal presence, femininity, sexuality and vulnerability. By working on a life size scale in this medium through installation in actual space, I hope to explore this.

In this regard I have examined interpretations of material as well as process within art making in the work created by artists such as Janine Antoni and Yinka Shonibare. I draw parallels to the work created by Zanele Muholi and Lolo Veleko as well as Shirin Neshat, which challenge expected representations of the female body and experience within particular cultural contexts. Similarly, the work I create seeks to encourage alternative modes of looking at the female body. [. . .]

[T]he necessity for a questioning of prevailing notions of the nature of Black Art or art made by Black people and therefore the very definitions of 'art' as we understand it [. . . follows from the persistence of a] tendency to homogenize Black and African Art, to apply Western criteria to the analysis and evaluation of art from Africa, and to be dismissive of it when it fails to conform to those criteria. Through drawing attention to the experiences of various Black Artists, particularly Black women, I highlight the diversity and some shifts in recent production in South Africa, and draw attention to the erroneous tendency to associate an essential Black identity with art production, that Blackness and Black Art be reduced to a single acceptable set of experiences, and that working in South Africa necessarily implies a historical political significance in the work.[5] [. . .]

Although Feminism may seem an essential aspect of my production, I have chosen not to focus on this area for a number of reasons. This term has most often been defined and used by middle-class White women and much of the earlier writing on this subject did not take into account the experience of Black women. Black Feminist writing that acknowledges this position is from the perspective of African American women and their views on the oppression and marginalisation they have, and to a degree still encounter. While a feminist reading of my work is not irrelevant, I have instead highlighted that through the use of my own body as a subject and object, I have taken control of representations of my body and therefore, hopefully influenced how it is seen by viewers of my installations. It is not my intention to present my work and experience in the context of oppression and marginalisation, or the female body as abject. [. . .]

The intention of the work I create is to evoke both presence and absence. This is achieved through the very literal absence of the mould I use to create each work as well as the physical form of the animal I have used. This work highlights both the presence and simultaneous absence of my Nguni heritage within my personal context. As mentioned previously, the information I have received about Nguni cultural practices has been a combination of oral accounts and brief encounters. I have not personally experienced a large portion of the elements of Nguni cultural life that may have informed some of the decisions I have made within my art making. The figures I have created are residual. They are residues of my process, the body of the cows I have used, the bodies of myself and [in some moulds] my mother: a repository for experience and memory.

NOTES

1. *West*: The 'Western World' refers to countries of Western Europe, the United States, Canada, Australia and New Zealand. Within the context of this document I highlight that West is no longer a term used just to indicate geographical location, but is used to describe European and Anglo-American hegemony within the reading and defining of art, history and culture.
2. *Nguni*: Nguni refers to both a group of clans and nations living in southeast Africa, and to a group of Bantu languages (Zulu, Xhosa, Swati, Phuti and Ndebele) spoken in southern Africa. In this paper I make reference to Nguni cultural practice as I understand my cultural heritage and have experienced it within my family context. My intention is not to attempt to speak for interpretations of Nguni cultural practices in other Nguni people's experience, or from an anthropological or ethnographic position.
3. *Inuit*: A member of any of several aboriginal peoples who live in coastal regions of the Canadian Arctic and in Greenland (Encarta World English Dictionary).
4. Discussion at Michaelis 29 March 2007.
5. Within this context I would like to highlight how I have been stereotyped and categorised through the use of words such as Black and African Artist. My intention is not to essentialise the experience or art of the artists I have used as examples. My use of terms such as Black and African Artist are as a result of the language necessary to emphisise the problematic nature of these stereotypes.

Chapter Seventeen

FROM "THE RENDERED MATERIAL OF FILM STOCK"

NICOLE SHUKIN

[For m]odern moving pictures to do more than trope animal mobility—that is, for cinema's animated effects to *literally* develop—they required the tangible supports of photographic and film stocks. It is here, in the material convolutions of film stock, that a transfer of life from animal body to technological media passes virtually without notice. To confront the animation effects of modern cinema with their carnal conditions and effects, one needs to tease out the animal ingredients of film stock via a material history of photographic gelatin. In 1873, a gelatin emulsion coating of "animal origin" was first widely adapted to photographic uses. Gelatin—aka "animal glue"—is a protein extracted from the skin, bones, and connective tissues of cattle, sheep, and pigs. As Samuel E. Sheppard wrote in *Gelatin in Photography* (1923): "As is commonly known, gelatin and its humbler relative, glue, are products of animal origin, the result of the action of hot water or steam upon certain tissues and structures of the body. . . . The actual material consists of the leavings of tanneries and slaughter-houses—i.e., trimmings, so-called skips, ears, cheek-pieces, pates, fleshings, etc." The suturing tissue of animal bodies is exchanged for what Sheppard calls the "physiological and biochemical unity" of image life in the duplicit, material-symbolic rendering of animals that helped to leverage cinema into historical existence (25). In the material convolutions of photographic and film stocks, in the viscosity of their "negative gelatin emulsions," resides an opaque politics of rendering (17). If we recall [Karl] Marx's use of the visceral metaphor of "mere jelly" to describe the abstract measure of exchange value, gelatin can be excavated as one site where the production of capitalist culture can be seen to always also involve the rendering of nature.

The coating of choice for photographic and film stocks today as it was at the turn of the century, gelatin binds light-sensitive agents to a base so that images can materialize. In 1884, when the word *film* was put into commercial circulation by George Eastman of the Eastman Dry Plate Company (soon to become the Eastman Kodak Company), the word "referred only to the gelatin coating upon the paper." Turn-of-the-century dialogues between Eastman and Thomas Edison led to the incessant finessing of film stocks capable of yielding specific visual effects (sharpness, high definition, transparency) to corroborate the immediacy and vitality of moving pictures. Even today, the Kodak corporation acknowledges that it is gelatin that is the veritable "Image Recorder."

Yet the manufacture of gelatin emulsions is shrouded in secrecy, historically involving a retreat into the darkroom to develop the writing with light that photography and film appear to magically execute. In an enigmatic bit of information proffered under the heading "Emulsion, the Image Recorder" on Kodak's Web page, the photochemical necessity of preparing sensitive gelatin emulsions in "total darkness" helps to obscure the already mystifying material conditions of image culture: "At this point, the remaining manufacturing steps must be performed in total darkness. Gelatin is dissolved in pure distilled water, and then solutions of potassium iodide and potassium bromide are carefully mixed with it. Silver nitrate solution is added to this heated mixture, and the desired light-sensitive silver halide . . . salts are precipitated as fine crystals." The incidental reliance on animal remains that Kodak fails to acknowledge in the cloaked science of gelatin manufacture is a fly in the ointment of the company's emulsion mystique, a repressed debt that can, nevertheless, through the active "attention" Brown theorizes, be disinterred to reopen a material politics of modern cinema. For modern cinema's mobilization and massification of image life is not only conditioned on time-motion sciences that take animals as organic metaphors of technological mobility; it is also materially contingent on what Sheppard referred to as "the leavings of tanneries and slaughter-houses."

A study of photographic and film stocks shows that prior to the invention of gelatin emulsions in the 1870s, the development of image life already relied heavily on albumen coatings derived from egg whites and animal blood. With the industrialization and popularization of image production pronounced by Eastman's emulsion-coating machines, his affordable portable cameras, and his film development services, however, the relation of film's mimetic effects to a material politics of animal protein changed both quantitatively and qualitatively. As Sheppard writes, "In 1884 the first machine for coating gelatino-bromide emulsion paper was built by Walker and Eastman, and the production of these papers was begun on a large scale" (18). In 1888, when the Kodak camera was introduced to the public, Eastman machines were busy coating "about six thousand feet of negative film a day" with photographic gelatin. It was film that Eastman Kodak also promised to develop for its customers—"You press the button, we do the rest"—encouraging miraculous rather than material knowledge around the popular production of images. By 1911, "in addition to its regular snapshot film, Kodak was manufacturing over eighty million feet of motion-picture stock annually." By the latter half of the twentieth century, the great "emulsion empires"—those of Kodak and Fuji Film—would measure their raw stock less in footages or mileages than in global lengths: "During a single five-day work week . . . workers at a Kodak film plant are able to coat enough 35 mm film to circle the globe." Yet the material means of cinema were simultaneously being rendered invisible beneath the moving image's fetishistic effect of immediacy.

It was not just film manufacturers who began ingeniously capitalizing on the remains of animal life flowing from industrialized slaughter around the turn of the century; North American entrepreneurs were widely experimenting with ways to incorporate the surplus of slaughter into material compounds capable of passing as genuine animal articles. An innovative mimetic material known as hemacite—a mix of animal blood and sawdust compressed under high pressure to form a virtually indestructible substance—imitated ebony and other precious substances without the prohibitive cost, rendered as it was from industrial waste products. Celluloid, though not composed of the "leavings" of slaughter, was among the efflorescence of synthetic materials being engineered to embody "a versatility and uniformity unknown to natural material," allowing them to be "molded into any desired form" through mass modes of production. Originally marketed by the Celluloid Manufacturing Company in the 1870s as a material capable of imitating ivory, tortoiseshell, coral, and amber, celluloid substituted for the look and feel of elephant tusks and other exotic parts of organic wild-life in luxury items such as hair combs, hand mirrors, and brooches. What Jeffrey Miekle calls celluloid's "power of mimicry" enabled it, as the Celluloid Manufacturing Company stated in an early advertising pamphlet, to assume "a thousand forms" and to pass as authentic so peerlessly as to "defy detection."

Beyond touting celluloid's mimetic power to pass as counterfeit for ivory or tortoiseshell, its manufacturers also argued a case for substituting celluloid for natural materials on affective grounds of wildlife conservation. The Celluloid Manufacturing Company declared that just "as petroleum came to the relief of the whale . . . [so] has celluloid given the elephant, the tortoise, and the coral insect a respite in their native haunts; and it will be no longer necessary to ransack the earth in pursuit of substances which are constantly growing scarcer." As Miekle notes, ivory was "the material [that celluloid] most imitated." In a Du Pont salesmen's handbook from 1919, the extinction of "great herds of elephants" was thus invoked in the marketing cause of celluloid (17). A logic of imitation persuasively articulated with a logic of wildlife conservation around the mimetic management of celluloid's artificiality. As Miekle remarks, "Comments such as those of Du Pont served primarily to associate celluloid with ideas of luxury and rarity, to suggest that the American housewife enjoyed comforts formerly available only in a sultan's harem. No evidence suggested a scarcity of ivory during the early twentieth century" (17).

In his search for a flexible film base that could replace cumbersome glass plates and liberate photography as a mass amateur pursuit, George Eastman saw more than just this mimetic potential in celluloid. In 1889, Eastman replaced glass plate and paper supports with thin, rollable strips of transparent nitrocellulose plastic, or celluloid film, supplying one of the missing material conditions of mass motion picture technology. Thomas Edison collaborated closely with Eastman in designing the Kinetoscope motion picture camera around the new rollable film, radically advancing the technological mimicry of continuous movement sought by early cinematographers. If a discourse of wildlife conservation buttressed celluloid's material bid to existence prior to its filmic adaptation, it would be articulated even more prominently to and through cultural discourses of photography and film, which pronounced a conservationist ideology in their call to shoot animals with a camera rather than with a gun (to go "Big Game

Hunting with a Kodak"). Étienne-Jules Marey's "chronophotographic gun," whose sequential filmic cartridges allowed him to shoot animal and bird studies in a manner that replaced the taking of life with its mimetic capture, explicitly heralded the substitution of the camera for the gun. Immuring wildlife on film was widely framed as a conservationist act; over a century later, the valorization of celluloid's conservationist logic still informs the cinematic theory of Lippit, who rearticulates film as a "virtual shelter for displaced animals."

Yet when Lippit proclaims that cinema preserves "the traces of an incorporated animality" (187), he celebrates film's sympathetic features at the cost of overlooking its pathological relationship to animal life. For onto a base of celluloid first pitched as a conservationist alternative to endangered animal tusks, horns, and shells, Eastman applied a second substance, a gelatin emulsion encrypting cinema's contradictory contingency on animal disassembly, one pivotal to its mimetic power to develop lifelike images. In the translucent physiology of modern film stock—in its celluloid base and its see-through gelatin coating—it is possible to discern the "two-layered" mimesis through which modern cinema simultaneously encrypts a sympathetic and a pathological relationship to animal life. Film thus marks a site where a contradictory logic of rendering is daringly, yet inconspicuously, flush.

Chapter Eighteen

INTERVIEW WITH HEIDE HATRY

On Skin and Meat

RON BROGLIO

RON BROGLIO: In *Heads and Tales* you use animal skin and body parts to fashion heads of women. You then photograph these and ask writers you admire to "select the image of one of my women and create a life for her." Did the writers know the heads were formed from animal parts? Did the animals' deaths affect your work and their writing?

HEIDE HATRY: The writers were made aware of the nature of my project and materials when I invited them to participate in making the book, and of course this fact would have to have some effect on their writing. I didn't really think of the question in just the way you pose it, but upon reflection I see that there are several stories in which killing an animal plays a part, though not uniformly in a horrific way, in fact at least once in a darkly and persistently comic way. As to how this affected my own work, the material I used was mostly offal, waste by-products of the slaughtering process, and therefore even more demeaned essences than meat, pelt or leather, and to me it lent a poignancy to the new creatures into which it was fashioned, which I sometimes imagine I see, especially in their sad or clouding eyes. Many of the stories in *Heads and Tales* do treat of death or violence or oppression, and I would have to surmise that the traces of violence in the scoring of the pigskin of which they are made, the occasional residues of subcutaneous blood, and the slight or sometimes greater eccentricity of the fabrication itself must, to some extent, have invoked such thoughts. And after all, in

FIGURE 18.1 Heide Hatry, *Madonna*, 2008. Silver Halide Photograph, 50 x 70 cm (30" x 20").
Source: Copyright Heide Hatry.

making the works, I did have in mind the history of violence that character-izes the universal experience of women, even if I didn't allude to that in my prospectus. [. . .]

RON BROGLIO: Skin acts as a surface between two worlds, a borderline between our "inner" world and the world outside. It is a site of vulnerability, a zone of events between inside and outside. How do you see your skin works as reflective of this borderline?

HEIDE HATRY: Your question allows me to discuss why I chose to connect my portraits to stories. This is because the skin reveals both and conceals what we have experienced, even to the extent of telling something of our inner lives, and I wanted the meaning of these objects to be deepened by verbal evocations of human experience. Although visual art invites interpretation and suggests meanings, it is fundamentally surface, and in determining that these works were to be given voice, I wanted to define a sphere of inner life for them.

In general, I think of the works I have created out of skin and animal parts as having a conceptual or meta-dimension that is determined by their material alone, and that sets them into a state of tension, or perhaps more properly, creates an irresolvable tension in their viewer, who believes himself to be looking at one thing and discovers he is looking at another, and this in itself exemplifies a borderline or liminal quality in the material.

RON BROGLIO: In your projects *Heads and Tales*, *Skin*, and *Meat After Meat Joy*, many of the works use skin and meat as media which have unique proper-ties; they are linked to bodies and identity and violence. How do the identity of the animal and the death of the animal to produce the material with which you work affect your art?

HEIDE HATRY: No animals are killed to produce the art works. The animal parts I use are waste products. Pretty much every part of an animal has some industrial application, but the skin and eyes are regarded as worthless, and I actually get them free at a slaughterhouse. Their only other use would be to be re-fed to other animals. The meat employed in all of the artworks exhib-ited in *Meat After Meat Joy* was a relatively negligible quantity, and I think that it served a purpose that animals would applaud if they were able, not to mention that their deaths in this case were not for nothing, or for pure consumption, but were meaningful. Although I could imagine art made of animal materials for which this question might be relevant, or could even be contextualised, it doesn't really seem to me to apply to my own, the apparent conflict notwithstanding. [. . .]

RON BROGLIO: You are, of course, familiar with Carol Adams' work including *The Sexual Politics of Meat*. She has delineated the link made by patriarchy between women and animals as well as women and meat or flesh for consumption. How has your work been influenced by Adams and/or similar writing and thinking?

HEIDE HATRY: Although my work has not been explicitly influenced by the writing of people like Carol Adams, Donna Haraway, Mary Midgley, et al., and I only came upon their books after having been well embarked upon the bodies of work in which I've employed animal products, I certainly acknowledge many general resonances and food, as it were, for thought, as well as plenty of differences. Even my personal discussions with feminist friends like Catharine A. MacKinnon, Eileen McDonagh, Thyrza Goodeve, and others, served rather to confirm than to determine the direction I am going with my work, though they certainly influenced me.

I believe today that my upbringing [on a pig farm], my experience with animals and women, and my observations influenced me most when it comes to the work: already as a child I connected the consumption of flesh with power and maleness (Adams says: "Meat eating is linked with virility, intelligence, courage, and material affluence. The "superior" sex requires and consumes more flesh") and this I experienced at home. My father and little brother got most of the meat. I saw that meat advertisements clearly spoke to male customers or to women who are going to feed these men. Adams says that Anna Kingsford (who happens to be one of the "characters" in *Heads and Tales*), and other early feminists in the 19th century, had already made a connection between flesh eating, domestic violence, and war. She says that these women saw the elimination of violence on the dinner table as a first and necessary step toward eliminating violence on the domestic "front," and ultimately between nations.

On our farm we gave our guard dog meat to make it more aggressive, and I have known people who have attributed episodes of "aggression" in others to an excess of meat in the diet.

In the U.S. 700,000 animals are slaughtered each hour, that is 11,500 each minute for human consumption. I wasn't aware of this crazy statistic as a child, but the fact that we bred these poor creatures in enormous numbers to kill and eat them was clear to me very early on when I accompanied my father to the slaughterhouse and saw hundreds of trucks filled with animals like ours waiting to be unloaded and killed.

I don't know how many people actually read books like those of Carol Adams. For me, an image leads to a faster and more immediate confrontation with these issues, though images do require words to transcend sense and enter consciousness.

RON BROGLIO: In 2008, you curated a show called *Meat After Meat Joy* which featured a number of artists whose work carries a similar concern along the nexus of identity, gender, power, and the corporeal flesh of humans (mainly women) and animals. The show reveals a striking number of artists working with meat as a medium. Could you explain the threads of similarity among the works, but also the differences: what are the unexpected different directions these artists have taken while using meat as a medium or item of inquiry.

HEIDE HATRY: The range of themes that meat as metaphor or meat as meat suggests is, as you might expect, a little narrow, even if extremely powerful. Works that question the meat and leather-goods industries intertwine quite naturally with investigations of the plight of workers, the de-humanization of technology, the perception of women by men, women's perception of themselves, the essence of animal and human life, violence, death, appearance and reality, surface and substance, the predication of life upon death. For me Jana Sterbak's *Flesh Dress for an Albino Anorectic* remains among the extraordinary and powerful works of contemporary art, simple in many ways though its subject is. And Betty Hirst's self-portrait, "obvious" though it seems to be, is something I cannot look at without feeling that it has said something so essential and yet so elusive that I cannot tear myself away from it. When I conceived the show, the first thing I thought of was Zhang Huan's *My New York*. It's a work that I still find rather perplexing and unsubmissive. There is some fairly overt iconography, but the tension of power and vulnerability embodied in one and the same iconographic component is an effect I find endlessly compelling. I suppose, though, that in the end, the work that I still find most provocative is Carolee Schneemann's *Meat Joy*—it's certainly the work that must have been historically most unexpected. It is ostensibly a work of Dionysian ecstasy, but the point might actually be that all of the blandishments of ecstasy are merely enticements to enslavement. The images of free and independent, "whole" women are inherently undermined by thraldom to meat, to killing and death. Or it may say that freedom is purchased at the cost of killing and death, that the worm is always already in the apple. Neither is very comforting, and the effect is that the work, whose surface seems so empowering, and so powerful in a straightforward sort of way, cannot be appropriated by the powers of any persuasion.

RON BROGLIO: I have often thought of meat as the moment when what remained hidden is opened up. The insides become exposed outsides. The depth of form becomes a surface and the depth of being becomes the thin lifelessness of an object exposed. Meat makes the insides visible, and through sight the body becomes knowable. And while meat serves as a means for us to take in the exposed flesh visually and mentally, it also marks the moment when the physical becomes consumable. Do you see these thematics in your work and/or the work of other artists working with animal flesh?

HEIDE HATRY: The dynamic of inner and outer, of appearance and reality, of surface and substance are all integral to my work and have informed it fairly self-consciously. The issues of identity and more recently, of what has been called "iconoplastic deconstruction" (a concept used by Paul Manfred Kaestner, to describe the strategy I've employed in the *Heads and Tales* works as well as in the work in a forthcoming project) are central to much of my work. I want the medium itself, as it gradually reveals itself to the viewer, to shake our common responses to things, to make us reconsider givens that we normally process pre-critically, and to put the viewer in the grasp of a sort of physical aporia, to be forced to conjure with the tension between appearance and reality, to transcend the state of "viewer" and actually experience, and think.

Chapter Nineteen

ON SOME LIMITS OF MATERIALITY IN ART HISTORY

JAMES ELKINS

In July 2008, I hosted the second annual Stone Summer Theory Institute, a book series that will eventually involve over 500 scholars, artists, curators, and others in discussions about unresolved issues in contemporary art. The topic for July 2008 was the question, "What is an image?" [. . .] Naturally, given the question "What is an image?" the assembled faculty and students spent time on etymology. [. . .] We agreed, provisionally, in a working distinction between *picture* and *image*, where—following English usage—*picture* denotes a physical object, and *image* denotes a memory, ideal, idea, or notion of a picture. The distinction proved to be helpful because some of the participants were more interested in images than pictures: W.J.T. Mitchell, for example, had a lot to say about the ways that images of the Twin Towers in New York City, or political caricatures, travel across media. In those explorations he was less concerned with the physical form of the pictures, and more with the things that were said about them. Other participants, however, were more interested in pictures than images. [. . .]

Still, *picture* and *image* are only heuristic categories, and in the course of the week-long event many different kinds of connections were explored. One three-hour session was especially illuminating: a seminar led by Jacqueline Lichtenstein, on and around the subject of image, picture, and painting. Throughout the week, the relation of painting to the other two terms was problematic and unresolved. To some people, it seemed best to speak about painting as an historically specific practice, associated with the last five centuries in the West. In that way of thinking, painting has become increasingly marginal, and is not appropriate as an exemplar for images as a whole. But to others, a painting is the central example of an image, and the discourse on painting has intimately informed the theorization of images from the middle ages onward. As a scholar of eighteenth- and nineteenth-century painting, Lichtenstein has a special interest in painting as a way to think about both pictures and images, and she also has an interest in what makes paintings different from other kinds of pictures and from disembodied images. So for the duration of her seminar, the group was invited to consider the materiality or physicality of painting as an indispensable element.

The participants were not agreed on the importance of materiality—that much could be expected—but they were also far from agreed on what should count as materiality. Lichtenstein cited detailed descriptions by Huysmans, Diderot, and Baudelaire, emphasizing their interest in the sometimes illegible detail that paintings offer when they are seen from very close up. She said that if we consider the texts on painting produced by art history, very few are on what she would consider painting: the textures, colors, and lines. She asked how we describe spots, patches, finger marks, and dots, and she observed that the long tradition of *ut pictura poesis* had made it easier to write about images than pictures—and by implication, easier to write about pictures than paintings.[1] We then talked for a while about the difference between embodied marks in painting and disembodied "marks" on a computer screen, and about Jacques Rancière and whether his writings on painting are an indication that he is theorizing pictures or paintings, rather than images. On these and other topics our conversation was fluid and fluent, and there were no major objections: a consensus might have been that art history and visual studies can become more attentive to materiality, but that the possibility of writing attentively about a painting's physical form has been inherent in Western art writing since the generation of Diderot.

Problems began to emerge, however, when the conversation turned to the extent and limits of art history's potential attention to materiality. How much materiality can appear in an art historical text? I mentioned my book *What Painting Is*, which offers full-page details of portions of paintings that are on the order of 70 mm across, and very detailed, mark-by-mark analyses of them.[2] That book is flawed, I said, and it has been rightly criticized, for giving up the *history* of oil painting in order to talk in such myopic detail. When you get that close to a painting, and pay careful attention to each barely visible mark, stray brush hair, fingerprint, and scratch, you find it is nearly impossible to connect your observations to art historical accounts of the paintings. *Nearly impossible*, I said, but not completely impossible. The problem with *What Painting Is* isn't that there is no meaning to very tiny portions of paintings, or that history has to be left completely behind when you look so closely at oil paintings. The problem is that it becomes excruciatingly difficult to keep talking or writing when you are looking very closely. And yet it is never impossible. The ideas come much more slowly—this is the *slowness of the studio*, which I will consider below—and they are hard to attach to other people's meanings (to the whole history of writing on, say, Monet or Sassetta or Rembrandt). They begin to sound eccentric, forced, or willful. I think of that book as an extreme case, a limit case, of what Lichtenstein said about the lack of books on painting.

[. . . T]he interest that art historians and others have in materiality *has no inner logic* that prevents it from paying closer and closer attention to a picture's materiality. There is no account of the materiality of physicality of an artwork that contains an argument about the limits of historical or critical attention to materiality, and therefore there is no reason not to press on, taking physicality as seriously as possible, spending as much time with it as possible, finding as many words for it as possible. The fact that historians and others do not do so demonstrates, I think, a *fear of materiality*. The "purely" or "merely" physical or material is conceived as a domain that is somehow outside of historical interpretation, or even outside of rational and critical attention. It is assigned to *making*, to the realm of art production, and therefore it is set safely apart from historical, theoretical, and critical accounts. [. . . We limit ourselves with] an anxiety about what we could say, and an interest in keeping the status quo. In art history, it is a *topos*, a commonplace, to assert that the discipline is interested in materiality and physicality. But it is a *fact*, a unpleasant one, that the overwhelming majority of art historians and critics do not want to explore beyond the point where writing becomes difficult. [. . .]

Academia is a very fast place. In the sciences, equations can be written hour after hour as fast as the instructor can manage. I have been in science classes where a fifty-minute lecture was enough to fill three fifteen-foot blackboards ten times over with graphs and equations. In the humanities, thoughts can flash by in blinding succession. A single conversation can stoke a research project for a year, and a seminar can become a pummeling succession of brilliant insights. This speed has consequences for the kinds of questions that can be asked about materiality.[3]

The studio, by contrast, can be overwhelmingly slow. Objects get in the way: large things are difficult to move, viscous substances are hard to control. Artists have two fundamental choices: either they optimize their methods and media so they can make things more efficiently, or they stick with what they have and learn to think at its level. The division is not exclusive, but it cuts deep. My impression is that art historians tend to think that artists regard their studios as tools, with no more affection than the historians have for their computers. In large measure I think the art historical opinion is wrongheaded, and it excuses art historians from looking into the day-to-day workings of the studio, where materiality is encountered in ways that are not always amenable to the conceptual speed of scholarship.

The challenge for a newcomer to artists' studios is to try to think at the speed and in the rhythm that is right for a given medium and purpose. Art historians who are new to the studio can find their minds racing like the engines of cars stuck in the ice. After a time they may notice that their thoughts are ill–matched to the objects around them, but it can be difficult to figure out how to pay attention in a more appropriate manner. Watching an artist, or making art, nothing may happen for long periods of time, and even when something does take place, it may not be immediately clear what it was, or whether it might be important.

To some degree the problem occurs in any medium, but the situation may be strongest in the visual arts. Few people have had the experience of starting to work on a large marble block, where ten minutes of hard work will only yield a pitiful dent. A dab of paint may cost an artist several minutes' work, adjusting the color, the thickness, and the load on the brush— but it may only represent a few leaves on one tree in a landscape of trees.

To a philosopher, this might not seem to be an issue at all. If ideas come more slowly in the studio, maybe the thing to do is wait, and collect insights and concepts that have accumulated over a long interval. Take the sum total of insights gained over a month in the studio, compress it, and it is ready for analysis. Conceived this way, slowness amounts to nothing more than an annoying impediment. An hour in the studio would be like an hour with a phlegmatic teacher.

But consider some things that slowness means. Slowness feels like work. For the first few days, someone used to academic discourse may find studio work stultifying. A typical art history student, exposed to the studio, wants to try everything, and learn the studio in a day or two, as if it were a book that could be expertly skimmed and condensed for future use. The experience can be unpleasant and disappointing in a particular way: it may start to feel like manual labor. It may begin to attract all the feelings that pervade ordinary work: the materiality of the studio will look dull, repetitive, dirty, and insufficiently rewarding. Class consciousness also pervades many people's first experiences of the studio. It is common to find students imagining that the studio exists in two modes: either a kind of underpaid work or, in the case of established artists, a heavenly opportunity for self-expression. Both the utopian and the dystopian readings are colored by largely inappropriate projections from the world of manual labor. On the other hand, studio work is labor in many respects, and slowness is one of its principal traits.

Slowness is painful. It follows that the experience causes anguish: nothing, it seems, is being learned, and no thought can find expression without being dragged through a purgatory of recalcitrant materials. For the first time in some students' lives, their hands seem clumsy. In effect, a baptism in the studio can be like returning to infancy: the eye sees something it likes (say, the contour of a model's neck), but the hand simply cannot follow the shape on paper. The student sees something graceful, and her hand draws something awful, and it happens over and over. Like an infant in a crib making wild gestures at a suspended toy, the experience can become intolerably frustrating. Studio art can become a kind of chronic, low-level pain, where the mind is continuously chafing against something it cannot have. Academic thinking—the running equations, the scintillating conversations—aim to be as free of that pain as possible. Our conversations in the Stone Summer Theory Institute were nearly seamless: nothing interrupted the flow of words, and when we ran out of ideas on one topic, we quickly shifted to another. It was automatic and unthinking: but it would not normally be possible in the studio. Materiality is something that gets in the way of thinking as well as looking. Slow thoughts cannot be sped up, and thinking slowly is thinking differently.

NOTES

1. I am paraphrasing because as I write this (summer 2008), the transcript has not yet been reviewed and edited by the participants.
2. Elkins, *What Painting Is* (New York: Routledge, 1999).
3. In *Pictures, And the Words that Fail Them* (Cambridge: Cambridge University Press, 1998), I argue that virtually all art historical interpretation moves too quickly. Another book, *Our Beautiful, Dry, and Distant Texts: Art History as Writing*, second printing, with a new Preface (New York: Routledge, 2000), is an attempt to draw attention to the qualities of art historical writing that proceed from overly rapid interpretation.

Chapter Twenty

ELEPHANTS IN THE ROOM

Animal Studies and Art

GIOVANNI ALOI

VISIBILITY, INVISIBILITY, AND MATERIALITY

It is worth noting that not only art materials have been a conspicuous "elephant in the room" of animal studies, but that the new animal presence in contemporary art has equally been poorly addressed by art history. Most regularly, art historical discussion of Damien Hirst, Joseph Beuys, Oleg Kulik, and Mat Collishaw have reduced animal presence in the work of these artists to the analysis of symbolic meaning or formalism. This approach is clearly flawed. This sidelining of animal-oriented critique in mainstream art historical analysis is indeed problematic, yet I'd like to propose that this phenomenon may be caused by a fear art historians have to shift the analytical framework from a semantic one to an ethical one according to which the ethical sphere may obliterate the artistic merit of the work itself. Beyond the shadow of sheer disciplinary anthropocentrism, it is even likely that this bypassing of animal-oriented critique in history of art may be led by the inherent difficulties involved in mediating different agendas in the complex attempt of doing justice to all.

As confirmed by James Elkins, art history has traditionally taken interest in the materiality of works of art on a general and abstract level.[1] This has been predominantly caused by a reliance on phenomenology, especially capitalizing on Merleau-Ponty, Sartre, and Husserl. However, Elkins

FIGURE 20.1 Damien Hirst, *Liberation*, 2019. Butterflies in household gloss on canvas. 184cm diameter
Source: Copyright Damien Hirst and Science Ltd. All rights reserved, DACS/Artimage 2019. Photo: Prudence Cuming Associates Ltd.

emphasizes that the changing scenery of contemporary artistic production is one in which the materiality of a work of art can no longer be ignored. He also acknowledges that it is a kind of anxiety to prevent us from seriously embracing this task. This anxiety, Elkins argues, is exacerbated by an inherent interest in keeping the status quo and a fear of what one may say.[2] "In art history, it is a topos, a commonplace to assert that the discipline is interested in materiality and physicality. But it is a fact, an unpleasant one, that the overwhelming majority of art historians and critics do not want to explore beyond the point where writing becomes more difficult".[3]

In light of these emerging preoccupations with materiality in the field of art and animal studies, I argue that taking the materiality of contemporary art, as well as that of classical painting, seriously may mean, at least from an animal studies perspective, to also acknowledge concealed animal deaths: the animal renderings which made the representation itself possible. Those who find the incorporation of a visible dead animal body in a work of contemporary art should indeed give a thought to the animal deaths that are normally embedded in a classical painting. In other words, if one finds Hirst's work unethical predominantly because it involves a dead animal, one should also be compelled to explain why the same criteria may not apply to a work of art from five hundred years ago that contains hundreds of different concealed dead animals.

TRANSUBSTANTIATION IN CLASSICAL PAINTING

The term transubstantiation, one etymologically linked to the Catholic Church, implies the transformation of one material into another. Transubstantiation played a key role in the miraculous—the possibility of transcending the boundaries and essence of materiality which manifested the greatness of God through its ability to subvert physical laws. It is possible to argue that classical painting has implicitly relied on the processes of transubstantiation tor the purpose of producing images in which the 'material *paint*,' had to be transformed into another material, at least mimetically. Thus in professionally executed classical paintings, blue paint becomes water in the sea, pink hues of paint become human flesh and greens, purples, and reds become velvety or silky fabrics. Beneath this first order of transubstantiation lies however a second and more hidden one related to [Nicole] Shukin's conception of rendering: a form of transubstantiation involving animal death. It now seems appropriate to identify the animals that were regularly rendered tor the purpose of producing many of the images we admire today. It is generally known that during the Renaissance, increased commerce with India and the discovery of America led to the introduction of new red pigments derived from scale insects. *Coccus cacti*, a scale insect parasitizing cacti leaves was dried and crushed for the purpose of producing a red dye.[4] *Kermes vermillio*, and *Kerria lacca*, scale insects of different species were used in similar ways. Of course, it is important to remember that scale insects are culturally considered parasites—too many of them would harm agricultural production, therefore, their harvesting and killing has never posed ethical problems. However, scale insects are not the only animals to have been used in the making of paintings. *Purpura patula* or *Purpura capillus*, a mollusk once common in the Mediterranean was used to produce a purple hue that was extremely expensive.[5] The colour was extracted from a small cyst in the mollusk and according to the Windsor and Newton historical archive, huge quantities were required for the production of the dye. "In 1908, P. Friedlander collected just 1.4 grams of pure dye from 12.000 mollusks".[6] Whether we care or not for the deaths of mollusks, (another animal that does not return the gaze) my concern here is more directly related to the environmental impact that such practices must have had on the ecosystems from which the animals were removed. *Winsor and Newton's* archive states that "spoil heaps of the shells can still be seen on the sites of ancient dye works around the Mediterranean."[7] Attempting to visualize the amount of mollusks killed for the purpose of producing such meager amount of pigment constitutes a challenge in itself—evaluating the disastrous ecological impact such practices may have borne upon local ecosystems appears equally difficult.

Besides mollusks, eggs also constituted a common ingredient used in the mixing of pigments. First in what was called 'egg tempera' during the middle ages in Italy and other areas in Europe and thereafter in the Renaissance, until the widespread adoption of oil paint in the early 1500s. Egg slowed down the pigments' drying times allowing artists to better apply colour and to gain more control over layering of different hues. At times, beeswax was also used for similar ends.[8] Gelatinous extracts from the bladders of sturgeons were generally used as a mixing agent in oil paint, whilst fish glue was also used in some countries.[9]

Perhaps less known to the non-specialist is that rabbits also made their way into classical painting as a priming agent.[10] Rabbit bones, tendons, and cartilage would be boiled down for the purpose of producing glue which was applied to the canvas prior to paint. It prepared its surface to receive the pigment and to deal with the humidity of the applied colour. It is important here to note that in Italy and central Europe alike, rabbits were regularly cooked for food, rather than being exclusively kept as pets as it happens today in other countries. Alternatively, glue extracted from horse hooves also served a similar role. And of course, having focused so much on the materiality of painting itself, it would be wrong to forget the mammals that were killed for the purpose of producing paintbrushes. Hairs and bristles of horses, boars, rabbits, hogs, oxen, squirrels, goats, and badgers were routinely used to produce a vast range of brushes available in different degrees of size and softness.[11]

As an art historian/visual cultures scholar, I cannot or afford to ignore these animal killings just because they took place in the past and because the animal bodies involved have been rendered invisible. It is thus for this reason that at the same time I cannot vehemently condemn the use of animals in contemporary art without acknowledging an underling hypocrisy. This is the conundrum that art historians engaging in animal studies should carefully consider. The vast majority of artistic production in western art has always involved the killing and rendering of animals. And it is important to stress that animal-killing that happened in the past, matters just as much as that taking place today.[12]

NOTES

1. Elkins, J. (2008) 'On Some Limits of Materiality in Art History, 31: Das Magazin des Instituts fur Theorie [Zurich] 12 pp. 25–30. Special Issue Neuner, S. and Gelshorn, J. (eds.) Taktilität: Sinneserfahrung als Grenzerfahrung, p.25
2. Ibid
3. Ibid
4. Church, A. H. (1901) *The Chemistry of Prints and Painting*, (London: Seeley Company) p.185
5. Ibid, p.302
6. Winsor & Newton, 'Articles and Inspiration' [online] <http://www.winsornewton.com/uk/discover/articles-andinspiration [Accessed on 12th August 2014]
7. Ibid
8. Elkins, J. (2000) What Painting Is, (Abingdon: Taylor and Francis), p.18
9. Ibid

10. Ibid

11. Genttens, R. J. and Stout, G. L. Stout (2012) *Painting Materials: A Short Encyclopedia*, (Chelmsford: Courier Corporation), p.281.

12. We are reminded of this by groups of animal rights oriented scholars who rightly abhor the death of Topsy the elephant, which was electrocuted in 1903 to advertise the efficiency of DC electrical current systems, and of other case studies that are usually recovered from past histories to document the unfairness that has dominated human-animal relations. Think of the animal cruelty committed by the Romans in the Coliseum, or the hoards of animals slaughtered at Smithfield Market in London during the Victorian period. Animal Studies critiques have addressed these instances condemning events and participants despite the historical distance that separates us from them.

Chapter Twenty-One

FROM *SECOND SKINS*

The Body Narratives of Transsexuality

JAY PROSSER

In December 1993 "Orlan: Omnipresence" brought to the Sandra Gering Gallery in New York the latest work of the French surgical performance artist, Orlan, This consisted in the surgical reconstruction of her face to resemble a computer composite of five canonical representations of beautiful women (the Mona Lisa and Botticelli's Venus among them). At the exhibition a video of the operation, originally relayed live to multiple international art galleries, showed a surgical team fitted out in black robes and conical hats performing on Orlan's laid-out body. The video of the surgery and its live broadcast, as Julia Epstein observes, "literaliz[ed] the term 'operating theater.'" Underlining this theatricality, a surgeon's bloody robe stretched and pinned to the wall at Gering's bore the legend, "The body is but a costume." To be sure, by her own account, Orlan seems to divest herself of her lineaments with an ease in keeping with this figure: "Skin is a mask of strangeness, and by refiguring my face, I feel I'm actually taking off a mask." Yet like the robe's disavowal of the body's materiality, Orlan's image for the superficiality of her face only raises anxious questions about the meaning of bodily matter for identity. If skin is a mask, where is the self in relation to the body's surface? Deeper than the skin (underneath the mask)? Or not "in" the flesh at all? In her surgical performance of the body (this was I think her sixth set of procedures), in her literalization of the body as a costume,

Orlan appeared to provide an insane personification of the poststructuralist insistence on the absolute constructedness of the body.

Contrary to the robe's and Orlan's assertions, the body's materiality (its fleshiness, its nonplasticity, and its nonperformativity) was anyway much in evidence elsewhere in the gallery: in the gruesome video itself; in the photographs of Orlan's face, much swollen, bruised, and misshapen, which served as a daily record of her very gradual postsurgical recovery; and (evidently a recovery not yet completed) in Orlan herself, (omni)present at the gallery the day I went, her face mostly hidden behind dramatic big dark glasses, what wasn't, still puffy and luminous, oddly large. In the Q&A following the artist's talk, after mentioning the work I was then beginning on transsexuality, I asked Orlan about the relation of body and identity in her work. Did she feel any sense of identity transformation, of an internal shifting, as her face underwent its successive alterations? Was the transformation really only skin deep? (I wondered what it was like to wake up to a different face each morning; I wondered how she sustained herself in the face—literally—of such change.) Skimming over the substance of my question (there were problems in translation) but picking up my reference to transsexuality, Orlan replied simply that she felt like "une transsexuelle femme-à-femme." It was a striking reformulation. But what was the import of transsexuality here? On the one hand, eliding the element of sex change but nonetheless suggesting a total identity (ex)change (she changed from one woman to another), her identification with a substantial transsexual transition implied that something of herself was indeed invested in the surgery, that the transformations were not simply skin deep. On the other hand, the readiness of her embrace of transsexuality and the ease with which transsexuality translated into a context that made of surgery a spectacle brought to the surface a commonplace assumption about transsexuality: that is, that transsexuality is precisely a phenomenon of the body's surface. In the cultural imagination that figure of the body as costume is surely welded most firmly to the transsexual. The transsexual changes sexed parts like a set of clothes, treats the body as tractable, provisional, immaterial: "For transsexuals a book may be read by its cover, and the bodily frame is thought of as another article of clothing, to be retouched at will." If the Orlan/transsexual analogy could have worked either way—to substantiate Orlan's transformation or to unsubstantiate (transubstantiate?) the transsexual's—what is the status of the body for transsexuals? Does sex reassignment suggest the body as a surface in which the self is substantially invested or conversely the body's substance as superficial to the self? What does transsexuality, the fact that subjects do seek radically to change their sex, convey about sex, identity, and the flesh?

Upon sex reassignment surgery, upon assumptions concerning its mechanics and effects, pivot popular attitudes to transsexuality. More than the potentially dramatic somatic effects of the long-term hormone therapy that necessarily precedes it, sex reassignment surgery is considered the hinge upon which the transsexual's "transsex" turns: the magical moment of "sex change." At the same time contemporary conceptualizations of sex make it difficult to believe that surgery, through the simple excision and restructuring of body parts, can miraculously and wholly alchemize one sex into "the other." Sex is currently ascribed a complex of meanings that push the category beyond the surface of the body. For a start, in science sex is no longer located monolithically in the genitals but disseminated through the inscrutable parts of the body: the gonads, the chromosomes, even the brain—parts of the body that cannot be exchanged in sex reassignment. On the basis of this multiplication and encrypting of sex, the transsexual can alter sex only partially and superficially, only in the limited sense of hormonal and genital sex. Second, our belief in the importance of the cultural and psychic in identity formation has left us wary of reducing sex to the body *tout court*. "Gender" has made it routine to ask how much of sex is socialization, cultural construction, and personal history. How can surgical intervention into biological material alter the accretion of this sociocultural matter, the experiences that make up our lives as men and women? Third, since feminism has complicated the status of difference in sexual difference (antithesis or likeness? difference from or difference within?), isn't the naturalization of sexual difference into a binary twoness anyway a cultural construct? Ann Fausto-Sterling argues that even medical narratives of sex reveal the dimorphic sex model as arbitrary. The transsexual would seem to assume a binary difference that doesn't even exist in biology: how, then, can s/he cross a space that is not clearly there? Finally—and most important since this constitutes the theoretical zeitgeist—if sex as much as gender is performative, an effect of our doing not a fact of our being ("gender all along"), how can we conceive of the transsexual as intervening in sex at all? If there is no sex left over, no immanent sexed part to the self that is not already gender, what substance is there for the transsexual to change?

Because sex has become irreducible not only to the sex organs accessible to surgical remolding but to the body itself, the transsexual's attempted sex reassignment may serve to illustrate the very failure of sexual difference. Elizabeth Grosz deploys the transsexual to this effect. Conceiving of sexual difference as "a problematic . . . entail[ing] a certain failure of knowledge to bridge the gap, the interval, between the sexes," she claims: "At best the transsexual can live out his fantasy of femininity—a fantasy that in itself is usually disappointed with the rather crude transformations effected by surgical and chemical interventions. The transsexual may look like a woman but can never feel like or be a woman." Looking like a woman but not really one, yet, after the "crude transformations" have "disappointed" his "fantasy" of gender, hardly looking like a man, the transsexual as transmogrified, hermaphroditic prodigy falls into that very space/time ("gap," "interval") of sexual difference. This "gap" is not only between man and woman but between signifier and referent: it is in this Lacanian sense (the fact that the signifiers of man and woman can never fully or fixedly inscribe themselves on referential bodies) that sexual difference is said to fail. In her Lacanian reading of transsexuality, Catherine Millot argues that the transsexual's quest for sex reassignment is a psychotic refusal to recognize the law of the symbolic that makes us subjects—that is, that the referent *is* symbolic, that sexual difference is a matter of signification only. Following Millot therefore, Parveen Adams reads Orlan's reformulation of transsexuality (the exhibition I attended was televised) to suggest Orlan as the better transsexual. Where the transsexual, in attempting to move substantively from one sex to the other, would seek to render literal a difference that is representational, Orlan's performative female-to-female transition "transform[s] the confident existence of one sex . . . towards the gap in representation which signifies sexual difference." *She* keeps open the gap, or rather reveals that the referent *only* figures: "[A]n image trapped in the body of a woman," Orlan demonstrates that "there is nothing beneath the mask." Ironically, this poststructuralist deliteralization of sex (its detachment from referentiality) can often seem like a further mystification of sex. Irreducible to the body, by definition indefinable, sex has become in excess, that which we cannot "know" about gender; as Grosz illustrates, "There remains something ungraspable, something outside, unpredictable, and uncontainable about the other sex for each sex."

Yet what is the status of the body's surface that the transsexual in chang-ing sex reconfigures? Is our corporeal outside simply a "mask," so detach-able from, so insubstantial for the self? [. . .]

From the prevalent perspective in gender theory the transsexual's story of becoming sexed can only appear naively overdetermined. Butler asserts that if "there is no body prior to its marking[,] . . . we can never tell the story of how it is a body comes to be marked by the category of sex." Relating first how the body comes to be marked by sex wrongly, then how it comes to be marked correctly, transsexual narratives take up poststructuralism's untellable story. What makes it possible for a female-to-male transsexual to name the somatic material (skin, tissue, and nerves) transplanted from his forearm or his abdomen to his groin "my penis," or for a male-to-female transsexual to name the inverted remains of her penis "my vagina" is a refiguring of the sexed body that takes place along corporeal, psychic, and symbolic axes. Gendered becoming, becoming a man or a woman, occurs for the transsexual at these points of intersection, complex crossings for sure but the investment of sex in the flesh is undeniable. Narratives that immerse us (subject and reader alike) in the bodily matter of sexual differ-ence, transsexual autobiographies challenge theory's cynicism over iden-tity's embodiment. In that s/he seeks to align sex with gender identification; in that the somatic progression toward these goals of sexed embodiment constitutes the transsexual narrative, the transsexual does not approach the body as an immaterial provisional surround but, on the contrary, as the very "seat" of the self. For if the body were but a costume, consider: why the life quest to alter its contours?

Chapter Twenty-Two

HUNTING AND GATHERING AS WAYS OF PERCEIVING THE ENVIRONMENT

TIM INGOLD

In his classic study of the Mbuti Pygmies of the Ituri Forest, Colin Turnbull observes that the people recognize their dependence on the forest that surrounds them by referring to it as "Father" or "Mother." They do so "because, as they say, it gives them food, warmth, shelter and clothing, just like their parents," and moreover, "like their parents, [it] gives them affection."[1] This form of reference, and the analogy it establishes between the most intimate relations of human kinship and the equally intimate relations between human persons and the nonhuman environment, is by no means unique to the Mbuti.[2] Precisely similar observations have been made among other hunter-gatherers of the tropical forest, in widely separate regions of the world. For example, among the Batek Negritos of Malaysia, according to Kirk Endicott, the forest environment "is not just the physical setting in which they live, but a world made for them in which they have a well-defined part to play. They see themselves as involved in an intimate relationship of interdependence with the plants, animals and *hala'* (including the deities) that inhabit their world."[3] The *hala'* are the creator beings who brought the forest world into existence for the people, who protect and care for it, and who provide its human dwellers with nourishment. And again, among the Nayaka, forest-dwelling hunter-gatherers of Tamil Nadu, South India, Nurit Bird-David found a similar attitude: "Nayaka look on the forest as they do on a mother or father. For them, it is not something 'out there' that responds mechanically or passively but like a parent, it provides food unconditionally to its children."[4] Nayaka refer to both the spirits that inhabit the landscape and the spirits of their own predecessors by terms that translate as "big father" and "big mother" and to themselves in relation to these spirits as sons and daughters.

What are we to make of this? [. . .]

In the specific case with which we are concerned, hunter-gatherers' material interactions with the forest environment are said to be modeled on the interpersonal relations of parenting and sharing: the former, assigned to the domain of nature, establish the object; the latter, assigned to the domain of society, provide the schema. But this means that actions and events that are constitutive of the social domain must be representative of the natural. When, for example, the child begs its mother for a morsel of food, that communicative gesture is itself a constitutive moment in the development of the mother-child relationship, and the same is true for the action of the mother in fulfilling the request. Parenting is not a construction that is projected *onto* acts of this kind, it rather subsists *in* them, in the nurture and affection bestowed by adults on their offspring. Likewise, the give and take of food beyond the narrow context of parent-child ties is constitutive of relations of sharing, relations that subsist in the mutuality and companionship of persons in intimate social groups.[5] [. . .]

That the perception of the social world is grounded in the direct, mutually attentive involvement of self and other in shared contexts of experience, prior to its representation in terms of received conceptual schemata, is now well established. But in Western anthropological and psychological discourse, such involvement continues to be apprehended within the terms of the orthodox dualisms of subject and object, persons and things. Rendered as "intersubjectivity," it is taken to be the constitutive quality of the social domain *as against* the object world of nature, a domain open to human beings but not to nonhuman kinds.[6] Thus, according to Trevarthen and Logotheti, "human cultural intelligence is seen to be founded on a level of engagement of minds, or intersubjectivity, such as no other species has or can acquire."[7] In the hunter-gatherer economy of knowledge, by contrast, it is as entire persons, not as disembodied minds, that human beings engage with one another and, moreover, with nonhuman beings as well. They do so as beings *in* a world, not as minds that, excluded from a given reality, find themselves in the common predicament of having to make sense of it. To coin a term, the constitutive quality of their world is not intersubjectivity but *interagentivity*. To speak of the forest as a parent is not, then, to model object relations in terms of primary intersubjectivity, but to recognize that at root, the constitutive quality of intimate relations with nonhuman and human components of the environment is one and the same.

NOTES

1. Turnbull 1965:19.
2. Subsequent ethnographic work among the Mbuti has, it should be noted, cast considerable doubt on the authenticity of Turnbull's somewhat "romantic" account. Thus, Grinker (1992) fails to find indigenous conceptions that would correspond to the feeling for the forest that Turnbull imputes to the Mbuti. And Ichikawa (1992) observes that Mbuti attitudes toward the forest are, in reality, decidedly ambivalent: the forest is held to be the home of destructive as well as benevolent powers. But such ambivalence is equally characteristic of intimate relations in the human domain, which also have their undercurrent of negativity. However, by addressing the forest as "Father," Ichikawa states, Mbuti "are appealing to it for the benevolence normally expected from a parent" (1992:41).
3. Endicott 1979:82.
4. Bird-David 1990:190.
5. Cf. Price 1975; Ingold 1986:116–117.
6. Willis 1990:11–12.
7. Trevarthen and Logotheti 1989:167.

REFERENCES

Bird-David, N. 1990. "The Giving Environment: Another Perspective on the Economic System of Gatherer-Hunters." *Current Anthropology* 31:189–196.

Endicott, K. 1979. *Batek Negrito Religion*. Oxford: Clarendon Press.

Grinker, R. R. 1992. Comment on Nurit Bird-David, "Beyond 'The Original Affluent Society.'" *Current Anthropology* 33, no. 1: 39.

Ichikawa, M. 1992. Comment on Nurit Bird-David, "Beyond 'The Original Affluent Society.'" *Current Anthropology* 33, no. 1: 40–41.

Ingold, T. 1986. *The Appropriation of Nature*. Manchester: Manchester University Press.

Price, J. A. 1975. "Sharing: The Integration of Intimate Economies." *Anthropologica* 17:3–27.

Trevarthen, C. and K. Logotheti. 1989. "Child in Society, Society in Children: The Nature of Basic Trust." In *Societies at Peace*, ed. S. Howell and R. Willis, 165–186. London: Routledge.

Turnbull, C. M. 1965. *Wayward Servants: The Two Worlds of the African Pygmies*. London: Eyre and Spottiswoode.

Willis, R. 1990. "Introduction." In *Signifying Animals: Human Meaning in the Natural World*, ed. R. Willis, 1–24. London: Unwin Hyman.

Chapter Twenty-Three

SUPER-NATURAL FUTURES

One Possible Dialogue Between Afrofuturism and the Anthropocene

ANGELA LAST

Two types of invitations seem to be fluttering into my inbox with increasing frequency, for talks and exhibitions on the Anthropocene and Afrofuturism respectively. At first sight, the two might not have much in common, apart from the fact that both imaginaries deal with far pasts and futures: the proposed new geologic era of the Anthropocene has become a provocation to re-think the human as a geophysical agent; Afrofuturism (re)imagines African (and especially African diaspora) pasts and futures through flamboyant scifi and spiritual aesthetics. However, looking at the common theme of the cosmic and its role as both physical origin and culturally marked space, a dialogue could start around the question: who (or what) makes the future?

Here, Afrofuturism does not provide answers, but possibilities. Importantly, it challenges white (anthropocenic?) expectations of the future in which disaster is associated with racialised victims and crafty white survivors. It is such inscriptions that Afrofuturism messes with. The Egyptian aesthetics of Sun Ra and Ellen Gallagher, for example, exemplify the historical struggle over cultural legacies and the construction of 'high culture' and primitivism. Although often humorous in nature, the Egyptian imagery points to questions about whom constructions of Africa continue to serve and how they can be rewritten. The origin as well as the necessity of the term 'Afrofuturism' underscore the fact that the 'African' and African

FIGURE 23.1. Ellen Gallagher, installation view of *Pomp-Bang*, 2003. Plasticine, ink and paper mounted on canvas, 244 x 488 cm.
Source: Museum of Contemporary Art Chicago, Joseph and Jory Shapiro Fund by exchange and restricted gift of Sara Szold. Photo by Aya Garcia.

diaspora have routinely been excluded from 'modern' and techno-futurist visions. Here I am reminded of Octavia Butler's response to a white science fiction author who argued that there was no necessity for Black people to appear in their novels, since statements about the Other can be made through aliens.

In many ways, the Anthropocene discourse, too, practices inversion as a strategy to unsettle visions of modernity and to search for new models of human agency. Although scientists have not been able to agree on a potential beginning for the proposed new era, most of them have to do with consequences of imperialism (nuclear war, ancient empires, colonisation of the Americas etc). It could be argued that imperialism is still an issue today— but when the oil is used up, the water polluted and the temperature up, our role as a geologic force could be unsatisfactorily short. Again, we have to ask how far science is in the service of (economic) imperialism? What 'modernity' do they embody? Do 'subaltern modernities' perhaps reflect a more beneficial vision of modernity? It is interesting to note that some of the most interesting proposals seem to have been excluded from the 'main-stream' and have been consigned to the area of 'post-colonial ecologies' (unless they are suddenly seen as the 'magic bullet' from 'outer space'). I am thinking here especially of French-Caribbean discussions of political ecology (e.g. Daniel Maximin, Edouard Glissant, Suzanne and Aimé Césaire, Maryse Condé, etc.).

In an inversion of stereotypes, some Afrofuturist commentators highlight the 'primitivism' of a science that seeks to classify the 'primitive', pointing to mainstream science's contribution to racism and genocide at various moments in history. Further, although Afrofuturism has been accused of having 'nothing to do with Africa, and everything to do with cyberculture in the West' (Bristow), this 'remixed' African component has become regarded as a valuable challenge, whether it is reimagining community against the reality of erasure, the contestation of 'development' or a conservative notion of progress (Auma Obama in Okpako). Why could certain 'African' models of living—real or 'invented'—not hold the key to what we want to develop towards? While there is a danger of imagining a coherent 'Afro' within Afrofuturism, there is also the possibility of a 'strategic essentialism' to perform criticism. The corresponding Anthropocene question might be put as "what could the geo" be and do? The logic seems to be that if the human can be a geologic force, how else is human life geophysical—and how could this perspective lead to a more constructive reframing of politics and the social? Especially since, thanks to climate change, the stability of the 'meteorological White middle class' (as a recent German TV satire described Europe) might become seriously unsettled. . . .

For me, at this moment in time, the work of Ellen Gallagher best synthesises the dialogue between Anthropocene and Afrofuturism. Experiencing her retrospective at the Tate Modern in person, I was struck by what I experienced as a 'hypermaterialisation' of layers and layers of material and meaning. Robin Kelly describes his encounter with Ellen Gallagher's work as 'confounding': '[t]o confound is not simply to confuse, but to surprise or perplex by challenging received wisdom. It also means to mix up or fail to discern differences between things.' I don't think any term could be more appropriate. To me, Gallagher's shifts between meanings of medicine

FIGURE 23.2. Ellen Gallagher, *IGBT*, 2008. Gesso, gold leaf, ink, varnish and cut paper on canvas. 202 x 188 cm / 79 1/2 x 74 inches.
Source: Courtesy of the artist and Houser and Wirth.

and wig adverts, 'high' and 'low' art/culture references, 'nature' (I especially love the title 'Double Natural') and 'blackness', marine creatures, minstrel imagery, ambiguous organic shapes and political pamphlets rendered tangible the multiple ways in which people are being materialised and enlisted as part of social and economic production: overworked and stuck in a job you cannot get out of? Pop a pill. More 'organic' than society's ideal? Neighbours throwing bombs at your house? Buy a wig. Keep calm and carry on. The sheer ridiculousness of the enterprise as well as our complicity in it becomes apparent. Does Gallagher suggest any way out? It seemed to me that she was perhaps implying that the path towards more productive forms of materialisation may lie not only in realising the ridiculousness, but to start from it. Geology and politics? Ridiculous! Africans in space? Ridiculous! A reversal of development hierarchies? Ridiculous! Or is it?

Chapter Twenty-Four

RHYTHMS OF RELATION

Black Popular Music and Mobile Technologies

ALEXANDER G. WEHELIYE

Much of the critical literature about cellular telephones tends to focus on how radically this technology has altered communicative patterns at the node of public and private through its mobility and how people use cell phones to distinguish themselves from others or project images of themselves as hip teenagers or successful businessmen in a Veblenesque or Bourdiuesque fashion. [. . .] While those aspects clearly remain important in any considerations of technology, too often the tactile or haptic dimensions of these machines remain muted. How can we think about cell phones as communicative devices without losing sight and sound of their ringtones, vibrate modes, visual displays, touch screens, keypads, and so forth, as well as the feel and color of the material the machines are made of?

Many critics have noted how mobile communication reduces the nonlinguistic aspects of the communicative performance between the two or more speakers given that they appear to each other only as disembodied voices and/or snippets of text (email, SMS, mobile chat, for example) [. . .]. Nevertheless, these forms of interaction also buttress the non-face-to-face tête-à-tête, for instance through the different environments (temporal, geographic, social, etc.) the speakers inhabit and the various textures (sonic, haptic, visual, olfactory, etc.) of the mobile devices. Accordingly, body-to-body communication does not vanish in mobile communication but (re)materializes in both the participants' respective location and in the apparatus itself (Fortunati 2005). Put simply, mobile devices are bodies too, even if they exist chiefly in relation to and in symbiosis with humans. Given the ubiquity of mobile devices in the western world and across the globe, it would behoove us to conceptualize them not merely as disembodied tools that facilitate pure communication but also devise languages that allow for the analysis of the "fuzzy" and textural dimensions of mobile communication and the different apparatuses in which it is bodied forth.

For my purposes, contemporary black popular music not only presents sonic redactions of techno-ecologies, but more importantly their transposition into the realms of sensation via rhythm. These musical formations stage the "rush" of itinerant information technologies, what Anna Everett has referred to as "digital plentitude." Instead of merely focusing on the communicational dimensions of these machines, contemporary R&B unearths the aspects of technology above, beyond, and between the transmission of zeros and ones, highlighting, for instance, a body registering a pager set to vibrate mode. Brian Massumi elucidates the different modalities through which humans experience the world, differentiating "perception," "[which refers] to object oriented experience" from "sensation," "[which refers to] 'the perception of perception,' or self-referential experience. Sensation pertains to the stoppage- and stasis-tending dimension of reality. . . . Sensation pertains to the dimension of passage, or the continuity of immediate experience. . . . Perception is segmenting and capable of precision; sensation is unfolding and constitutively vague." Conveying sensation is crucial for it locates the import of technologies not merely in the contents they transmit or their socio-political significance, but also in the textural provenances of these machines, which are a considerable part of their allure and utility while oftentimes eluding the grip of critical discourse. [. . .] Whereas scholarly discussions tend to focus on the perception of mobile technologies, (black) popular music intensifies their sensation: the textural relay and relation between human bodies and machines. [. . .]

I will now turn to the British TV series *Metrosexuality* (1999) to draw attention to the rhythmic representation of mobile technologies in a chiefly ocular medium. In *Metrosexuality* much of the social interaction between the characters takes place on mobile and sedentary telephones, and phone conversations constitute at least half of the screen time. In the very first scene after the opening credits, we are introduced to teenager Kwame, who is desperately trying to reunite his divorced fathers Max and Jordan. Before Kwame makes a visual entrance on the screen, we witness a fast-paced montage of the telephone call Kwame places on his mobile. Rather than showing Kwame dialing his father's number, however, the screen is taken up by a series of accelerated motion images featuring city streets and buildings that are soundtracked by swishing sounds and accelerated recordings of mobile dial and ringing tones. Moreover, the camera angles are frequently irregular, which only adds to the perplexity engendered by these shots, especially since these shots also function as an introduction to Metrosexuality. The expedited noises and visual montage come to an abrupt halt with the tone of Max's mobile as he answers Kwame's call while sitting in a hair salon. Then, the editing crosscuts between Kwame's position on the streets of Noting Hill (the lettering on screen reads "In the heart of Noting Hill . . .") and Max's location at the salon as up-tempo dance music plays in the background. In this part of the sequence the camera circles restlessly around Kwame as he moves around and speaks to his father, while a stable camera frames a medium close-up of Max's face.

Once the phone conversation between the two has ended, we cut to a close-up of Kwame's hands as he dials papa Jordan's number, which is followed by another fast-motion montage that depicts the rapid travel of information over cellular networks via the rhythmic editing of image and sound. Jordan takes Kwame's call on a grey cordless phone whilst working in a recording studio with mid-tempo bass heavy music emanating from the studio speakers. In his conversations with his fathers, Kwame tells both that the other parent has failed to pick him up from soccer practice, and, as a result, Max and Jordan arrive at Kwame's location at the same time, while Kwame and his two best friends watch them interact at a distance. Sadly, Max and Jordan do not reconcile as Kwame had hoped in devising this elaborate ruse. In Jordan's portion of this tripartite interaction, the diegetic music, the telephone, and Jordan's clothing provide a muted contrast (monochrome, largely grey clothing, enclosed space, only the bass of the music is audible, etc.) to the brash, colorful, and buoyant sounds and colors that structure the shots featuring Kwame (canary yellow hip-hop outfit, electric blue cellular phone, lots of movement, etc.) and Max (red mobile phone, blond dreadlocks, red flowery outfit, etc.).

There are many instances like this over the course of the show's narrative that imagine how aural information traverses space via the deployment of highly accelerated and rapidly intercut images accompanied by swishing and ringing noises to accentuate the velocity of the montage. Here, velocity registers as the intensification of sensation, because the viewer is forced to bear witness to the duration of its escalation. The collages of the telephone calls in *Metrosexuality* punctuate the triangulated visual and sonic flow between the different locales/characters, channeling the rush mobile communication in ways that are specific to the medium of television; they also set in motion a rhythmic "poetics of relation" at the juncture of mobile devices and humans.

Nicola Green's treatment of rhythm accents the different temporal structures of mobile technology use, distinguishing between three modalities of mobile rhythm: "the rhythms of mobile use; the rhythms of integrating mobile use into everyday life; and the rhythms of relation between use in everyday life and institutional social change" (2002, 285). The examples discussed in this chapter add another rhythmic layer to the relational complexities of mobile time by initially removing mobile technologies from everyday life. Wrested from the vagaries of the quotidian and interfaced with pop songs or televisual narratives, these machines have radically different functions, moving, to put it in schematic terms, from practical use to aesthetic sensation. Surely, both of these aspects already commingle before their musicalization, and in this way, it is a shift not in kind but in degree and intensity that amplifies those rhythmic dimensions beside and below routine information transmission. Moreover, once they have entered into rhythmic relations with other matters and forces, the textural facets of mobile technologies reenter the annals of everyday life, becoming integral to these devices' allure and functionality. According to Gilles Deleuze, "rhythm . . . is more profound than vision, hearing, etc. . . . What is ultimate is thus the relation between sensation and rhythm, which places in each sensation the levels and domains through which it passes. . . . Sensation is not qualitative and qualified, but has only an intensive reality, which no longer determines within itself representative elements, but allotropic variations." The instances of mobile rhythm analyzed above produce the polymorph variations mentioned by Deleuze in their emphasis on the diverse rhythms of the technological and the human, hinting at an embodied relational theory of mobile technologies that accents their communicative and aesthetic facets.

As a conceptual tool and a mode of apprehending the world "rhythm" mobilizes "the processes of bringing-into-relation" that are fundamental to any social formation and/or object but are habitually neglected in favor of their stagnant counterparts. Still, these models of rhythm (and Glissant's notion of relation) do not simply replace the metronomic beat of the inert and unchanging with sheer flux; instead they dwell in the uneven territory at the junction of mobile use, everyday life, institutional social change, and aesthetics. Indeed, rhythm names and transacts the dialectical liaison of these at times opposing forces, making them constitutive of the objects or practices they envelop. Therefore, rhythm produces the multifaceted processes through which mobile technologies (along with a host of other technologies and rituals) come into being as consuming textural, sonic, and haptic relations, or in Henri Lefebvre's phrasing: "To grasp a rhythm it is necessary to have been *grasped* by it. . . ." Taken together, the cell phone rings, the pager sounds, Drake's BlackBerry authorship, ringtone rap, the repeated sung vociferations of ring, ring, ring, call me, 2-way, LOL, smiley face, and blackberry, as well as the optico-sonic overflow of *Metrosexuality* boost the mobile sensations of communication technologies through the conduit of rhythm. The aforementioned rhythmifications might appear auxiliary, but they tap into facets central to the existence and utility of mobile technologies that do not register on the metronomic radar of many critical dialects. If, as John Urry remarks, "humans are sensuous, corporeal, technologically extended and *mobile* beings," then cellular telephones, because they are highly mobile and facilitate interpersonal contact, operate as prime indicators of what it means to be human at this point in history (original emphasis). The sonic incorporation of mobile technologies into popular music extends and remixes these machines' anthropomorphic bass line, and, as a result embodies the rhythmic relation of all technologies.

Chapter Twenty-Five

PROLIFERATION, EXTINCTION, AND AN ANTHROPOCENE AESTHETIC

MYRA HIRD

Th[e] Anthropocene aesthetic, which allows us to "move on and see nothing," [. . .] explains why rampant pollution in great urban cities such as New York, London, and Paris during and since the Industrial Revolution was not viewed as a catastrophe or even an unintended but necessary consequence of capitalism's expansion but was rather understood as a material visualization of the power, scale, acceleration, and *success* of capitalism's conquest of nature. Monet and other artists depicted industrialism's flourishing pollution—London smog, soot-covered houses, blackened sludge-filled rivers—in paintings such as *Impression: Sun Rising* (1873). In his analysis, Mirzoeff draws our attention to Monet's depiction of his own hometown of Le Havre in Normandy, which was at the time France's central port for transatlantic passenger shipping. In this painting we see the long-established rowing boats of premodernity dwarfed by industrial cranes and coal smoke billowing from steamers. Indeed, suggests Mirzoeff, it is the unique color of the yellow coal smoke combined with the blue morning light and red rising sun that makes this painting so visually remarkable.[3] This pollution, like the soot covering buildings in early twentieth-century British cities like Bradford was viewed as a verification of society's progress in industrializing.

Similarly, the middens of premodernity that grew in scale and diversity to vast trash heaps encroaching on urban landscapes were perceived as a

FIGURE 25.1. Claude Monet, *Impression Sunrise*, 1872, oil on canvas, 48 cm x 63 cm (18.8 in. x 24.8 in.).
Source: public domain.

testament to the progress of capitalist venture in what would become an emerging Anthropocene aesthetic. Take for instance E. H. Dixon's famous watercolor, the *Great Dust Heap* (1837), at King's Cross in London, which depicted an enormous garbage dump in the shape of the Alps, surrounded by urban slum dwellings, a few allotments, and a smallpox hospital. Carts loaded with more detritus are being cast onto the burgeoning heap. So well known was this garbage dump that it appeared in Charles Dickens's *Our Mutual Friend* (1865) [. . .,] illustrat[ing] an Enlightenment aesthetic in which pollution signifies economic prosperity and industriousness. One household's discards were the scavenger's spoils, to be picked over, collected, and reinserted into the circuits of capital.[4] *Where there's muck, there's brass.*[5] [. . .]

Today's Anthropocene aesthetic, with its roots in the Enlightenment conquest of nature and territory, colonization, biopolitics and hygiene, and invasion ecology visualizes landfills' teeming microbial masses safely

stowed and contained within engineered megalandfills: nature destrati-
fied, utilized, and restratified. The earth gives up its resources—fossil fuels,
minerals, rocks, water, and so on—and, through geo-bio relations humans
imagine and engineer, welcomes back our detritus and indeed turns it into
a resource for human use.[6] Microbes are now enlisted in relations of calcu-
lation, control, and, increasingly, services in the form of oil spill–cleanup
operations, carbon sinks, and the consumption of waste to produce meth-
ane. Capitalist enterprise is even exploring the potential of landfill mining.
Through an Anthropocene aesthetic, we visualize our waste as not there:
invisibly restratified, covered over, and reutilized into "natural spaces"
while at the same time enlisted into capitalist regimes of profit and circulation (Hird forthcoming).

[. . . A]t the limits of the Anthropocene, the future cannot be visual-
ized: It is an unknown aesthetic in excess of scientific prediction, human
agency, and good will. [. . .] Put another way, there is an imprescriptibility
to the Anthropocene—a reckless quality. An unintended stumbling into
something we don't understand, are not able to predict, and are not able
to control. [. . .]

What could define an Anthropocene antiaesthetic is an acknowledgment of the profound implications that bacteria may be generating new life
forms not registered by humans *and* that this is what the microcosmos has
been doing for the past 3.5 billion years. Landfills are not simply standing
reserves for humans to dump their waste into and then exhume. And this,
I think, is one of the major points about the Anthropocene—that humans
are now contributing to, making their mark, as a geological force, and that
this force is not so much from a godlike positionality of consciousness and
control but must be added to the list of proliferations and extinctions with
unintended and unknown consequences. And further, that the power relationship—if there is one—is squarely in favor of the microcosmos. [. . .]

There is a runaway quality to this Anthropocene aesthetic: that
nothing—no patch of land, sea, or air—escapes the potentiality of capital's
perpetual reach. Waste "management," then, signifies not only attempts to
contain capital's fallout but to refuse it. And it is precisely in this refusal
that the Anthropocene's anti-aesthetic manifests. This antiaesthetic is not
subsumed within the aesthetic; it is not an aesthetic subset. It occurs when
the sensorium "can no longer make sense of what is presented to it. We cannot articulate what we perceive, namely, that the climate is wrong—too hot,

too dry, too wet, or all of the above. Any suggestion to this effect is at once challenged." Thus, perhaps what characterizes an Anthropocene aesthetic is a heightened anxious slippage between visualizations of the conquest of nature and the realization of our vulnerability *as* nature within a volatile and agentic environment: an aesthetic of solar panels orbiting the earth and an antiaesthetic of leaking, exploding, seeping, and combusting landfills.

Chapter Twenty-Six

INTERVIEW WITH GRAHAM HARMAN

On Art and Ecology

ZANE CERPINA

ZANE CERPINA: [. . . M]aybe you can explain how Object Oriented Ontology [OOO] can help us to understand the world we live in better and if it can help us to deal with possible future scenarios? Can it guide us through the age of the Anthropocene?

GRAHAM HARMAN: The initial motivation of OOO was the same thing as with many philosophers: namely, we need to begin with the widest possible category. That is what we do in philosophy. And since the modern distinction between subject and object still haunts contemporary philosophy, with its assumption that the human is a radically different ontological kind from all other entities, our first task is to flatten this distinction. I actually prefer the term "object" as the flat term that covers both humans and non-humans, simply because I see my thinking as building on the work of the Austrians from Brentano through Husserl. Some observers are critical of this term "object" and think I should change it, [but[I'm more or less married to it now. [. . .]

History itself is becoming a matter of objects. Sometimes we encounter the quarrel between those who think that great individuals shape history and those who think that the collective mass is a more important force. The problem is that these two such opposed views are fixated on people as the moving force in history. But history is increasingly shaped by technological objects and consumer entities that are much more important and famous than their human creators. I've seen the World Wide Web change my own life and everyone else's over the past twenty years. We can be polite and give Tim Berners-Lee some deserved credit for this, but he is not the household name that Napoleon and Thomas Edison were, even though his invention is known to everybody. [. . .]

Let's turn now to art, which has always been Anthropocene as well. If all humans (along with whatever animals are capable of aesthetic experience) were exterminated, I am confident in saying that there would be no art. Thus, human participation is necessary for art. But once again, it doesn't follow that art is nothing more than whatever explicit impact it has on humans. An artwork resists our first interpretations, or has effects different from what the artist intended. This point would never have occurred to me if not that someone asked me in 2012: "What would an art without humans look like?" The question confused me at first, but after a few weeks of thought I realized it was a meaningless question, based on the overly literal notion that since Speculative Realist philosophy is interested in the world as it is beyond human access to it, therefore we must be trying to expunge humans from every corner of the universe. This is an absurd notion for which I blame, primarily, the overly literal minds at Urbanomic Publishing, who continue to promulgate falsehoods such as "realism means that science is more important than the humanities." Hardly. The real exists everywhere, including in the purely human domains. There is no reason to get rid of the human in order to take reality seriously.

ZANE CERPINA: You said that we are ingredients to art rather than being observers. But what is art's role as an ingredient in human understanding of the world?

GRAHAM HARMAN: I would say rather that we are also observers of art, but that our observations do not exhaust the artwork, which refuses to reveal itself entirely to the observer. In some ways art has never been stronger. There are artists almost anywhere you go, and a great many of them are doing something interesting. You can find them pretty much anywhere on the globe without even looking very hard. And yet I don't sense a strong conception among artists of what an artist is supposed to be doing. Maybe that's useful in a way, since in the modernist period there was perhaps an overly polished and premature self-understanding that guided the art of that period. But these days it is very unclear where art ends and sociology or anthropology begin. The blurring of artificial boundaries is an activity that, in our time, always has a good press. Yet I'm not sure that it's deserved. At a certain point, you need to gain individual or collective clarity about what you're doing. I am hopeful that in next decade or so we will start to have a clearer vision of where things are headed in the arts.

Though I'm not entirely on board with the formalist conception of art as divorced from the society and politics of its time, politicization is a constant danger, precisely because our sphere of political thinking has become so banal. There's a sort of "Lowest Common Denominator Leftism" that everyone in the arts is obliged to endorse. We must all oppose American and especially Israeli imperialism. We must express grave worry about the surveillance society and the destruction of the environment. We must bemoan the treatment of immigrants and refugees. Well, I can't really disagree with any of this. As a citizen I will accept these views. But why use up valuable art-time to preach these already processed and adopted standard political ideas to each other? The chances of contemporary art successfully spearheading any fresh new political principles is close to zero. We're just regurgitating a 19th century idealist discourse, and by choosing "neo-liberalism" as our recurrent target we're not being as honest as the old Marxists when they said "capitalism." By "idealist" what I mean here is the notion that the human mind is basically alienated, and needs to be liberated from this alienation. And while it's true that there are places where liberation from oppression is badly needed, I reject the idea that this depicts the human condition more generally. That's because I don't think freedom is what we really want. We don't really want to be free human subjects: in fact, we would rather be objects than subjects. We would rather be a particular thing rather than some vague free human subject that can be anything.

ZANE CERPINA: You mentioned previously that art does not give solutions, but is more a way of knowledge making. Do you think that artists who focus on contemporary problems, such as the refugee crisis in Syria or global warming, can give the society new ways to perceive and deal with these issues?

GRAHAM HARMAN: I am skeptical toward the idea that either art or philosophy should be dealing with the social problems of the moment, because then it is reduced to making the public aware of truths that we think we have already mastered. Art then is reduced to a public propaganda, however humane and admirable its specific goals may seem. Again, I am not entirely a formalist, and I don't think that social content is entirely irrelevant in art. And yet, art cannot provide a great solution, just as it can not provide knowledge. If what you need is knowledge, art is not the best place to look. Instead, please look first to science, or even to Wikipedia. When looking at art, you should be looking instead for an aesthetic surprise of some sort, some new way of looking at things[, . . .] primarily an aesthetic experience rather than a scientific one.[. . .] Art is a form of cognition without being a form of knowledge, and philosophy is in the same position. Philosophy is not a knowledge. In part, [OOO] is trying to recover Socrates' energetic sense of this. [. . .]

ZANE CERPINA: You are also using ideas from Marshall McLuhan in your philosophy. How do you think technologies affect our culture and thinking in the current times?

GRAHAM HARMAN: I was pleased to hear [. . .] that you appreciate Marshal McLuhan, because so many people do not. This is especially true in the UK, where Raymond Williams was perhaps the most prominent author who poisoned the soil for McLuhan. In the UK he is often attacked as a "technological determinist," though this is demonstrably untrue. In the United States his critics speak in different terms, picking on details: one critic doesn't like the distinction between hot and cold media, and another rejects the idea of media as extensions of the human body. But as McLuhan used to say in his lectures: "If you don't like that idea, I have others!" You can think what you like about McLuhan, but he was one of the great "depth theorists" of the twentieth century along with Freud, Heidegger, and Clement Greenberg. By "depth theory" I mean the idea that surface content is trivial in comparison with its hidden background conditions. This, too, has its limits, but it was nonetheless one of the great discoveries of the twentieth century. OOO starts from this contempt for the surface but does not end there. To push such twentieth-century depth theory another step, one needs to realize that, paradoxically, the surface is where everything in the depth is triggered. Causation, for example, happens at the most trivial layer of existence, yet it has so many consequences. So that even though OOO is widely considered a theory of withdrawn objects (and for good reason), it is about to flip into the opposite, into a theory of how the surface is triggered.

ZANE CERPINA: Thinking about interdisciplinarity. You are often invited to give talks for art and architecture students and also in other fields, not only in philosophy. How do you see the importance of mixing different fields? Of being transdisciplinary?

GRAHAM HARMAN: I think if you try too consciously to mix fields, it results in a kind of flavorless mush. I think it is important that if mixing happens, it has been a direct result of hard work in your home discipline, and was largely unintentional. Otherwise, I could not be happier, could not be more reassured about my work, than when other disciplines show an interest in it. Sometimes philosophers (generally not successful ones) attack me by saying that only other disciplines are interested in me. But I'm not sure why philosophers should be proud when no one reads their work but themselves.

Chapter Twenty-Seven

FROM *DARK ECOLOGY*

TIMOTHY MORTON

Remember Earth clearly. Thinking outside the Neolithic box would involve seeing and talking at a magnitude we humanists find embarrassing or ridiculous or politically suspect. Perhaps it is completely outlandish: thinking this way is easily marginalized as an activity for loons. We can find examples, but they are indeed marginal. We might for instance find them in the insights of psychedelic drug-fueled depression exemplified in the middle-period work of the British techno group Orbital (active since 1989). The video for Orbital's "The Box" is a miracle of juxtaposed timescales. A lonely wanderer played by Tilda Swinton holds a position for a very long time. A camera films her and what happens around her. Then the film is sped up, so that the wanderer appears to be walking through a megacity while cars and people rush around her at breakneck speed. The physical difficulty of the dancer's role is breathtaking, which performs the difficulty of thinking on more than one scale at once: the thinking that ecological awareness demands.

The dancer stops outside a cheap electronics store. She watches televisions in the window. Unbeknownst to the passersby, since it is happening on such a slow timescale relative to them, secret messages are flashing on the screen. Only the isolated wanderer can see them: she functions in a temporal scope sufficient to read the messages that perhaps to others appear only as minuscule flickers. One has to pause the video to read the evocative sequence oneself:

REMEMBER EARTH CLEARLY
BAD
DAMAGED
BATTERED
PLANET
FRAYED
DUSTBOWL
COMPROMISED
WAKE UP
MONSTERS EXIST

It's a sinister, paranoid moment of ecological awareness. What is the monster? Sophocles encapsulated it already in the astonishing Second Chorus of his Theban play *Antigone: Of the many disturbing beings, man is the most disturbing.* Why? Because he plows, and because he is aware of how this plowing disturbs Earth. "DUSTBOWL" obviously references the disaster of agricultural feedback loops. We are disturbed by our disturbance—and we don't stop: seeing "MONSTERS EXIST" on a TV screen in a shop window is like the fantasy of seeing a monstrous face in the mirror when you pass by in the dark.

Imagine *seeing* on more than one timescale—just as geology and climate science *think* on more than one. Imagine for a moment that the phenomenon-thing gap were closed and that you could see everything. This is what is happening to the woman in *The Box.* The lonely walker perceives the phrase "MONSTERS EXIST" on a television screen that no one else can see: they would require the scaled-up temporality at which she is living to see it. This is like being able to see hyperobjects. Why is this disturbing? Because *you are already living* on more than one timescale. Ecological awareness is disorienting precisely because of these multiple scales. We sense that there *are* monsters even if we can't see them directly.

There's a monster in the dark mirror, and you are a cone in one of its eyes. When you are sufficiently creeped out by the human species, you see something even bigger than the Anthropocene looming in the background, hiding in plain sight in the prose of Thomas Hardy, the piles of fruit in the supermarket, the gigantic parking lots, the suicide rate. What on Earth is this structure that looms even larger than the age of steam and oil? Isn't it enough that we have to deal with cars and drills? Hardy provides a wide-screen way of seeing agricultural production, sufficient for glimpsing not only the immiseration of women in particular and the rural working class in general at a specific time and place but also the gigantic machinery of agriculture: not just specific machines, but *the machine that is agriculture as such*, a machine that predates Industrial Age machinery. Before the web of fate began to be woven on a power loom, machinery was already whirring away.

Chapter Twenty-Eight

FROM WHAT IS THE MEASURE OF NOTHINGNESS?

Infinity, Virtuality, Justice

KAREN BARAD

Nothingness. The void. An absence of matter. The blank page. Utter silence. No thing, no thought, no awareness. Complete ontological insensibility.

Shall we utter some words about nothingness? What is there to say? How to begin? How can anything be said about nothing without violating its very nature, perhaps even its conditions of possibility? Isn't any utterance about nothingness always already a performative breach of that which one means to address? Have we not already said too much simply in pronouncing its name?

Perhaps we should let the emptiness speak for itself.

At the very least, listening to nothing would seem to require exquisite attention to every subtle detail. Suppose we had a finely tuned, ultrasensitive instrument that we could use to zoom in on and tune in to the nuances and subtleties of nothingness.[1] But what would it mean to zoom in on nothingness, to look and listen with ever-increasing sensitivity and acuity, to move to finer and finer scales of detail of . . .? Alas, it is difficult to conceive how one would orient oneself regarding such a task. What defines scale in the void? What is the metric of emptiness? What is the measure of nothingness? How can we approach it?[2]

On the face of it, these questions seem vacuous, but there may be more here than meets the eye. Consider, first, setting up the condition for the experiment: we begin with a vacuum. Now, if a vacuum is the absence of everything, of all matter, how can we be sure that we have nothing at hand? We'll need to do a measurement to confirm this. We could shine a flashlight on the vacuum, or use some other probe, but that would introduce at least one photon (quantum of light) onto the scene, thereby destroying the very conditions we seek. Like turning up the light to see the darkness, this situation is reminiscent of the mutually exclusive conditions of im/possibility that are at issue in Niels Bohr's interpretation of quantum physics.

Measurements, including practices such as zooming in or examining something with a probe, don't just happen (in the abstract)—they require specific measurement apparatuses. Measurements are agential practices, which are not simply revelatory but performative: they help constitute and are a constitutive part of what is being measured.[3] In other words, measurements are *intra-actions* (not interactions): the agencies of observation are inseparable from that which is observed. Measurements are world-making: matter and meaning do not preexist, but rather are co-constituted via measurement intra-actions.

If the measurement intra-action plays a constitutive role in what is measured, then it matters how something is explored. In fact, this is born out empirically in experiments with matter (and energy): when electrons (or light) are measured using one kind of apparatus, they are waves; if they are measured in a complementary way, they are particles. Notice that what we're talking about here is not simply some object *reacting* differently to different probings but *being* differently. What is at issue is the very nature of nature. A quantum ontology deconstructs the classical one: there are no pre-existing individual objects with determinate boundaries and properties that precede some interaction, nor are there any concepts with determinate meanings that could be used to describe their behavior; rather, determinate boundaries and properties of objects-within-phenomena, and determinate contingent meanings, are enacted through specific intra-actions, where *phenomena* are the ontological inseparability of intra-acting agencies. Measurements are material-discursive practices of mattering. And phenomena are contingent configurations of mattering. At the heart of quantum physics is an inherent ontological indeterminacy. This indeterminacy is only ever partially resolved in the materialization of specific phenomena: determinacy, as materially enacted in the very constitution of a phenomenon, always entails constitutive exclusions (that which must remain indeterminate). Now, it's one thing for *matter* to materialize differently according to different measurement practices, but is there some way in which the specificity of measurement practices matters if we're measuring the *void*, when the void is presumably nothing?

Complementarity.[4] Contingency. Indeterminacy. Inseparability. Any attempt to say something, anything, even about nothing, and we find ourselves always already immersed in the play of quantum in/determinacy.

Questions of the nature of measurement—or, more broadly, intra-actions—are at the core of quantum physics. Intra-actions are practices of making a difference, of cutting together-apart, entangling-differentiating (one move) in the making of phenomena. Phenomena—entanglements of matter/ing across spacetimes—are not in the world, but *of* the world. Importantly, intra-actions are not limited to human-based measurement practices. Indeed, the issues at stake in exploring the vacuum are not merely questions of human exploratory practices in the quest for knowledge, but are thought to be ontologically poignant matters that go to the very nature of matter itself.

When it comes to the quantum vacuum, as with all quantum phenomena, ontological indeterminacy (not epistemological uncertainty) is at the heart of (the) matter . . . and no matter. Indeed, is it not rather the very nature of existence that is at issue, or rather nonexistence, or rather the conditions of im/possibilities for non/existence? . . . Or maybe that's the very question the vacuum keeps asking itself. Maybe the ongoing questioning of itself is what generates, or rather *is*, the structure of nothingness. The vacuum is no doubt doing its own experiments with non/being.[5]

In/determinacy is not the state of a thing, but an unending dynamism. The play of in/determinacy accounts for the un/doings of no/thingness.

From the point of view of classical physics, the vacuum has no matter and no energy. But the quantum principle of ontological indeterminacy calls the existence of such a zero-energy, zero-matter state into question, or rather, makes it into a question with no decidable answer. Not a settled matter, or rather, no matter. And if the energy of the vacuum is not determinately zero, it isn't determinately empty. In fact, this indeterminacy is responsible not only for the void not being nothing (while not being something), but it may in fact be the source of all that is, a womb that births existence. Birth and death are not the sole prerogative of the animate world. "Inanimate" beings also have finite lives. "Particles can be born and particles can die," explains one physicist. In fact, "it is a matter of birth, life, and death that requires the development of a new subject in physics, that of quantum field theory. . . . Quantum field theory is a response to the ephemeral nature of life."[6]

Quantum field theory (QFT) was invented in the 1920s, and its development continues to this day.[7] It is a theory that combines insights from the classical field theory of electromagnetism (mid-nineteenth century), special relativity (1905), and quantum mechanics (1920s). QFT takes us to a deeper level of understanding of the quantum vacuum and its implications. According to QFT, the vacuum can't be determinately nothing because the indeterminacy principle allows for fluctuations *of* the quantum vacuum.[8] How can we understand "vacuum fluctuations"? First, it is necessary to know a few things about what physicists mean by the notion of a field.

A *field* is something that has a physical quantity associated with every point in spacetime.[9] Let's consider a very simple example of a field: an infinite drumhead that can be assigned a time-varying displacement value at each point in space. If the drumhead is not vibrating, then it is completely flat and has the same value everywhere—let's call this the zero value, corresponding to no displacement. If a drummer now taps the drumhead, it vibrates, and waves of energy flow outward from where it is tapped. In this case, the field values vary in space and time as the displacement wave moves across the surface. Thus far we have a classical field theory, with a perfectly still drumhead representing the classical vacuum (or zero-energy state), and a vibrating drumhead representing a nonzero-energy state. Now we add quantum physics. Quantizing the field means that only certain discrete vibrational states exist. (If you're not used to thinking about different vibrational modes of a drum, it may be easier to visualize a stringed instrument with only a discrete set of standing waves, or harmonics, possible.) Now we add special relativity, in particular, the insight that matter and energy are equivalent ($E = mc^2$). Since vibrations of the field carry energy, and only a discrete set of energy states can exist, and a mass value can be assigned to each energy state, then we can see that a field vibrating at a particular frequency or energy is equivalent to the existence of particles of matter with a particular mass. This correspondence between quantum particles and quantized fields is the cornerstone of QFT.

Now let's return to our question: what is a vacuum fluctuation? Using the drum example, the quantum vacuum would correspond to a state where the average value of the displacements is zero everywhere, that is, there's no drummer tapping the drum. And yet the stillness of the drumhead is not assured, or rather, there is no determinate fact of the matter as to whether or not the drumhead is perfectly still, even in the absence of all external disturbances, including drumming. In other words, vacuum fluctuations are the indeterminate vibrations of the vacuum or zero-energy state.

Putting this point in the complementary language of particles rather than fields, we can understand vacuum fluctuations in terms of the existence of virtual particles: *virtual particles are quanta of the vacuum fluctuations*. That is, *virtual particles are quantized indeterminacies-in-action*. Admittedly, this is difficult to imagine, even more so than the account that is usually given. According to the usual lore, virtual particles are very short-lived entities that come into and out of existence so quickly that they can't be detected, and hence are not real, not in the same sense as actual particles. But this way of putting it entails the wrong temporality and ontology. *Virtuality* is not a speedy return, a popping into and out of existence with great rapidity, but rather *the indeterminacy of being/nonbeing, a ghostly non/existence*. In other words, the common portrayal of quantum vacuum fluctuations as an arena of covert virtual activity—particle-antiparticle pairs rapidly coming into and out of existence, getting away with something for nothing if only it happens fast enough that we can't know about it, that is, that we can't actually count any divergences from pure nothingness, like a banker playing fast and loose with accounts, taking money out and paying it back before anyone notices anything missing from the ledger—is of questionable validity. The void is not a financial wheeler-dealer, an ethically questionable, shadowy character.[10] Rather, the void is a spectral realm with a ghostly existence. Not even nothing can be free of ghosts.[11] Virtual particles do not traffic in a metaphysics of presence. They do not exist in space and time. They are ghostly non/existences that teeter on the edge of the infinitely thin blade between being and nonbeing. They speak of indeterminacy. Or rather, no determinate words are spoken by the vacuum, only a speaking silence that is neither silence nor speech, but the conditions of im/possibility for non/existence. There are an infinite number of im/possibilities, but not everything is possible. The vacuum isn't empty, but neither is there any/thing in it. Hence, we can see that indeterminacy is key not only to the existence of matter but also to its nonexistence, or rather, it is the key to the play of non/existence.

Virtual particles are not in the void but *of* the void. They are on the razor edge of non/being. The void is a lively tension, a desiring orientation toward being/becoming. The vacuum is flush with yearning, bursting with innumerable imaginings of what could be. The quiet cacophony of different frequencies, pitches, tempos, melodies, noises, pentatonic scales, cries, blasts, sirens, sighs, syncopations, quarter tones, allegros, ragas, bebops, hip-hops, whimpers, whines, screams, are threaded through the silence, ready to erupt, but simultaneously crosscut by a disruption, dissipating, dispersing the would-be sound into non/being, an indeterminate symphony of voices. The blank page teeming with the desires of would-be traces of every symbol, equation, word, book, library, punctuation mark, vowel, diagram, scribble, inscription, graphic, letter, inkblot, as they yearn toward expression. A jubilation of emptiness.

Don't for a minute think that there are no material effects of yearning and imagining. Virtual particles are experimenting with the im/possibilities of non/being, but that doesn't mean they aren't real, on the contrary. Consider this recent headline: "It's Confirmed: Matter Is Merely Vacuum Fluctuations."[12] The article explains that most of the mass of protons and neutrons (which constitute the nucleus and therefore the bulk of an atom) is due not to its constituent particles (the quarks), which only account for 1 percent of its mass, but rather to contributions from virtual particles. Let's try to understand this better. Consider an individual particle. According to classical physics, a particle can stand on its own. We simply place a particle in the void—a Democritean delight. But according to QFT, a physical particle, even a (presumedly) structureless point particle like an electron, does not simply reside in the vacuum as an independent entity, but rather is inseparable from the vacuum. The electron is a structureless point particle "dressed" with its intra-actions with virtual particles: it intra-acts with itself (and with other particles) through the mediated exchange of virtual particles. (For example, an electron may intra-act with itself through the exchange of a virtual photon, or some other virtual particle, and that virtual particle may further engage in other virtual intraactions, and so on.) Not every intra-action is possible, but the number of possibilities is infinite. In fact, the energy-mass of this infinite number of virtual intra-actions makes an infinite contribution to the mass of the electron. But how can this be when the mass of a physical electron is clearly finite (indeed, it's pretty darn small from our perspective)? The explanation physicists give is that the lone ("bare") point particle's contribution is infinite as well (infinitely negative due to the negative charge of the electron), and when the two infinities (that of the bare electron and that of the vacuum self-energy) are properly added together, the sum is a finite number, and not just any finite number but the one that matches the empirical value of the mass of the electron![13] In other words, an electron is not just "itself" but includes a "cloud" of an indeterminate number of virtual particles. All this may seem like a farfetched story, but it turns out that vacuum fluctuations have direct measurable consequences (e.g., Lamb shift, Casimir effect, the anomalous magnetic moment of the electron).[14]

So even the smallest bits of matter are an enormous multitude. Each "individual" is made up of all possible histories of virtual intra-actions with all Others. Indeterminacy is an un/doing of identity that unsettles the very foundations of non/being. Together with Derrida we might then say: "identity . . . can only affirm itself as identity to itself by opening itself to the hospitality of a difference from itself or of a difference with itself. Condition of the self, such a difference *from* and *with* itself would then be its very thing . . . the stranger at home."[15] Individuals are infinitely indebted to all Others, where indebtedness is not about a debt that follows or results from a trans/action, but rather, a debt that is the condition of possibility of giving/receiving.

Ontological indeterminacy, a radical openness, an infinity of possibilities, is at the core of mattering. How strange that indeterminacy, in its infinite openness, is the condition for the possibility of all structures in their dynamically reconfiguring in/stabilities. Matter in its iterative materialization is a dynamic play of in/determinacy. Matter is never a settled matter. It is always already radically open. Closure can't be secured when the conditions of im/possibilities and lived indeterminacies are integral, not supplementary, to what matter is.

Nothingness is not absence, but the infinite plentitude of openness. Infinities are not mere mathematical idealizations, but incarnate marks of in/determinacy. Infinities are a constitutive part of all material "finities," or perhaps more aptly, "af/finities" (*affinities*, from the Latin, "related to or bordering on; connection, relationship"). Representation has confessed its shortcomings throughout history: unable to convey even the palest shadow of the Infinite, it has resigned itself to incompetence in dealing with the transcendent, cursing our finitude. But if we listen carefully, we can hear the whispered murmurings of infinity immanent in even the smallest details. Infinity is the ongoing material reconfiguring of nothingness; and finity is not its flattened and foreshortened projection on a cave wall, but an infinite richness. The idea of finitude as lack is lacking. The presumed lack of ability of the finite to hold the infinite in its finite manifestation seems empirically unfounded, and cuts short the infinite agential resources of undecidability/indeterminacy that are always already at play. Infinity and nothingness are not the termination points defining a line. Infinity and nothingness are infinitely threaded through one another so that every infinitesimal bit of one always already contains the other. The possibilities for justice-to-come reside in every morsel of finitude.

> To be oneself is first of all to have a skin of one's own and, secondly, to use it as a space in which one can experience sensations.
> —DIDIER ANZIEU, *THE SKIN EGO*

> The layer which I really needed to take off was what can only be described as a second skin. But no matter how hot or how cold or how uncomfortable it makes you feel, you cannot get it off. I yearned for the pure relief you get from ripping off some really uncomfortable piece of clothing, except, I couldn't because that last layer was me.
> —RAYMOND THOMPSON, *WHAT TOOK YOU SO LONG?*

> Why should the area of the skin, which guarantees a human being's existence in space, be most despised and left to the tender mercies of the senses?
> —YUKIO MISHIMA, *SUN AND STEEL*

NOTES

1. Throughout the paper, I invoke, and sometimes mix, different modalities of sensing as a way of gesturing toward the multiplicity of possibilities for sensing the insensible, including the possibility of synesthetic expression and its detection. Scientific evidence of the stimulation of synesthetic experience through sensory deprivation is at least evocative in this context. See, for example, the review by Pegah Afra, Michael Funke, and Fumisuke Matsuo, "Acquired Auditory-Visual Synesthesia: A Window to Early Cross-Modal Sensory Interactions," *Psychology Research and Behavior Management* 2 (2009), pp. 31–37; and David Brang and V. S. Ramachandran, "Survival of the Synesthesia Gene: Why Do People Hear Colors and Taste Words?" *PLoS Biol* 9, no. 11: e1001205. doi:10.1371/journal.pbio.1001205.

2. While I begin this essay with the idea of zooming in on nothingness, I don't want the reader to misunderstand and think that indeterminacy, or rather, the play of in/determinacies, is limited to the domain of the small. On the contrary, the play of indeterminacies is ontologically prior to notions of scale and, more generally, space and time. It's just that with current technologies they are more easily detected on relatively small scales.

3. For a detailed discussion of measurement in quantum physics see Karen Barad, *Meeting the Universe Halfway: Quantum Physics and the Entanglement of Matter and Meaning* (Durham, N. C.: Duke University Press, 2007).

4. Bohr's notion of complementarity does not follow the colloquial usage. By "complementarity" he means simultaneously "mutually exclusive" and "mutually necessary."

5. In *Meeting the Universe Halfway* (see note 3), I argue that questions of epistemology are not separate from those of ontology. And knowing is not the sole prerogative of humans. In fact, I suggest a reworking of *knowing* (even as it applies to humans) in light of quantum physics. In any case, it is easy to see that "zooming in" is not a uniquely human activity. For example, the larvae of sunburst diving beetles come equipped with bifocal lenses. And light emitted from the sun, that is, photons of different frequencies, and other particles too, are capable of probing different length scales without any human assistance.

6. A. Zee, *Quantum Field Theory in a Nutshell*, 2nd ed. (Princeton, N. J.: Princeton University Press, 2010 [orig. 2003]), pp. 3–4.

7. See Silvan S. Schweber, *QED and the Men Who Made It* (Princeton, N. J.: Princeton University Press, 1994).

8. That is, it allows for fluctuations around a value of zero for its energy.

9. For example, the specific pattern made by iron filings lining up in the presence of a magnet can be understood as the marks of a specific magnetic field configuration.

10. The story that so often gets told about the existence of virtual particles is that it is a direct result of Heisenberg's uncertainty principle. But the energy-time "uncertainty" (*sic*) principle is far from a settled issue. Notably, recent research supports the interpretation of this relation in terms of indeterminacy rather than uncertainty. That is, what is at issue is "objective [ontological] indeterminacy" (Paul Busch), not epistemological uncertainty. See, for example, Paul Busch, "The Time-Energy Uncertainty Relation," in *Time in Quantum Mechanics*, ed. Juan Gonzalo Muga, Rafael Sala Mayato, and Íñigo L. Egusquiza, 2nd ed. (Berlin: Springer, 2008 [orig. 2002]). See also Barad, *Meeting the Universe Halfway* (see note 3), for a detailed account of the differences in interpretation marked by questions of uncertainty (Heisenberg) versus indeterminacy (Bohr).

11. For materialist readings of Derrida's "hauntology" (as opposed to "ontology"), see Karen Barad, "Quantum Entanglements and Hauntological Relations of Inheritance: Dis/continuities, SpaceTime Enfoldings, and Justice-to-Come," *Derrida Today* 3, no. 2 (2010), pp. 240–68; Vicki Kirby, *Quantum Anthropologies: Life at Large* (Durham, N. C.: Duke University Press, 2011); and Astrid Schrader, "Responding to *Pfiesteria piscicida* (the Fish Killer): Phantomatic Ontologies, Indeterminacy, and Responsibility in Toxic Microbiology," *Social Studies of Science* 40, no. 2 (April 2010), pp. 275–306.

12. Stephen Battersby, *New Scientist*, November 20, 2008. www.newscientist.com/article/dn16095-its-confirmed-matter-is-merely-vacuum-fluctuations.html (accessed February 2012).

13. It may help to remember that not all infinities are the same size. For example, the number of real numbers (an uncountably infinite set) is larger than the number of integers (a countably infinite set).
14. Wikipedia has relatively accessible explanations of these phenomena.
15. Jacques Derrida, *Aporias* (Stanford: Stanford University Press, 1993), p. 10.

PART III

Registering Interconnectedness

Chapter Twenty-Nine

INTERVIEW WITH KATHY HIGH

Something We Are Responsible To

JESSICA ULLRICH

JESSICA ULLRICH: You often engage with life sciences and nature/culture boundaries. In your multimedia installation *Embracing Animal* you brought questions of kinship into dialogue with high-tech animal husbandry by working with transgenic lab rats who were microinjected with human DNA. Few people feel sympathy for rats, yet you seem to identify with transgenic rats. Could you explain why that is?

KATHY HIGH: I was reading Deleuze and Guattari's *Thousand Plateaus* as I started this work in 2004. Of course, like many others, I was grappling with the concepts in the heady chapter "Becoming Animal". This whole idea of *becoming* was another way to think through our relations with animals and other things (such as cells, microbes, and molecules). I was also taken with Donna Haraway's description of the OncoMouse TM as her sibling from *Modest Witness.* . . . I began this project very naively—which was proba-bly the best way to do it. I had never even handled a rat before I started *Embracing Animal*. I was curious to reverse engineer—if you will—the idea of pharmaceuticals developed for my own illnesses. In previous video work done with the NYC collective Paper Tiger Television (*Just Say Yes: Kathy High Looks at Marketing Legal Drugs* 1990), I had co-produced a video about the pharmaceutical industry and how they manipulate the market and use persuasion to sell their products. So I had an interest in the critique of "big Pharmas". This project started out that way. But it became quite different

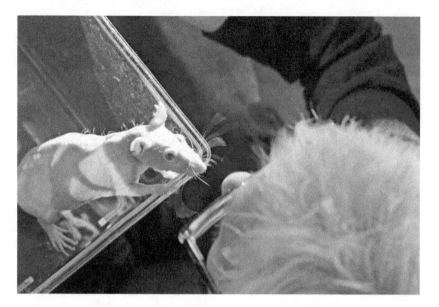

FIGURE 29.1. Kathy High, *Embracing Animal*, 2004-06.
Source: Photo by Olivia Robinson, copyright Kathy High.

once I started to really consider the lab animals used to conduct the research. And then the whole notion of *transgenic* was super sci-fi to me. Eduardo Kac had done art with transgenics that was very inspiring. And yet his Alba bunny project was frustrating as, in the end, Alba remained in the lab. *Embracing Animal* was in some ways a response to that project. It was not that I liked rats. I was simply curious as to what transgenics meant in an embodied way, and how these animals reacted to their condition. Literally. And how would the rats behave if they had alternative choices? Because I had been dealing with chronic disease for much of my life, and I felt so trapped by the conventional medical system. I fought to seek out alternative medicines—alternative and more holistic ways to understand my illness and my diseased body. I wondered if research could be conducted with these rats that could also be "alternative." [. . .] I was scared of the rats when I met them and unsure of what to do with them. But over time, I found them to be incredibly smart and curious—and also sick. The more I looked into lab rats the more fascinated I became with their history as standardized animal products. The fact that they existed in this kind of limbo in the USA where they are not exactly considered as animals under the law (not that they don't receive good care by their lab technicians and researchers), and that these rats were transgenic—somewhere between human and animal, made them poetic creatures to me. Liminal. Caught in inbetweenness. I think as a queer and a feminist I identified with that notion as well.

JESSICA ULLRICH: You treated the rats holistically and took care of them in many different ways. In 1982 Carol Gilligan developed the *Ethics of Care*, a strain of moral philosophy that emphasized the relations of concrete individuals, the maintenance of connections, responsiveness, and the satisfaction of needs. It opposed or complemented the justice framework in ethics that relies more on an abstract conception of morals focusing on the application of general rules of conduct and the fair resolution of conflicting interests. Would you situate yourself within a theoretical (and practical) framework of ethics of care and what do you think about the gendering of such a concept?

KATHY HIGH: I agree with Gilligan's ideas although it is easy to see the gendering of this concept. I agree with her specificity because I also believe in the personal, the individual action, the actual manifestation of ideas, ideologies, and ethics. Embodiment and materialism is key to understanding concepts for me—otherwise my head is just in the clouds all the time. I should note that Irina Aristarkhova has also written about the notion of hospitality and she has been criticized about the gendering of this idea too. I think that ideas from new materialism may help to think through this gender bias. If we consider caring for an actual tangible animal, or person, or object, then it is manifest as something we are responsible to. This relationality can be enacted by anyone. At MASS MoCA—where I had my longest exhibition of this work—the rats were on display for 10 months. I gave them an enriched housing situation with climbing areas and different environments to play in. They had really good care at the museum by the curators, interns, and especially the night watchman, Mike Weber. They had veterinary care. The rats were adored by the staff and brought out the best in them all! And the rats came home in the end.

JESSICA ULLRICH: You have characterized the animals in your work as "collaborators" and as "sisters". The terminology reminds me of Haraway who called Oncomouse her sibling. Would you also consider the animals to be co-authors of your art and could you elaborate a little bit on the agency of your rats?

KATHY HIGH: I understand that the relationship between myself and the rats was not "equal". Of course, there were power dynamics as I was the one in control of their destiny. And, yes, I was moved by Haraway's writing about the Oncomouse and that inspired my thinking about my relationship to these particular HLA B27 rat models. But I do have to give them credit for their work—as they were more than contributors. They created this project as well. I feel that I gave them a platform to perform in. They took advantage of the situation and thrived. I took huge risks with them exposing them to this environment. These are creatures that typically would never leave a very controlled laboratory setting. I had a theory that exposing them to different environments and giving them a varied diet would help to strengthen their immune systems. Also much more room to explore. They took advantage of it all and did very well, learning how to play—and heal. They took control of their new situation and had more agency. [. . .]

JESSICA ULLRICH: Some of your work is very personal. For example with *Embracing Animal* you made your Crohn's disease public, and your own pets feature regularly in some of your videos. How important is it for you to separate your private life and your art or is there no need for you to do so?

KATHY HIGH: I had not really thought about the "outing" of my Crohn's disease when presenting *Embracing Animal*. But it ended up being helpful. This is an invisible disease and not talked about very much—unless you have it! Many people have talked to me about their own Crohn's disease after my disclosure. I think that a lot of it has to do with discussion of our bodies—diseased bodies, bodies in a living space, our bodies in relation to other nonhuman bodies. Art often comes from a very personal place. "The personal is political." As a feminist it is important for me to use my life as an example of how I practice my politics. So, I do think my personal life is very close to my artwork—and more so as time goes on. Hopefully my private stories give people an entry to the work. [. . .]

JESSICA ULLRICH: With *Trans-Tamagotchi* you developed a computer game in which people can care for virtual transgenic animals. In other works you document playing rats. Many philosophers have highlighted the close relationship of art and play. Thomas Seboek for example regards play as the precursor of art and in more recent times Dario Martinelli stresses the close relationship of lying, playing and aesthetics. A play can offer experiences just as an artwork and both have the power to transform the involved beings.

How important is the notion of play for you, especially when it comes to interspecies communication?

KATHY HIGH: I fell in love with art as a young child. I grew up outside of Philadelphia and went on a school trip early on to the Philadelphia Museum of Art. While my classmates were looking at some early American abstract paintings, I snuck off to the Marcel Duchamp room. There I found one of Duchamp's last pieces *Etant Donné*. As you walk into the room there is a wooden door on one side with two peepholes in the door. The peepholes were dark from the facial oil of many people looking thought them, and they smelled musty and very animal-like. Beyond the peepholes was a mysterious and wondrous diorama of a (anonymous) naked woman lying on a cliff holding a lantern with and a waterfall in the far background. This work had a profound effect on me. I was scared and delighted by it—and somehow I found it very funny. I had no idea what it was, but the absurdity of it touched me. Duchamp's use of the absurd in many of his works taught me how to be playful in my own projects. Also, growing up I was told by my family that I shouldn't be an artist. So, I have always felt a bit naughty making art. It was the one thing I did where I could work with taboo subjects, take risks—and be provocative and playful. Besides, animals—who I find endlessly funny— taught me to play, be playful, and to be more creative.

JESSICA ULLRICH: For the interdisciplinary art + science experiment *Blood Wars* you investigate the human immune systems, in states of both health and disease, by staging a tournament between different individual's white blood cells in a petri dish. The blood dueling picks up the understanding of the immune system as a defense system, but it also claims to demystify irrational notions associated with blood. Could you explain this a little bit further?

KATHY HIGH: I think that we ascribe blood with mystical powers. It is used in ritual, we talk about "pure bloods", we have blood brothers/sisters by joining our blood, etc. I was interested in looking at how blood—which is culturally revered—is infused with meaning and significance. In the case of *Blood Wars*, we had people compete against each other using the medium of their own white blood cells. *Blood Wars* plays off the aggressive, military language used when speaking about the immune system. I adopted the format of the FIFA World Cup, a highly competitive sports play-off, modeling the immune system on sports rivalries in order to exaggerate this use of fighting metaphors and to bring attention to this communication. Ultimately, I want to

FIGURE 29.2. Kathy High, *Rat Laughter*, work in progress, 2000.
Source: Copyright Kathy High.

think about the immune system as a cooperative team, an alliance, and redirect this semantic about immunology to draw on terms that are more about adaptation, mediation and negotiation.

JESSICA ULLRICH: You often focus the indistinguishableness of humans and other animals. Has the notion of becoming animal by Deleuze/Guattari been an inspiration for your work or are there other ideas on posthumanism that have been (more) important for you?

KATHY HIGH: I think that Deleuze and Guattari have been really inspiring for sure. Particularly in exciting my imagination. I often read philosophy to help in my creative process. I found that Deleuze and Guattari offered useful ways to talk about animal human relations. But I have found others too such as Donna Haraway, Cary Wolfe, Timothy Morton, Steve Baker, Ron Broglio, and recently I (happily) discovered the work of Vinciane Despret. There are too many to list. I am a pragmatist and so I like works that are grounded in actual practices to question our ways of thinking through these theories. I have also been inspired by the new feminist materialists such as Astrida Neimanis, and anthropologists such as Eben Kirksey, who coined the term "multispecies ethnography", as well as artists Bryndis Snaebjörnsdóttir and Mark Wilson, Lee Deigaard, Terrike Haapoja, Oliver Kellhammer, and many others. There is a way we need to think about our situated-ness in relation to non-humans. Now that we are faced with the very real dangers of climate change, the larger picture of how interspecies relations matter take on an urgency and essential meaning. [. . .]

Chapter Thirty

FROM WRITING MACHINES

N. KATHERINE HAYLES

Among the best known and most beloved artists' books is Tom Phillips's *A Humument*. Like other works in the genre, *A Humument* interrogates the material properties of the book and mobilizes them as resources for signification. Its specificity as a technotext comes from its origins in a pre-existing book. Intrigued by William Burroughs' cut-ups, Phillips liked the idea of operating on source texts to make entirely new documents. To create *A Humument*, he took an obscure Victorian novel by William Mallock entitled *A Human Document*, bought by chance because it met his criterion of costing no more than three pence, and "treated" it by covering over the pages with images that left only a few of the original words visible.

Through curious serendipity, his treatment of Mallock's text re-inscribes Mallock's own strategies; Mallock in his "Introduction" creates a persona who agrees to edit a scrapbook of journals, letters, and memorabilia of two recently deceased lovers. These documents are hyper-textual, for though "some single thread of narrative, in a feminine handwriting, ran through the whole volume," this was "broken by pages of letters, by scraps of poetry, and various other documents" in a masculine hand (Mallock, p. 4). The editor believes that this profusion of materials disqualifies the scrapbook from being a novel. Uncannily anticipating contemporary descriptions of hypertext narrative, he asserts that "as they stand they are not a story in any literary sense; though they enable us, or rather force us, to construct one out of them for ourselves" (p. 8).

The story that emerges from his recasting of this hypertextual profusion focuses on Grenville, a poet-philosopher turned finance officer, who feels himself on the threshold of a highly successful career in government, complete with a wealthy prospective wife. But before this bright future can materialize, love shakes him around, turning him toward an uncertain future with the unhappily married Irma. The novel attempts to resist its own stultifying conventionality in the editor's positive view of the lovers' illicit liaison—but these resistances, precisely because he regards them as so daring, merely underscore his conservatism. [. . .]

These strategies share a double impulse. On the one hand, they posit precursor texts that embody a hypertextual proliferation of narratives, signified by a diversity of material forms and incomplete or erasable marks. On the other hand, the novel's project is to suppress this unruly complexity, smoothing many conflicting paths into one coherent narrative. This double impulse takes thematic expression through the editor's professed desire to rebel against the "rules" dictating that characters (particularly women) should have only moral thoughts, and his equally strong aversion to the frankness of Zola's *Nana*, which he sees as a moral aberration. His resistance to rules is encoded as the hypertextual proliferation of unruly and multiple narratives, whereas his anxiety about where this might lead is enacted through scenes of writing that over-write previous inscriptions to make them more tractable, predictable, and coherent—which is to say, make them a novel rather than a hypertext.

In "treating" Mallock's novel, Phillips creates an artist's book that seeks to bring into view again this suppressed hypertextual profusion. The opening page proclaims:

Most of the treatment consists not of coining new words but obliterating ones that already exist, as if to silence the rationalizing consciousness of narrator and editor so that the murmurs of hypertextual resistance to coherent narrative can be heard. Page 178 illustrates the technique; here a page from Mallock's text has been torn, burnt around the edges, and stained in the middle, making most of the text illegible. More typical is page 17, where the few phrases left visible are joined by "rivers" consisting of white spaces between Mallock's words. Visually these rivers of white space trickle down the page, often branching into multiple pathways. Other devices creating hypertextual profusion are leaky borders, which visually separate the page into multiple narrative levels and also transgress this separation, suggesting that distinctions between character, narrator and author are less ontological categories than contingent boundaries susceptible to multiple reconfiguration. Additional hypertextual effects are achieved through interplays between word and image.

All these strategies are on display on page 17, where a central gray rectangle, colored to suggest three-dimensional texture, is placed on a field of variegated yellow, itself centered on another rectangle of variegated tan. The placement of the gray block suggests a page surrounded by margins, which in turn becomes a page in Phillips's text surrounded by the white margins of his book. This arrangement is further complicated by the rivers that run through the borders, as well as by the lexias that extend beyond the outermost yellow field and intrude into the margin's white space, thus suggesting that even the page as Phillips defines it is a boundary to be transgressed. On this page there are several possible sequences in which to read the spatially dispersed words:

> —a repetition that enacts the narrative multiplicity of hypertext and also gently mocks it, since the words are all the same, differing only in their placements within the image. The attentive reader can make out some of Mallock's text through the covering paint, and this effect offers another possible reading sequence.

The text on this page illustrates the nature of the narrative. Broken and reassembled, the prose achieves the compression of poetry, becoming allusive and metaphoric rather than sequentially coherent:

> The ambiguity of the hypertextual rivers makes it possible to read these lines as if the *REFERENT* for "makes me ill" is the critic's name on a label, in which case malady and cure spring from the same source, a bottle of "art/ art." Twelve pages earlier comes page 5, which seems to comment on this strategy:

Here the comparison with Mallock is especially illuminating. The lines were reworked from the editor's "Introduction," in which he criticizes Irma's style as she strives to make a single narrative out of her diverse materials. Despite himself, the editor admires her "baffled and crippled sentences, her abrupt transitions, and odd lapses of grammar," for though these "could hardly be said to constitute a good description of what she professed to have felt, seemed to be more than that:—they seemed to be a visible witness of its reality, as if her language had been broken by it, like a forest broken by a storm, or as if it were some living tissue, wounded and quivering with sensation" (p. 5).

Yet it is this very hypertextual intensity that the editor smoothes away in his putative recasting. From this smoothed language Phillips, by obliterating most of the editor's words, recovers a sense of the broken language that supposedly underlies it, making the coherent text speak of the "attempt to cripple," a phrase that can be taken to apply to the editor rather than the editor's judgment of Irma's faulty style. Similarly, it is now not Irma's wounded sensations that are "quivering," but the fabric of the perceptual world itself, "reality broken by quivering peculiarities." The strategy of uncovering the putative hypertext underlying Mallock's novel is beautifully captured in "poken," a fractured word that both alludes to the "spoken" of Mallock's text and the evocative, broken language it supposedly covers over.

Contributing to the recovery of hypertextual profusion is the rich interplay between subtext and context, word and image. Running across a visual bend in page 5 are the words:

naming as well as illustrating Phillips' hypertextual breaking of Mallock's page. Also on this page are the squiggly lines that run in rows across the "page" as it is defined by the yellow margins (and then deconstructed as a page by being set within white margins, which recontextualize the page as the leaf in Phillips' text). These squiggles clearly resemble writing—perhaps the handwriting of the journal the editor recasts. Significantly, this writing is illegible as words, transformed into the image or representation of writing rather than writing itself. A similar technique appears on page 83, where the text in the upper right river names:

a scene that the white squiggles against the dark background seem to enact, although again they are illegible as words and function instead as visual representations of verbal marks. Commenting on this interplay of word and image in his *Curriculum Vitae* series, Phillips makes an observation equally relevant to *A Humument*: "Once more I emphasize the fact that I regard texts as images in their own right: treated as they are here with words ghosted behind words to form a (literal) subtext they are all the more image for being doubly text." [. . .]

These strategies make us freshly aware that the character is never self-evidently on the page; they also construct Toge as an alter ego for Phillips. As Paschal points out, the alert reader can see signs of Phillips everywhere. On page 44, a scrawl on a brick wall announces "Tom [w]as here," along with the "X" repeated throughout his Terminal Greys series and recurring so frequently in his work that it can be regarded as his "mark." The page forcibly reminds us that Toge exists only insofar as he is created by a human author who inscribes durable ink marks on a flat fiber surface and a reader who interacts with the hook as material object. In *A Humument*, the page is never allowed to disappear by serving only as the portal to an imagined world as it does with realistic fiction. In many ways and on many levels, *A Humument* insists on its materiality.

Chapter Thirty-One

FROM UNEXPRESS THE EXPRESSIBLE

CHUS MARTÍNEZ

Art cannot be reduced to some external meaning or truth that we know in advance. Art is thinking but is not theory. The world's reality resides in art, and it is inseparable from art's investigative procedure, which seeks to expose how the forces, the different compounds of elements—material and conceptual—interact in order to produce a certain effect.

The nineteenth-century invention of the constitutional State was an attempt to link the public sphere to an idea of law. It guarantees its citizens certain basic rights—something that amounts to establishing the public sphere by way of identifying the public character of every act of reason. By linking law to rational debate in this way, the idea of the State as a top-down dominating force is abolished.

The bourgeois public sphere depends on particular social and economic factors that are unique to the eighteenth and nineteenth centuries. Jürgen Habermas borrows the term "civil society" from Hegel to denote the sphere of production and exchange of goods that forms part of the private realm and is distinct from the State. Hence, civil society is essentially the economy: it operates according to its own laws but is able to represent its interests to the State through the public sphere, whose lifeblood it purports to be. Actions that were part of the private, of the *oikos*—the house—started to be part of the public domain as activities formerly confined to the household framework emerged into the public sphere; the economic activity of the civil society was oriented toward the public commodity market, and hence both internal and external to the State.

"Public" relates to public authority, the State; "private" relates to the economy, the society, and the family. "Public" and "private" are defined and separated in terms of law and institutions. The public sphere exists as an extension of the private world that in this way moves into the public domain. "Public" relates to the State but also means "open to all." This amalgam, then, somewhat paradoxically transforms the public into a critical judge that regulates access to, and the constitution of, its principal inclusivity.

Rational-critical debate occurred in the eighteenth-century public sphere between members of a property-owning, educated, reading, and reasoning public. It centered on literary questions and on political issues, like the public authority of the State. The key shift in the modern world is the loss of apparent distinction between the private and public spheres: only with the development of a modern State and economy did public and private assume their currently recognized forms. Interest groups on both sides started to operate together, resulting in a societal complex that, following Habermas, reduced the possibility of a true public debate. The decline of rational, meaningful argument is among Habermas' major criticisms of the modern State.

Chapter Thirty-Two

INTRODUCTION TO NOCTURNAL FABULATIONS

Ecology, Vitality, and Opacity in the Cinema of Apichatpong Weerasethakul

ERIN MANNING

A conversation to come is one that invents interlocutors, one that refuses to know in advance where the encounter will lead. [Gilles] Deleuze calls this a minoritarian discourse: "We must catch someone fabulating, catch them 'in the act' of fabulating. Then a minoritarian discourse, with two or many speakers, takes shape . . . To catch fabulation in the act is to seize the movement of the constitution of a people. A people never preexists (translation modified)."

[. . . T]he work of the cinematographer Apichatpong Weerasethakul [. . . inspires me to ask] *what else* might be at stake in setting up the conditions for collaboration across two genres—cinema and writing[, . . .] *what else* this uneasy interstice of image-thought can look like when it moves onto the page[?] This thinking-with can be understood as an engagement with how the films of Apichatpong themselves propose collective ecologies of thought and how these ecologies foreground new ways of seeing the image as a movement of thought. This gesture of thinking with and across image and text, of being moved by a work that intercesses two discrete but intertwined perceptual processes, developing vocabulary not to "explain" the work but to reactivate it by other means, proposes a wholly different ethos of engagement. [. . . T]here is always a sense, in watching his films, that he is a participant in a process that has yet to quite unfold, and that his work is, before all else, dedicated to a people (and a conversation) yet to come.

Apichatpong describes his work as "open cinema", and often seems at odds with questions interviewers pose, uneasy with their probing into plot sequence and intentionality: "Sometimes you don't need to understand everything to appreciate a certain beauty," he tells one interviewer. "And I think the film operates in the same way. It's like tapping into someone's mind. The thinking pattern is quite random, jumping here and there like a monkey." In another interview: "I believe that cinema has its own life," and then, when the interviewer prods a bit more: "Yeah, but the more I explain, the more the movie loses its mystery so I think I should stop! [. . .] [I]t's the mood and the feeling that matters to me."

With some filmmakers, one might have the sense of these being anti-intellectual attempts to avoid taking a stance—"you just have to feel it—as I can't explain it" a stand-in for "the artist has an intuition that comes from outside the everyday and defies explanation." This is not what is at stake with Apichatpong, for his films do always take a stance, and he does not shy away from complex conceptual-aesthetic issues. But he does trouble language, especially the kind of language that would like to frame experience, his effort more directed toward the complexity of what feeling can do at the edges of ineffability. Here feeling is not so much outside of language as *with* its uneasy telling, the plot not carried by the tenor of an emotion that orients the image as by the affective tonality of a thinking-feeling that resists stable time signatures. Language is made uneasy precisely because it does not easily speak in the cacophony of time unmoored. What is felt in Apichatpong's work, what matters in the feeling, is carried forth by an image that cannot quite be left behind in the explaining. To explain the work, to categorize it sequentially, as interviewers (and critics) are wont to do, is to misunderstand how its movements undermine any kind of linear telling. It is to underestimate what the image can do. [. . .]

For how we perceive really matters in Apichatpong's works: "everything matters, [. . .] you're not really looking forward to the finished work but looking forward to every moment; enjoying every moment." What is unusual, however, is that this mattering isn't primarily inward-looking: the image's thinking-feeling does not begin and end here, in this cinematic experiment, in this plot sequence.

Before I used to think of film as maybe just one project. With my process being finishing it piece by piece, before moving on to different themes or interests. But lately I think of film like satellites: surrounding this ongoing universe; even building that universe. So when I finished *Cemetery of Splendour*, it wasn't really finished. It's almost like a platform, to move onto another work that can be built from it. But it all ends up being one piece; all together." [. . .]

To be an intercessor is to *participate* in this relational platform, not to *mediate* it. It is to recognize how the immediacy of an encounter with an image, with a movement of thought, or better yet, with the intervals of thought-images yet to come, affects what it means to perceive. Intercessors change the norms of contact. Changing the norms of contact is always a creative gesture: there is no intercessor that would exist once and for all, nor is there a creative act that can flourish without intercession. "Fictive or real, animated or inanimate, one must make one's intercessors. It is a series. If you don't form a series, even completely imaginary, you are lost. I need my intercessors to express myself, and they would never be able to express themselves without me: we are always many at work, even when you don't see it" (translation modified).

To act is to have been intercessed, to have been moved by conditions beyond the frame of an encounter predetermined. A creative act, it must be underscored, is not something that belongs to me: the work is activated in a field of relation that is always lively with intercessions. And so to seek to know a work is to be curious about how it has been intercessed.

Chapter Thirty-Three

POSTHUMAN PERFORMANCE

LUCIAN GOMOLL

Orlan's disruption of the classical, normative, and essentialized female body often generated connections between her art practice and the theoretical work of Donna Haraway. In relation to Haraway's "A Cyborg Manifesto: Science, Technology, and Socialist-Feminism in the Late Twentieth Century" first written in 1986 and widely republished thereafter, Orlan is sometimes called an embodiment of the hybrid and monstrous cyborg. But it is an association that the artist seems to welcome over the mad, radically freakish, non-human, or less fashionable figures of abnormality. Both call their work blasphemous.[1] Haraway's manifesto proposed groundwork for a new feminist subject unbound by binaries or essentialisms, and instead enacts a subjectivity that extends and is metonymized outside of the traditional limits of the body. Orlan performed many of these ideas directly, especially when developing her concept of omnipresence through which digital technologies unfurled her consciousness transnationally to various art institutions like the Pompidou Center. In *Omnipresence*, those watching in Paris could see Orlan being operated on in New York, and hear audience members participating from other global locations like Toronto. While bestowing on Orlan a God-like quality, *Omniprescence* also agreed with some of the basic concepts from Haraway's cyborg manifesto because it emphasized an expansion of consciousness that is not imprisoned by any fixed categories of identity.

FIGURE 33.1. Orlan and Cimier ancien de danse Ejaban Nigeria et visage Euro-Stéphanoise, *Self Hybridisation*, 2000. Digital photograph, colour print, 125 x 156 cm, Saint Etienne, Musée d'Art Moderne de Saint-Etienne Métropole.
Source: Photograph Cliff Shain, Standard Bank Public domain. CC BY-SA 2.0.

The connections discussed above seem promising, yet it is important to note how the latter sections of Haraway's essay often go unmentioned in favor of a more trendy and techno-fetishizing vision.[2] This is true to the extent that some scholars seriously misrepresent "A Cyborg Manifesto," such as the misconception that it argues for the total disappearance of gender or difference.[3] Haraway's emphasis on the strategic alliances formed by women of color feminists is just as, if not more, fundamental to her theory of cyborg feminism as the technological aspects. These are ideas that begin to complicate Orlan's oeuvre in addition to my discussions of the artist's carnivalesque style and her claims to sanity. For example, Haraway foregrounds Chela Sandoval's strategies for women of color who enact coalitions based on affinity rather than identity, characterizing them as cyborg activity and a "potent formulation for feminists out of the worldwide development of anti-colonialist discourse; that is to say, discourse dissolving the 'West' and its highest product—the one who is not animal, barbarian, or woman; man, that is, the author of a cosmos called history.

As Orientalism is deconstructed politically and semiotically, the identities of the occident destabilize, including those of feminists."[4] Re-attending to transnational and postcolonial feminism in Haraway's manifesto reveals that it is not cosmetic surgery that is Orlan's core problematic (as some feminists would have previously argued). The underlying "progress" of avant-gardism and European notions of the racialized self/Other are the conditions that make it possible for her to reductively engage with non-Western cultural practices.

Orlan's Orientalism is not adequately theorized as part of her status as a posthuman artist. These problematics are less evident in the surgeries and are much more apparent in her meta-narratives about them, especially in *Carnal Art*, and the subsequent *Self-Hybridization* series for which Orlan digitally transposes her face onto images that supposedly indicate radically different notions of beauty from other civilizations. Her self-hybridizations sometimes approach two-dimensional minstrelsy, especially those series based on non-ancient African (2000–2003) and American Indian (2005–2008) cultures. Images, such as that of the Ejagha headdress that is appropriated for one of Orlan's *Self-Hybridizations*, take for granted the static and visual aspects of such an object not meant to be seen predominantly in stasis. Elisabeth Cameron explains that, "by themselves they [photos of African masks] do not communicate either the movement and meaning—and the sheer wonder and fun—of a performance, or the interplay between men and women, masked and unmasked."[5] Orlan's digital adaptations naturalize a Western tendency to devalue or ignore performances by fetishizing visual form according to European art standards. In these ways, the post-surgery images are similar to works by modernist avant-garde artists who have mined so-called primitive cultures for artistic inspiration, like Picasso, Gauguin, and countless others. Orlan treads on thin ice with her later projects, threatening to undermine the efficacy of her earlier works during which she did not engage racial and cultural differences quite so flippantly. These images are not attempts at feminist strategic alliance. Orlan cites recent or contemporary non-Western peoples who practice various forms of body modification in *Carnal Art*, but too often she frames them as examples of past cultural practices and denies their coevalness.[6] Thus she reinscribes non-Western cultures as "primitive" in a cultural-aesthetic (and aestheticized) hierarchy traceable to the beginnings of European humanism and modernism.

I consider Orlan's works to be groundbreaking as they continue to provoke uncanny responses twenty years after they were first staged.[7] Even if I
do grow uncomfortable when she talks about the Maya, her work nonetheless has come to represent ideas about posthuman art and technology that
persisted for an entire decade. But to avoid repeating Orlan's mistakes, I turn
again to Haraway, who has more recently theorized companion species and
other ways of relating between different beings, recasting the cyborg as but
one figure in a web of many other types of relationships.[8] With Haraway, we
can see how the cyborg or posthuman might not only exist as a single species connected to and expanding with inorganic materials, but also important are our interactions with other living and non-living things. Haraway's
work decenters the human from all directions, and troubles what was posed
as the fantasy of "pure decision" that some progress-oriented narratives of
cybernetics would have us believe is possible, and was applied to Orlan's
and Stelarc's work by Jane Goodall.[9] By now, artists and theorists have been
expanding and violating the human beyond posthuman parameters of the
1990s, meriting a further exploration of examples from the last ten years
that may present to us other ways to act as ethical posthumans. [. . .] I knot
them together under the category of *posthuman performance* in an attempt
to synthesize the productive contributions of both posthuman and posthumanist theories, and to insist on a radical politics and relationality for this
type of practice. The category is therefore not exhaustive or limiting, nor is
it faithful to either discourse. Instead the concept is a point of intersection
for possibilities in discourse and being. [. . .]

In *Destination Culture* (1998) Barbara Kirshenblatt-Gimblett observes
that displays of people always enact a "semiotic seesaw" between opposing meanings, such as animal/human, self/Other, and living/dead.[10] This
dynamic is a legacy that persists in exhibitions, despite the suppression of
histories that recall how people were exhibited in the West since the early
nineteenth century. Most of the persons who performed at that time were
framed as cultural exotics or as freaks, which Rosemarie Garland-Thomson
says allowed the audience to formulate the normative human in relation
to what it was not.[11] As such, they functioned as constitutive others to the
liberal human and contributed to its normalization. By the twentieth century, these displays were banished from the exhibitionary circuit due to a
combination of city laws pertaining to "decency" and massive opposition
from museum professionals.[12] The reintroduction of live performance in

the museum did not occur in the exhibitionary circuit until many decades later.[13] I am particularly interested in artists who not only engage the body and performance in their works, but whose works call upon the nineteenth century displays and provoke similar interactivities while inverting the power play in order to disrupt traditional constructs of "the human."

Narcissister is one such performer. The image that appears on the first page of this essay features her in full costume, posing with an artificially reconfigured body that has two tall imposing heads and hybridized Victorian-Asian style clothing. Prosthetic elements of her costume include the heads as well as the exposed breasts that are inconsistent shades of flesh. As an organic-inorganic monstrosity, Narcissister's abnormal corpus is ambiguous and resists any fixed social categories like "the individual," racial categories, and even essentialized notions of gender, considering all parts that might signify femininity are inorganic (including her breasts) and metonymic. Narcissister is a classically trained dancer whose works range from proscenium performances (usually dances), to film, to situational interactive works. Her trademark is the use of mannequin parts, and particularly an ethnically-ambiguous mask. Thus her performances always enact a hybridization and enlivening of plasticity—plasticity in terms of both art and of mannequin—while the person underneath remains mysterious in terms of gender, race, and authorship. The shadowy third head appearing in the first image metaphorizes a lack of an essential identity or core to her performances: how we read her body depends on our recognition of signs related to race, gender, and corporeal normativity, but any essence remains mysterious, anonymous, shadowy, a negativity. [. . .] Narcissister shows us through the use of prosthetics that the posthuman need not be exclusively cybernetic, as she just as effectively expands through the enlivening of non-digital body parts. Instead, her postuman performance relies on metonymic and relational expansionism. [. . .]

Recently, Narcissister has begun a quite brilliant project of expanding her prostheticized body through the participation of multiple performers, marked by a common mask, allowing for variable interruptions of the classical or normative body. While this project, entitled "Narcissister is You," has thus far only involved others taking photographs with the mask, the artist may consider performative contributions that disrupt self/other relationships of race, gender, and so on, unraveling the threads of relating and selfhood that are wound so tightly around the normative human in the liberal humanist tradition.

The self-proclaimed "experimental sideshow" performances of *La Pocha Nostra* also interrogate the roles of posthuman or techno-subjects in nationalist, racialized, and gendered discourses. *La Pocha* contributors, which include a core troupe that collaborates with artists transnationally, have written important manifestos that are very much in line with what I propose to be posthuman performance in this article.[14] Particularly important are their construction of "ethno-cyborgs," as opposed to characters, and "living dioramas" as opposed to the proscenium theatre—both rearticulations of traditional western theatrical structures. These performance models interrogate traditional divisions between actor/character, actor/audience, stage/seating, and are potentially more interactive. *La Pocha's* structural transformations of theatrical conventions are not new, as so-called modernist avant-garde movements have attempted to change them for decades. However, *La Pocha* collaborators do not ignore the influences of both minoritarian subjects and intercultural histories that are still regularly erased from (or devalued in) the histories of performance art and avant-gardism.[15] Unlike Orlan, the troupe does not consider comprehensibility or sanity to be a necessarily desirable outcome of their works. In fact, indecipherability is sometimes used strategically by the artists, to provoke audience curiosity, and also to protect themselves from any foreclosing descriptions of what they are doing. As such, we might call their work *refractory art*, a term coined by Nelly Richard for works that function "as a 'tenacious negation' and as a 'deviation from a route that preceded' it."[16]

La Pocha Nostra performances very often include old video footage of non-Westerners who were appropriated by Europeans and Euro-Americans, and these twentieth century films maintained much of the nineteenth century visual language that framed people who performed in exhibitions as exotic. Through live interactive performances and technological enhancements, images from previous displays of nonwestern peoples are interrogated and transformed. Such is the case in the performance series entitled *Corpo/Ilicito: The Post-Human Society*. The stunning action "6.9" featured an ensemble of performers donned in costumes related to military and technological violence, indigenous hybridized accoutrements, and who engaged with each other in speechless, almost disembodied power-plays, in proximity to a looping projection of old racist films. Cross-species promiscuities were suggested by hybridizing costume, such as a swine mask, as well as the ceremonial feeding of a banana to Gómez-Peña.[17] The latter gesture recalls his previous invocation of this offering in the 1992–3 performance *Two Undiscovered Amerindians*, and its associations with monkeys and the jungle (and by extension "primitive" humans as older exhibitions of live persons would have suggested). Of course, invisible to our liberal-humanist trained eyes will be the many microbes that keep each performer alive and are already on stage with them. *Corpo/Ilicito* interweaves both posthuman and posthumanist figures, all while invoking legacies of racism, violence, nakedness, and incomprehensibility knotted to performances of the "illicit" body throughout history. [. . .]

Thus far I have turned to Narcissister and *La Pocha Nostra* for models that complicate existing expressions of the posthuman with anti-racist and historically engaged practices. The actors in such performances disrupt the normalized white human, but, nonetheless, for the most part all the actors remain human. Keeping theories from the posthumanities also in mind, we might imagine what those performers might accomplish by engaging non-human species in their work as well. [. . .]

In looking to recent examples that may contribute to the practice I am calling posthuman performance, I am particularly drawn to projects like Basia Irland's *Hydrolibros* and *Ice Books* (2008), the latter which suggest an "ecological language" in sculpted frozen river water. The *Ice Books* melt, sprout, and nurture non-human life in the gallery space.[18] In a project such as this, the species performing are of an entirely different biological kingdom (and phylum if it attracts insects), directed by a human but with an understanding that one is not in total control of the process. Indeed, the work complicates a definition of what can count as performance because it is not a human who is staged in this ephemeral and transformative type of bio art in the gallery. Irland describes her process, "I work with stream ecologists, biologists, and botanists to ascertain the best seeds for each specific riparian zone. When the plants regenerate and grow along the bank, they help sequester carbon, hold the banks in place, and provide shelter for riverside creatures."[19] Irland's sprouts are therefore intended to participate in relations with other species in and out of traditional art contexts. Indeed, by bringing plants and perhaps other species into the museum and gallery, she disrupts the usual rules of inside/outside where humans are normally the only beings allowed into these spaces. She describes the process of her work in and out of the space of exhibition, "at eye level, on a metal grate above a trough, an Ice Book is placed and allowed to melt during the opening. After a week or so the seeds released into the trough during the melt, sprout in the water provided by the ice, creating a micro-ecosystem in the gallery. The sprouts are then taken to the river to float downstream, completing a cycle."[20] For Irland, neither the art exhibition nor a permanent collection is the final destination for her work. Instead, these sites are but one point on an itinerary for traveling beings who not only engage with us, but are destined to travel much farther with the facilitation of Irland and several of her audience members.[21]

In related projects, the Critical Art Ensemble (CAE) with other artists such as Beatriz da Costa and Shyhshiun Shyu have developed interventions such as *Free Range Grain* (2003–4) that stage non-human performances in the gallery space, as well as the omnipresent transmissions of participants outside of the gallery. CAE calls the work "a live, performative action. CAE/da Costa/Shyu has constructed a portable, public lab to test foods for the more common genetic modifications. People bring us foods that they find suspect for whatever reason, and we test them over a 72-hour period to see if their suspicions are justified. While we will not be able to say conclusively that a given food is genetically modified (although we can offer strong probability as whether it is), we can test for conclusive negatives, and we can bring issues of food purity into the realm of public discourse."[22] Process-based works like *Free Range Grain* incorporate posthuman articulations between people and technologies, with posthumanist interest in our relationships to other species. In this case, the point of interest is uncovering whether or not humans were involved in the engineering of our food sources, as well as the ethical problems that surround this type of relationship. We might imagine the other possibilities for engaging with multi-species posthuman performance that involve both digital interactivities and non-human species as integral to the work. [. . .]

To engender a new era of exhibition and performance that liberates us from institutions like the museum that interpellate us through fixed identities, we must contend with the figures of posthuman performance to arrive at the mysterious realms of possibility for radical relationality in the galleries beyond. Here identified, the tools for such praxis are readily available.

NOTES

1. See Donna Haraway, "A Cyborg Manifesto: Science, Technology, and Socialist-Feminism in the Late Twentieth Century." In *Simians, Cyborgs, and Women: The Reinvention of Nature* (New York: Routledge, 1990): 149. See also Alyda Faber, "Saint Orlan: Ritual as Violent Spectacle and Cultural Criticism." In *The Performance Studies Reader*, edited by Henry Bial (New York: Routledge, 2007): 109.

2. I make this statement based on my own experiences engaging with Haraway's work before becoming her student. Nicholas Gane discusses with Haraway the tendencies to "drop the feminism" in her manifesto in an interview, "When We Have Never Been Human, What Is to Be Done?" in *Theory Culture Society* Vol. 23 (2006): 136.

3. See, for example, Ken Gonzales-Day, "Choloborg; or, The Disappearing Latino Body." In *Art Journal*, Vol. 60, No. 1 (Spring, 2001): 23 and 26. Gonzales-Day actually claims that Haraway argues for the disappearance of gender and that she does address race in her manifesto. To clarify, Haraway is not arguing for the disappearance of gender, but for the unfixing of social identity categories and for coalition building that is inspired by women of color feminists with a strong commitment to anti-racism.

4. Haraway (1990): 156.

5. Elisabeth Cameron, "Men Portraying Women: Representations in African Masks." *African Arts*, Vol. 31, No. 2(Spring, 1998):72–79.

6. As Johannes Fabian writes, supposedly primitive or exotic non-Westerners come to represent past stages of human evolution paradoxically in the present. See Johannes Fabian, *Time and the Other: How Anthropology Makes Its Object* (New York: Columbia University Press, 2002).

7. I screen the *Carnal Art* documentary in various classes and am always struck by the unexpected responses from my students, such as squirming, covering of the eyes, leaving the room, and even nausea.

8. Donna Haraway, *The Companion Species Manifesto.* (Chicago: Prickly Paradigm Press, 2003):4.

9. Jane Goodall, "An Order of Pure Decision: Un-Natural Selection in the Work of Stelarc and Orlan." In *Body & Society* Vol. 5 No. 2–3 (June 1999): 149–170.

10. Barbara Kirshenblatt-Gimblett, *Destination Culture: Tourism, Museums, and Heritage.* (Berkeley: University of California Press, 1998): 34–47.

11. Rosemarie Garland-Thomson, E*xtraordinary Bodies: Figuring Physical Disability in American Culture and Literature.* (New York: Columbia University Press, 1996): 59.

12. See my forthcoming article on this history, "Interactivity and Displays of Difference in the Nineteenth Century" (tentative title, subject to change). See also Susan Schweik, The Ugly Laws: Disability in Public (New York: NYU Press, 2009).

13. In the 1960s and 70s, performance artists presented their bodies and processes as mediums for their work, often to critique the institutional practices that produced the "dead" space of the museum. Performance did not "return" to the museum until the 1980s.

14. See http://www.pochanostra.com/downloads/pocha_manifesto.doc, last accessed April 2011.

15. Roselee Goldberg, who frames the Futurists as the first performance artists. See Goldberg, *Performance Art: From Futurism to the Present* (New York: Thames &

Hudson, 2001). Coco Fusco challenges this genealogy by insisting we also acknowledge the centuries of people who were put on display before European artists arrived at performance art in their practice. See Coco Fusco, "The Other History of Cultural Performance." In *English is Broken Here Notes on Cultural Fusion in the Americas.* (New York: The New Press, 1995): 37–64.

16. Inspired by Walter Benjamin, theorist Nelly Richard uses the term refractory to describe a type of art that emerged during the Chilean Pinochet dictatorship. It is a type of artistic practice that attempts to be completely useless for the purposes of fascism or totalitarian systems.

17. I see this as an opening in the performances, rather than an example of multi-species collaboration. We might imagine how La Pocha's interventions might play out if they involve other species beyond those that make up "individual" human bodies.

18. Donna Haraway introduced me to Irland's work in May 2010.

19. See http://www.basiairland.com/recent-projects/ice-books.html, last accessed April 2011.

20. From artist's website, http://www.basiairland.com/recent-projects/ice-books.html, last accessed April 2011.

21. Irland's website states, "In June 2009, after showing the receding/reseeding video documentary at the Albuquerque Museum, about sixty participants boarded a bus and arrived at the Rio Grande to witness and help launch eleven Ice Books." http://www.basiairland.com/recent-projects/ice-books.html, last accessed April 2011.

22. http://www.critical-art.net/FRG.html, last accessed April 2011.

Chapter Thirty-Four

CRITICAL RELATIONALITY

Queer, Indigenous, and Multispecies Belonging
Beyond Settler Sex and Nature

KIM TALLBEAR AND ANGELA WILLEY

This special issue of *Imaginations* was conceived to document, provoke, [Our] special issue of theorize, and imagine relations between humans, and between humans and other-than-humans, that go beyond and trouble normative categories of nature, sex, and love. Such categories manifest, for example, in settler-colonial forms of kin, kind, and relating that are hierarchical, anthropocentric, capitalocentric, and hetero- and homonormative. Activists, artists, and scholars have rigorously critiqued family forms legitimated by state-sanctioned marriage and naturalized by neo-Darwinian narratives of belonging centered around biological reproduction and which treat land, women, and children as property, yet such forms remain as relational ideals. The so-called natural is always paramount in settler ideas of appropriate ways to relate, control, and allocate rights and resources that reproduce structural inequities.

If we are to move beyond the reproduction of the dyadic family's scripting and privileged status, we need to understand nature differently. We need to rethink sex as the central organizing principle of human sociality, the human as the only important unit of relational ethics, and the white supremacist settler and other colonial cultural scripts as ethical measures of belonging through which the naturalized ideal of the family emerged historically (McClintock 1995, Carter 2008, Carter 2007, Cott 2002, Denial 2013, Morgensen 2011, Franke 2015, TallBear 2018). Our ability to imagine nature and relationality differently are deeply enmeshed, and this imaginative work is vital to the re-worlding before us.

Another set of generative influences that spur this issue of *Imaginations* are the frameworks of ecosexuality and Indigenous Studies relational frameworks, including Indigenous eco-erotics. Performance artists Beth Stephens' and Annie Sprinkles' ecosexual approach—Earth as lover rather than Earth as mother—has a global following (Stephens and Sprinkle 2019, Theobald 2017). Their art and activism—like Audre Lorde's "erotic"—prompt us to deconstruct the concept of "sexuality." Ecosexuality is theoretically generative for an Indigenous Studies analysis of sex and relations, precisely because it is not necessary for Indigenous people who have much longer-standing intimate relational frameworks to guide relations with lands and waters. To that end, Turtle Mountain Chippewa scholar Melissa Nelson writes on Indigenous eco-erotics that do not limit the notion of erotic relations to sex. Nelson foregrounds Indigenous stories and frameworks of relationality between humans and nonhumans (Nelson in Barker 2017). Finally, the critical analyses of Indigenous Studies scholar and anthropologist, David Delgado Shorter, challenge the objectification by anthropology of both Indigenous sexuality and spirituality. Instead he advocates for Indigenous analytical frameworks and emphasizes the circulation of power in order to disaggregate these objects into sets of relations between bodies, not all of them human and not all of them living (Shorter 2015 and 2016).

The writers and artists featured in this issue explore critical forms of relating that defy the raced, gendered, and genocidal kinship mandates of settler-colonial structures. In their textual and visual analyses and advocacy of critical theories, knowledges, and forms of relating, these thinkers and creators take inspiration from the potentially articulated fields of feminist, queer, and trans theory; Indigenous theory; disability and crip studies; critical race studies; science studies; animal studies; and performance studies. In their play with relations among various analytics, fields, and methodologies, they are often innovating new ways knowing and talking about relationality.

Twelve essays plus two book reviews constitute this special issue. Prominent theorists inform the thinking in these pages, but this issue features especially scholars and artists who are working in new, experimental ways to challenge normative ways of relating. Their archives and visions push understandings of queer, Indigenous, and multispecies belonging in exciting new directions.

As non-artist writers and scholars who seek to decolonize and disaggregate sexuality from an object out into sets of relations, Rebecca Anweiler's *Sexual/Nature* images compel us in their veering away from objectifying sex as a thing. Yet Anweiler does this by counter-intuitively focusing the artist's eye on bodily entanglements that to many observers signify the thingness of sexuality, for example hands or mouths on breasts, fingers and tongues on/in genitalia. The artist's statement notes and pushes back against a world and its human scientific and media gazes that have privileged heteronormative and biologically reproductive sex between not only humans, but also other-than-human animals as natural. At the same time, same-sex relations have been depicted as unnatural or perverse. We were delighted with how Anweiler's images and artist's statement playfully and seriously challenge what she sees as a perverse solidification of relations into the object of sex. So-called sex can then be ordered, scripted, managed, and controlled by the patriarchal white male human subjects who have traditionally gathered these relations into a narrow purview with their visualizing apparatuses (Haraway 2013). How unsexy! The boring straight sex that is scripted and standardized by the settler-colonial gaze is then used to obscure diverse, pleasurable ways of relating.

Emily Coon and Nicole Land, in *"iMessaging Friendship and Flesh,"* deploy a "Millennial feminist academic" writing method and build their paper through and around iMessage exchanges that nearly instantaneously cross 4,595 kilometres of land spanning Haudenosaunee and Anishinaabe peoples on one side of the continent and Coast and Straits Salish peoples on the other. The symbiotic relations that form their feminist ecosystem might serve as a metaphor for the centrality of relationality to our work. Jenny Reardon and Kim TallBear engaged in a Generation X feminist academic version of this collaboration one summer, years ago. They wrote *"Your DNA is Our History": Genomics, Anthropology, and the Construction of Whiteness as Property* (2012) by exchanging drafts daily via email. Their geographic distance facilitated an efficient writing process with the writing happening 16–20 hours a day. TallBear wrote from Berkeley, California and sent drafts to Reardon by 10 pm each night. That was 6 am in England where Reardon was writing. Reardon would add her edits and return the draft to TallBear by 5 pm England time, 9am California time. They sent drafts back and forth daily like this for several weeks.

While Reardon and TallBear wrote a more typical academic article less co-constitutively formed with the technology that carried words nearly instantaneously around the globe, their writing and friendship process, like Coon's and Land's process in both content and form, models the sort of relationship work usually imagined to belong to—and often seen as constitutive of—sexual/romantic relationships (Petrella 2007). The naturalization of settler monogamy depends as much upon distinguishing love from friendship and other forms of affinity as it does the pathologization of promiscuity or non-monogamy (Willey 2016, 72). The valuation of friendship as a site of intimacy, meaning-making, resource sharing, and transformation has the potential to unravel stories about the specialness of sex and to fuel our imaginations to rethink forms and structures that exceed the ideal of the settler family, which may sustain and remake us.

Coon and Land are also pulled along their path as they walk with curiosity and a sense of ethical adventure a lush citation-lined path through a forest populated by towering old-growth intellectuals, including Donna Haraway, Sandra Harding, Banu Subramaniam, and Mishuana Goeman. We hope that our mentors and colleagues will not mind us calling them "old growth." It is only a testament to their intellectual stature! Coon and Land also walk among brightly colored, resilient, and determined new growth springing up in light through the old growth canopy. The newer growth includes @apihtawikosisan, @kwetoday, @EricaVioletLee, @thesarahhunt, @RedIndianGirl and others. All are essential to this feminist intellectual ecosystem that also feeds their resurgent decolonial solidarity—their "Indigenous-settler friendship" filled with exchanges and mutual supports built through the technology of iMessage that arises from settler-colonial extractions and simultaneously works to circumvent and challenge them. This is, in short, the fundamental predicament of doing anti-colonial work within the colonial academy. We predict that this article will incite more (serious) playfulness in the writing of other re/insurgent Millennials who, rather than simply coming after us, are, like their co-constitutive technologies, coming *for* us.

Also working from within a colonial scientific field she challenges, plant scientist and artist Sophie Duncan constructs an "*(Un)Natural Archive*," an anti-colonial narrative that traces scientific explorations, discoveries, and the imposition of Latin names onto plants across time and space. Duncan demonstrates botany's co-constitution as a discipline with imperialism and colonialism spanning Rome to European invasions of the Americas. "*(Un)Natural Archive*" is punctuated with Duncan's original artworks that combine representations of plant and human bodies, sometimes with text. The series of images represent the imposition of human categories of race, gender, and otherness onto the plant world in ways that rescripted relations—both between humans and plants, and between plants and different lands—to coincide with colonial narratives of Eurocentric male exploration, discovery, and appropriation. The images are often built on top of old faded newspaper in which plants were pressed by collectors or onto magazine text in which romanticized tales of exploration are etched. Paradoxically, the images are richly splashed with primary and other colors, thus freshly analyzing the faded, but still dominant colonial archive of the "fathers of botany." Rarely is the taking-down of the "false god" of Objectivity such a delight to gaze upon.

"Ruximik Qak'u'x: Inescapable Relationalities in Grupo Sotz'il's Performance Practice" is a deeply collaborative multimedia essay. Maria Regina Firmino-Castillo, with Daniel Fernando Guarcax González (on behalf of Grupo Sotz'il), and Tohil Fidel Brito Bernal combine their use of video, still images, and text to offer a set of analytics for thinking relationality beyond settler sex and nature. The engagement of audio and visual sensorium supports the translational and analytic explication of rich understandings of knowing and being in intimate relation with nonhuman and human others. Beginning with the Iq'—life force—they map Kaqchikel epistemologies that unsettle human exceptionalism, the individual as knower, and the practice of knowing as one of domination. The methodology they enact suggests ways of knowing with and about our inextricable entanglements with one another. Relationality here is always already more-than-human and often dangerous.

Similarly, more-than-human relations ground Alexandra Halkias's "Tracking Love in the Wild." This piece offers a gentle, urgent narrative analysis accompanied by photographs of water, stone, bone, and a bit of plant matter. Halkias presents in the photographs "fluidity of form," thus conveying the related materiality of all entities, even those not considered to be living according to the definition of organismically-defined life foreground in Eurocentric disciplinary thought. The photographs of mostly lifeless objects punctuate the author's discussion of relevant multispecies, new materialist, queer, and Indigenous approaches to the relationality between human and nonhuman animals and also with geological matter. The bone adjacent to rock in one photograph also recalls relationality with ancestors, be they human or other-than-human relations now fossilized perhaps in both kinds of matter. In defense of her rejection of the stable boundary between human and animal, Halkias acknowledges that while human rights are powerful weapons for social justice, destabilizing that human/animal line may loop back to "erode the very ground that feeds these violations," violations that include mass incarceration and police violence against certain racialized human subjects. The essay then tracks across geographies from San Diego, New York, and Boston to Athens to depict dense emotional and intellectual ties between humans and nonhuman animals in several long-term relationships. Two of the most insightful tales of human-animal love are two articulated stories—the author's relationship with the cat Myrra (eventually euthanized after a very long life) and the three-way love between her friends, Eleni and Athena, and their dog baby, Bonnie. Bonnie also became ill and was euthanized just as Eleni and Athena's human babies (conceived with Danish sperm donors) were born. The essay drives home convincingly the idea that the relationality between humans and nonhumans is life-sustaining and in focusing on this cross-species sustenance we might diminish the importance of "natural difference" and disappear entirely "all social and political uses of 'the animal'" that ultimately do violence to so many beings, and to the planet.

Of course, the animal and notions of lesser evolution have been central to the articulation of race and racial science for centuries, and continue to be albeit in ways that seem more subtle from centuries past. Jennifer Hamilton's "From Bits to Bodies: Perfect Humans, Bioinformatic Visualizations, and Critical Relationality" focuses on "racialsexual formation," which is the idea that sexual dimorphism (the two-sex model) is inextricable from the development of racial categories since the 18th century. And while the biological reality of race is contested in genomic discourse, Hamilton argues that sexual dimorphism remains largely uncontested. Yet dimorphism is central to the de-animation of women and to placing them into a hierarchy below men. Hamilton anchors an analysis of contemporary genomics and its contribution to heteronormative racialsexual formation in the 2014 (not so) sarcastic assertion and bioinformatic visualization by a Berkeley computational biologist of the perfect human. The scientist referred to a legendary sixteenth century Taino (Puerto Rican) woman, Yuiza, who along with her conquistador lover, are considered in some nationalist narratives as the "great-great-grand grandparents of the Puerto Rican nation." Bringing together Indigenous, feminist, and queer theory that is critical of the role of heteronormative kinship in nation-making, Hamilton analyzes nationalist-cum-genomic narratives that are seemingly anti-racist and multicultural. But as is common in nationalist genomics discourse, the narrative and bioinformatic visualization of Yuiza is also grounded in longstanding eugenic thought and heterosexist modes of kinship.

While Hamilton reminds us of how enmeshed logics of heteronormativity and white supremacy are, others take up the limitations and possibilities of queerer notions of belonging. In "Digital Nomadism and Settler Desires: Racial Fantasies of Silicon Valley Imperialism," Erin McElroy tracks the flexibility of settler logics of belonging. McElroy offers a careful examination of discourses of freedom alongside the infrastructures that demand and enable the "digital nomad's" way of life. Despite a celebratory pretense of queering heteronormative values, like homeownership, using powerful images of protest against Airbnb, McElroy reads this figure as enacting settler politics through the displacement of others their reliance on short-term housing economies requires. The racial fantasy of a gypsy lifestyle occludes the realities of gentrification, white supremacy, and violence upon which this new subjectivity depends. Through this analysis, McElroy powerfully conveys that the queering of relationality must exceed the intimate priorities of the individual. We exist in relation with people we do not know. Critical relationality here might mean centering in our thinking the material conditions of possibility for our own constrained choices and the distribution of harms and benefits in which they are imbricated.

Conversely, Naveen Minai explores the disruption of settler epistemologies of time and space in " 'Who Gave Your Body Back to You?' Literary and Visual Cartographies of Erotic Sovereignty in the Poetry of Qwo-Li Driskill," which considers the conditions of possibility for decolonizing belonging. The imposition of settler genders and sexualities as a site of colonial violence (Rifkin) is thematized in Driskell's poetry through the concept of erotic sovereignty. Minai's reading highlights the exercise of

erotic sovereignty in Driskell's deployment of Cherokee meanings, including the relationship to land as a relation between lovers. The close reading
of the spatial and temporal disruptions of settler time and space (which
locate settler colonial violence in the past and Indigenous bodies apart
from Indigenous lands), offers rich and generative narrative resources for
reimagining belonging, beyond settler sex and nature.

Lindsay Nixon's critique of the disjuncture between Robert Mapplethorpe's treatment of white and Black subjects extends this analysis of the
racial conditions of possibility for the intelligibility of queer white settler
subjectivities. In "Distorted Love: Mapplethorpe, the Neo/Classical Sculptural Black Nude, and Visual Cultures of Transatlantic Enslavement," they
offer a careful analysis of Mapplethorpe's evocation of iconographies of the
transatlantic slave trade and critiques of these themes in his work, showing
how such images and symbols enact a queer necropolitics that depends
upon the devaluation of some lives for the revaluation of others. Through a
meditation on varied meanings of queerness in relation to Mapplethorpe's
celebrated photographic representations of queer bodies, Nixon conjures a
fragile kinship among queers to call for the accountability of our communities (unmarked) toward "Black queer kin."

Cleo Woelfle-Erskine takes up disparate imaginaries of kinship in his
analysis of settler-fish relations as a site for the production of gender, sexualities, and family. "Fishy Pleasures: Unsettling Fish Hatching and Fish
Catching on Pacific Frontiers" treats fish-relations as a naturecultural process, enabling Woelfe-Erskine's deep exploration of the coproduction of
"human nature" among more-than-human actors. A careful reading of the
visual production of settler relationality through fishing cultures unsettles
its neo-Darwinian claims on nature. The significance of the production of
land and fish as resource to the formation of heteronormative familial life
centers the non-human in our imaginaries of relational possibility. Woelfe-
Erskine stunningly renders the juxtaposition of settler and Indigenous
epistemologies of relation here in ways that make it clear that the project of
queering human-human love relations is inadequate to the task of reimagining belonging in truly transformative ways.

Extending and further exploring this insight, in "Pili'oha/Kinship: (Re)
Imagining Perceptions of Nature and More-than-human Relationality"
Kimberley Greeson offers a multispecies, autoethnographic exploration of
Native Hawaiian (Kanaka Maoli) perspectives on kinship. The centrality

of multispecies entanglements to Plioha—kinship—is at the heart of this methodological meditation. Drawing on naturecultural approaches, diffractive reading practices, and an authoethnographic thematization of experience, Greeson explores what it means to do decolonial feminist research. Learning to see and understand reciprocity among humans and the land, between humans and their more than human kin, and among non-human actors is key here not only to biodiversity, but to reimagining what it means to relate, to be related, to be in relationship.

Shifting our focus back to the ubiquity of reductionist notions of relationality, Jay Fields' digital art piece *Consumption* explores the ideal of sexual-romantic coupledom and the values that shape and are perpetuated by compulsory monogamy, the dyadic family structure at the center of settler sexuality. A meditation on the mundane interpersonal violence this system perpetuates, *Consumption* raises questions about power, desire, and the conditions of possibility for the inscription of monogamy in stories about human nature. What humans? In what contexts? Fields' visualization of monogamy offers a sharp juxtaposition to the romanticized naturalization of pairing off as the apex of human evolutionary and psychosocial development.

WORKS CITED

Carter, Julian B. *The Heart of Whiteness: Normal sexuality and race in America, 1880–1940.* Duke University Press, 2007.

Carter, Sarah. *The Importance of Being Monogamous: Marriage and Nation Building in Western Canada to 1915.* University of Alberta Press, 2008.

Cott, Nancy. *Public Vows: A History of Marriage and the Nation.*" Harvard University Press, 2002.

Denial, Catherine J. *Making Marriage: Husbands, Wives & the American State in Dakota & Ojibwe Country.* Minnesota Historical Society Press, 2013.

Franke, Katherine. *Wedlocked. The Perils of Marriage Equality.* NYU Press, 2015.

Haraway, Donna J. *Primate Visions: Gender, Race, and Nature in the World of Modern Science.* Routledge, 2013.

Lorde, Audre. "The Uses of the Erotic: The Erotic as Power." *The Lesbian and Gay Studies Reader,* edited by David M. Halperin, Henry Abelove, and Michele Aina Barale. Routledge, 1993, pp. 339–343.

McClintock, Anne. *Imperial Leather: Race, Gender, and Sexuality in the Colonial Contest.* Routledge, 1995.

Morgensen, Scott Lauria. *Spaces Between Us: Queer Settler Colonialism and Indigenous Decolonization.* University of Minnesota Press, 2011.

Nelson, Melissa. "Getting Dirty: The Eco-Eroticism of Women in Indigenous Oral Literatures." *Critically Sovereign: Indigenous Gender, Sexuality, and Feminist Studies,* edited by Joanne Barker. Duke University Press, 2017, pp. 229–260.

Petrella, Serena. "Ethical Sluts and Closet Polyamorists: Dissident Eroticism, Abject Subjects and the Normative Cycle in Self-Help Books on Free Love." *Sexual Politics of Desire and Belonging*, edited by Nick Rumens. Brill Rodopi, 2007, pp. 151–168.

Reardon, Jenny, and Kim TallBear. "Your DNA is *Our* History": Genomics, Anthropology, and the Construction of Whiteness as Property." *Current Anthropology* 53, S5, 2012, pp. S233–S245.

Shorter, David Delgado. "Sexuality." *The World of Indigenous North America*, edited by Robert Warrior. Routledge, 2015, pp. 487–505.

Shorter, David Delgado. "Spirituality." *The Oxford Handbook of American Indian History*, edited by Fred E. Hoxie, Oxford University Press, 2016, pp. 433–457.

Water Makes Us Wet: An Ecosexual Adventure. Directed by Stephens, Beth and Annie Sprinkle, Juno Films, 2019.

TallBear, Kim. "Making Love and Relations Beyond Settler Sexuality." *Make Kin, Not Babies*, edited by Donna Haraway and Adele Clark. Prickly Paradigm Press, 2018, pp. 145–164.

Theobald, Stephanie. "Nature is Your Lover, Not Your Mother: Meet Ecosexual Pioneer Annie Sprinkle." *The Guardian*, 15 May 2017.

Willey, Angela. *Undoing Monogamy: The Politics of Science and the Possibilities of Biology*. Duke University Press, 2016.

Chapter Thirty-Five

ECOSEX MANIFESTO

ELIZABETH M. STEPHENS & ANNIE M. SPRINKLE

(i) **WE ARE THE ECOSEXUALS.** The Earth is our lover. We are madly, passionately, and fiercely in love, and we are grateful for this relationship each and every day. In order to create a more mutual and sustainable relationship with the Earth, we collaborate with nature. We treat the Earth with kindness, respect and affection.

(ii) **WE MAKE LOVE WITH THE EARTH.** We are aquaphiles, teraphiles, pyrophiles and aerophiles. We shamelessly hug trees, massage the earth with our feet, and talk erotically to plants. We are skinny dippers, sun worshipers, and stargazers. We caress rocks, are pleasured by waterfalls, and admire the Earth's curves often. We make love with the Earth through our senses. We celebrate our E-spots. We are very dirty.

(iii) **WE ARE A RAPIDLY GROWING, GLOBAL, ECOSEX COMMUNITY.** This community includes artists, academics, sex workers, sexologists, healers, environmental activists, nature fetishists, gardeners, business people, therapists, lawyers, peace activists, eco-feminists, scientists, educators, (r)evolutionaries, critters and other entities from diverse walks of life. Some of us are SexEcologists, researching and exploring the places where sexology and ecology intersect in our culture. As consumers we aim to buy green, organic, and local. Whether on farms, at sea, in the woods, or in cities small and large, we connect and empathize with nature.

(iv) **WE ARE ECOSEX ACTIVISTS.** We will save the mountains, waters and skies by any means necessary, especially through love, joy and our powers of seduction. We will stop the rape, abuse and the poisoning of the Earth. We do not condone the use of violence, although we recognize that some ecosexuals may choose to fight those most guilty for destroying the Earth with public disobedience, anarchist and radical environmental activist strategies. We embrace the revolutionary tactics of art, music, poetry, humor, and sex. We work and play tirelessly for Earth justice and global peace.

(v) **ECOSEXUAL IS AN IDENTITY.** For some of us, being ecosexual is our primary (sexual) identity, whereas for others it is not. Ecosexuals can be LGBTQI, heterosexual, asexual, and/or Other. We invite and encourage ecosexuals to come out. We are everywhere. We are polymorphous and pollen-amorous, We educate people about ecosex culture, community and practices. We hold these truths to be self evident; that we are all part of, not separate from, nature. Thus all sex is ecosex. **The ecosex revolution wants YOU. Join us.**

(vi) **THE ECOSEX PLEDGE.** *I promise to love, honor and cherish you Earth, until death brings us closer together forever.*

Chapter Thirty-Six

INTERVIEW WITH JANE BENNETT
Vibrant Matters

PETER GRATTON

PETER GRATTON: What I should note straight off is that your book has gained a following among people in Continental philosophy working on what's called "speculative realism," and Graham Harman himself has said he wishes he had written this book. [. . .] What do you make of this historical moment where we have this (seemingly) wide return to the things themselves that your book marks?

JANE BENNETT: There is definitely something afoot, something about everyday (euro-american) life that is warning us to pay more attention to what we're doing. There is the call from our garbage: our private and public spaces—houses, apartments, streets, landfills, waterways—are filling up with junk, with vast quantities of disposables, plastic artifacts, old tv's and devices, clothes, bags, papers, bottles, bottles, bottles. The American television shows "Clean House" and "Hoarders" expose the more extreme versions of this mounting mountain of matter, but it's everywhere you look, including in the middle of the oceans: "SAN JUAN, Puerto Rico—Researchers [have discovered] . . . a swirl of confetti-like plastic debris stretching over a remote expanse of the Atlantic Ocean. The floating garbage [is] . . . similar to the so-called Great Pacific Garbage Patch, a phenomenon discovered a decade ago between Hawaii and California . . ." (Mike Melia, "A 2nd garbage patch, plastic soup seen in Atlantic," Associated Press, April 15, 2010).

A second kind of call is coming from the weather, from volcanos that stop flight traffic across Northern Europe and from hurricanes like Katrina that take down neighborhoods and maybe even George W. Bush. And 24 hour weather reporting and its disaster porn intensifies this call of the wild. (Timothy Morton's *The Ecological Thought* and his discussion of "hyperobjects" at contemporarycondition.blogspot.com are relevant here.)

For those of us who are philosophically-inclined, the response to such calls has been a renewed focus on objects, on an object-oriented ontology, or a renewed interest in materialisms—there have been in the last decade materialist turns in literary studies, anthropology, political theory, history. Part of this may be a pendulum swing in scholarship: a reaction to the good but overstated insights of social constructivist approaches.

PETER GRATTON: What my students and I liked best about your work is its sustained critique of "mechanism," which treats the things of the world as inert and determined. There's a danger to writing about this, since apparently it's okay to have a rather antiquated view of nature (circa Newton, or even before) but it's not okay to risk trying to describe the unruly world in all its messiness. Your book calls for a "strategic anthropomorphism" as means for thinking a non-determined materiality in and around human beings. Could you say more about the limits of this strategy and what it risks?

JANE BENNETT: A perhaps unnecessary caveat: while I think it's a mistake to allow "mechanism" to serve as a generalizable or all-purpose model for natural systems (a model that continues to linger in popular and social scientific imaginations), it would be foolish to deny that many assemblages function with a degree of regularity and repetition characteristic of machines. So, while Bergson and other philosophers of Becoming are right to draw attention to the creative element in evolution or to the capacity of physical systems to self-arrange in ways that defy prediction, I don't want to overstate the freedom, mobility, or fragility of the working groups that form in nature and culture.

One of the projects I'm working on now is to explore theorizations of the strange kind of structuration at work in what Michel Serres has described (in *The Birth of Physics* and *Genesis*) as "turbulent" systems. Here Graham Harman's critique (in *Prince of Networks*) of "lump ontology" (which he, perhaps too hastily, associates with Deleuze) highlights for me the relatively undertheorized quality of the question of formativity within philosophies of immanence, including the version at work in my *Vibrant Matter* book.

Harman makes me want to focus more carefully on the question of how it is that actants form and hold themselves together, both as individuals and as members of an assemblage. I want to get better at discerning the topography of Becoming, better at theorizing the "structural" quality of agentic assemblages. For the question of "structure"—or maybe that is the wrong word, and the phrase you suggest below is better, i.e., "linkages" between and within "open relations"—does seem to fall in the shadow of the alluring image of an ever-free becoming—the seductive appeal of Nietzsche's world of energetic flows, of Deleuze and Guattari's vibratory cosmos, of Bergson's creative evolution, of Michel Serres's "pandemonium of the gray sea." Inside a process of unending change, bodies and forces with duration are somehow emitted or excreted. But how? How, Serres asks, "is Venus born from the sea, how is time born from the noisy heavens?" (Genesis 26) What is this strange systematicity proper to a world of Becoming? What, for example, initiates this congealing that will undo itself? Is it possible to identify phases within this formativity, plateaus of differentiation? If so, do the phases/plateaus follow a temporal sequence? Or, does the process of formation inside Becoming require us to theorize a non-chronological kind of time? I think that your student's question: "How can we account for something like iterable structures in an assemblage theory?" is exactly the right question. I'm working on it!

With regard to the liabilities of the strategy of anthropomorphizing or allowing yourself to relax into resemblances between your-body-and-its-operations and the bodies-of-things-outside, I can think of at least three: it is easy to get carried away and 1) forget that analogies are slippery and often misleading because they can highlight (what turn out to be) insignificant or non-salient-to-the-task-at-hand resemblances, 2) forget that your body-and-its-operations is not an ideal or pinnacle of evolution, but just the body you have; 3) forget that the human body is itself a composite of many different it-bodies, including bacteria, viruses, metals, etc. and that when we recognize a resemblance between a human form and a nonhuman one, sometimes the connecting link is a shared *inorganicism*. I think that anthropomorphizing can be a valuable technique for building an ecological sensibility in oneself, but of course it is insufficient to the task.

PETER GRATTON: Your description of democracy, I think, gives us up to thinking of the "masses" or dêmos in an innovative way, since how the masses act, seemingly out of the blue (e.g., storming the Bastille), has thrown thinkers of individual free will and so on into fits for centuries. Could you talk more about the way this thinking could inform a look not just at the politics of matter (the way in which objects relate to one another) but also what we normally take politics to be?

JANE BENNETT: You ask another important and difficult question. Let me begin by saying something "Machiavellian," i.e., that political effectiveness requires choosing the right action and the right *style* of action at the right time, and to do this one must be alert to the role of impersonal (*fortuna*) as well as personal (human intentional) forces at work in "real time." The political strategy I pursue in order to enhance the prospects for "greener" modes of consumption and production is an *indirect* one: the story of vibrant matter I tell seeks to induce a greater attentiveness to the active power of things—a power that can impede, collaborate with, or compete with our desire to live better, healthier, even happier lives. Perhaps this new attentiveness will translate into more thoughtful and sustainable public policies. I am not sure that it will, but it is, I think, a possibility worth pursuing for a while. My political strategy is indirect because its target is not the macro-level politics of laws, policy, institutional change but the micro-politics of sensibility-formation. In the book, I also suggest that a heightened sensitivity to the agency of assemblages could translate into a national politics that was not so focused around a juridical model of moral responsibility, blame, and punishment. The hope is that the desire for scapegoats would be lessened as public recognition of the distributed nature of agency increased, and that politics would take on a less moralistic and a more pragmatic (in Dewey's sense of problem-solving) cast.

Chapter Thirty-Seven

INTERVIEW WITH PAULINE OLIVEROS

Listening to Cicadas

HELEN BULLARD

FIGURE 37.1. Pauline Oliveros playing accordion in her home garden. Leucadia, California, 1976 (photograph by Becky Cohen).

"Tell me what you hear right now . . ."

The sun is warm on us, but a fall breeze is picking through the canopy above, shaking down its music at us. Pauline Oliveros has just finished teaching this afternoon's Deep Listening class, and with the sun in my eyes I start to wonder if a field guide has ever been written to explain all the voices of the breathing wind, or the sighs and full-stops of urbanity . . .

whooooaaaarrrr-oooouww-sssshhhhhh

ch ch ch-ch-ch-chchchchch-tttttssssssssssssiiiiiiiiiiiiiiiiiiiiii. Pa. Pa. Pa.

"I hear the wind in the trees," I say, "and cicadas . . ."

Sshhhhhh-aaarrwwooooo-ppppppppppphhhhhhhhhaaarrrr

"and, passing traffic."

We are sitting at a wooden table under a poplar tree. It is mid-September, and this is my first proper conversation with Pauline Oliveros. [. . .]

[Composer John] Cage once said, *"Through Pauline Oliveros and Deep Listening I finally know what harmony is . . . It's about the pleasure of making music"* (1989). Well, it seems that Pauline takes a great pleasure in embracing all of the experiences that life provides. [. . .]

"I am an animal person too, you know!" she says, as she leans across that wooden table, under that poplar tree, in the fall sun.

Oliveros studied music everywhere in her life, from her mother and grandmother's piano playing to those soundscapes of Texas. She talks of animals in her book *Deep Listening A Composer's Sound Practice* "Animals are Deep Listeners. When you enter an environment where there are birds, insects or animals, they are listening to you completely. You are received." [. . .]

Among [her] broad archive of works, I would personally recommend *Bye Bye Butterfly*, commended by the *New York Times* as "the best piece of the 1960's" (and still staggeringly contemporary), and the hauntingly beautiful *Lear*, one of [the] tracks recorded in the cistern for the album *Deep Listening*, with a wonderful demonstration of that forty-five second reverb at the end. A wet, sucking, sticky, clicking, puttering of investigating animals creeps into the eerie reverberating forests of *Wolf/Loba*, from the album *Ghostdance*, and splits and judders and rises with strange crying electronic birds through canopies of frogs and ghosts. You have to listen, deeply, to appreciate Oliveros' orchestra: wild, captive, electronic animals, imaginary buildings in imaginary places. It is, in the deepest sense, "found sound." Perhaps Oliveros says it best and most simply herself: "You are part of the environment."[1] [. . .]

Seventeen years ago, Pauline and poet Mikhail Horowitz staged the first New York State Cicada Festival. This summer, to mark the re-emergence of the seventeen-year cicada, this festival will manifest again. Oliveros will be joined by David Rothenberg, among others, for a variety of arts and cicada events at various locations in New York State. Surrounded, hopefully, by the thick, high, full electric buzz of singing cicadas! And, *The Nubian Word for Flowers*, a new opera in collaboration with Ione, promises to stage a vast, enveloping, and ambitious sensory extravaganza in cities world-wide. An initial staging of one scene will happen in Los Angeles on June 1, 2013, with plans to move to New York City, Cairo, London and Khartoum in 2014. Opening with scenes of the vast and shifting cosmos, majestic oceans, and desert planes, *The Nubian Word for Flowers* tells the story of colonization and loss as the desert floods with high, turbulent night waters, under the construction of the Aswan Dam. It is about displacement, Egyptian armies, and the life of botanist, UK Secretary of War (1914–16), and repeatedly knighted Field Marshal of war, Lord Horatio Herbert Kitchener of Khartoum. It is an epic tale woven in flowers, oppression laced with stars and trance, phantoms and ghosts, landscapes and animals, voices and gold. Through immersive video and sound, cows and "elephants' infra sound radiating through sub-woofers, trumpeting and stampeding" (Oliveros).

I hear the wind in the trees.

whooooaaaarrrr-oooouww-sssshhhhhh,

ch ch ch-ch-ch-chchchchch-tttttsssssssssssssssiiiiiiiiiiiiiiiiiiiiiiii. Pa. Pa. Pa.

Sshhhhhh-aaarrwwooooo-pppppppppppphhhhhhhhhhaaarrrr

And cicadas, and passing traffic.

She leans back in the sun on our wooden bench, under that poplar tree.

"Yes," says Pauline Oliveros. "And all of these sounds work together; they are an orchestra! And once you hear it, you are *in* it!"

HELEN BULLARD: In your book, *Deep Listening: A Composer's Sound Practice*, you tell us that animals are Deep Listeners. Could you say a little more?

PAULINE OLIVEROS: [. . .] If *you* were living in the jungle, as our ancestors may have, *you'd* be listening!! You'd be listening for predators, you'd be listening for danger, you'd be listening for possible food sources—this is a very extensive part of being an animal; listening. Listening, though, is *not* so simple . . . this is more difficult to measure than just *hearing*. Hearing is different from listening, as I say in my book. Hearing is the mechanism for getting sound waves to the audio cortex so that they can be interpreted—so, the *interpreta-tion* and *decision making* that takes place; that is *listening*. [. . .]

So, in June, I'll be participating in a seventeen-year cicada festival that we [also] did seventeen years ago in Kingston, New York. As it was, we had to use a video of cicadas, but we're going to try this year—hopefully—to find live spots! There are a couple of naturalists (Spider Barbour and his wife), and they are going to take us on a tour to Eves Point, Socrates, New York, where they are supposed to be emerging. And, there are other parts of New York State where you can find these particular seventeen-year emergees."

HELEN BULLARD: When you write, it seems that everything is important in the soundscape; the dog, the jet plane, your jawbone—even conjured guests seem equal—the staircase, the bull; the whole world. Did you always hear the whole world?

PAULINE OLIVEROS: I believe we come into the world as deep listeners. We are already listening in the womb; the ear is the first sense organ to develop. So, we are listening already—*deeply!* So when we arrive in the world, we're rather prepared! That's why I say I think babies are the deepest listeners. But, what is the meaning? And how do you *listen* and interpret what it is that you're hearing? . . . I learned English, and later studied Spanish, and so I'm not a native speaker of Spanish, but I can speak a bit. And I have an ear for many different languages; can say phrases from many different languages . . . any-ways, so language co-opts our interests in the sounds of the world [at about six months], unless they're threatening.

So, our listening . . .

She breaks off, deep in thought.

. . . we have very *deep* feelings about sounds. And not always are they conscious, you know?

HELEN BULLARD: When *you* listen to animals, do *you* imagine becoming the animal in order to understand it better?

PAULINE OLIVEROS: Ah!

She chuckles again . . .

That is a wonderful question! Hmmm . . . I think that is a very special thing to do. And I think it is a Shamanic practice; I am not a Shaman, but I've certainly studied (or read) about shamanism, and I feel the ability to transmute your consciousness to another consciousness, or another being, is a very interesting practice. I can't say as I do that, but I recognize it. I have another piece, it's called *Angels and Demons*; it's a piece where a group, say, is asked to perform in the following way: you make the angels in the piece start to make long tones, and blend together these nice long tones on one breath, so it's kind of a drone-like thing that is quietly happening. But people who choose to be demons, need to go into this Shamanic state . . . or try . . . so that they can find the sound that they want to make that comes from the depths of their being. And then they can make any sound, whatever it is that they want to make to express that feeling. And the assumption is, with that instruction, that they might find sounds that are very loud and screamy, and different than what the angels are doing. And it might take all of their . . . all of their energy, to do it! If they really put themselves into it, you know. But the other part of the piece is that you can switch from being an angel to being a demon. (laughter). Or, from being a demon to being an angel; it takes a lot of energy to be a demon! Some people manage to get into it, and not want to stop being a demon!

Hearty, jolly laughter

Well, I guess that is an answer . . . of some kind. [. . .]

HELEN BULLARD: And will you be doing that in the cicada festival? You were saying you're able to mimic the cicada with your accordion . . .

PAULINE OLIVEROS: Well it's not about mimicry so much as it is about . . . an affective . . . sensational expression. Not trying to be a mimic.

HELEN BULLARD: It's more of a response . . .

PAULINE OLIVEROS: More of a response, yes.

HELEN BULLARD: I think my most silent moments have been between birds and animals; in moments of waiting. Do you find silence near animals?

PAULINE OLIVEROS: Oh, yeah! I think so! They can become extremely quiet as part of their defense, for one thing; their stillness and their ability to blend with the environment—

The sound of a beeping . . . like a camera timer . . . or a microwave from two rooms away . . .

Some of them actually by changing their looks—like the chameleon, for example. But I think that's a very important aspect of being an animal, and as a human I've certainly done that myself—tried to become invisible, you know? (Both laugh.) And the invisibility is stillness, and quiet, on my own part. So that can be profoundly silent.

[pause]

I mean "silent" . . . there is no such thing as silence. Because that would be zero vibrations as an absolute. And if there were zero vibrations we wouldn't be here at all! But that . . . it's the convergence toward that that I think of as silence.

HELEN BULLARD: Hmm. What was your most silent moment?

PAULINE OLIVEROS: Hmm . . . this is gonna take a little contemplation . . .

She laughs, leans back and closes her eyes . . . I listen.

Well, I had a moment on the throughway, going back home from RPI, it was about 2008, or 2009, or something, and I wasn't well. I was feeling not so good, and I . . . umm . . . I went to sleep at the wheel. And so then there was the sound of the grating on the side of the highway to wake you up, and it woke me up and I had an immediate reaction, you know, to stop going off the highway!

HELEN BULLARD: Yup.

PAULINE OLIVEROS: But then the car went into a spin. And it spun around and around and around, until I finally . . . it . . . I overturned, on the side of the road.

HELEN BULLARD: Ahuh.

PAULINE OLIVEROS: So I think there was that . . . in that *spin* . . .

(exhalation and slight laugh)

. . . that was kind of a very silent moment! As I experience this . . . this whole . . . uh, "circumstance."

HELEN BULLARD: Yup. Wow. Kind of a heightened awareness, I suppose.

PAULINE OLIVEROS: Yes, definitely! So . . . and that's, I think, when you have a heightened awareness, when you experience the most . . . *closest* to silence. So, I went over; overturned, but I was fine; I wasn't wearing my seatbelt, but I was perfectly balanced—I was ready to get out of the car, but some nurse had stopped, and she came and she took my head and she said "don't move!" She wouldn't let me move, and the ambulance arrived and they took me off to the hospital . . . my car was totaled.

HELEN BULLARD: But you were fine.

PAULINE OLIVEROS: Ya! *(slow laughter . . .)*

HELEN BULLARD: Traffic. Silence. It reminds me of that John Cage quote; "The Sound experience I prefer to all others, is the experience of silence. And the

silence almost everywhere in the world now, is traffic . . . if you listen to traffic, you see it is always different." Are your silences always different?

PAULINE OLIVEROS: Well, it's more appropriate to say "quiet." Both "quiet" and
"silence" are pejorative—they can be commands—we don't quite like to be
commanded . . . now what was the question?

Yes. I think so. As much as you would like to repeat an experience, you
really can't. There is always something a bit different. For me quiet is pleasurable, for the most part . . . although it can be ominous as well.

NOTE

1. Pauline Oliveros, "The Poetics of Environmental Sound," in *Software for People*
(Unpub Editions, 1983), 28.

Chapter Thirty-Eight

ANIMALS, NOSTALGIA AND ZIMBAWE'S RURAL LANDSCAPE IN THE POETRY OF CHENJERAI HOVE AND MUSAEMURA ZIMUNYA

SYNED MTHATIWA

In this chapter, I focus on the way nature and animal imagery are mobilised to express the poets' conceptualisation and construction of rural Zimbabwe and the Shona people's nature-culture. I argue that the presence of animals and other aspects of nature in the poetry reveals and highlights the Shona poeple's embeddedness in their ecology, and exposes the relationship between the poeple, their land, and the flora and fauna—a relationship spoilt by colonial and postcolonial exploitation of both humans and nature. The representation of animals and description of the landscape in the poetry also reveal the poets' ecological awareness and displeasure at the abuse and destruction of nature. The rural landscape, on the other hand, works as a metaphorical map of the poets' childhoods, real or imagined, and of their attempts at self-exploration and discovery, given that both poets subsequently chose to leave the rural world for Western education and the city.

To contextualize my argument, a brief overview of the Shona World-view regarding land and nature is necessary here. In Shona religious belief, land, whose (ultimate) owners are 'the tutelary spirit, *Mwari*', the creator, and the spirits of the ancestors who were buried in it, is considered sacred. Mickias Musiyiwa [. . .] gives more insight into what he refers to as the Shona land mythology, or Shona people's beliefs about the land, as expressed in the popular songs. The sanctity of the land among the Shona also obtains from the umbilical cords of the people buried in it. By virtue of 'his supposed connections with mythological founder-ancestors of his chiefdom,' the Shona believe that the ancestors bequeathed the land to the chief, who acts as a trustee and manages the land for all generations of people, the dead, the living and the unborn. This, therefore, presupposes group ownership of the land. That is, all generations of people (the living, the dead, and those yet to be born) in a particular chieftaincy own the land, whose overseer is the chief. It is not surprising, therefore, that, as Nisbert Taringa (2013: 204) observes, among the Shona 'land has no marketable value' and 'cannot be sold or transfered to another', given that the rights to the land are 'vested in cooperative groups that have overriding right over those of individuals'. This belief in the sacredness of the land means that certain taboos must be observed. Failure to do so is believe to anger the ancestors, which will lead to calamities being unleashed, such as droughts and epidemics. The taboos and prescribed behaviour have the effect of instilling an ecological sensibility in the people and conserving nature.[1]

However, Taringa cautions against romantacising the Shona attitudes to nature (and the past to which these attitudes mainly belong) as ecological, arguing that a critical examination of Shona worldviews reveals that the peoples' attitudes to nature are ambivalent and discriminative, and are 'primarily about power and relation with spirits than with ecological issues in the scientific sense.' Whereas some aspects of nature are respected and conserved among Shona, others are abused and exploited. For Taringa, this exploitation and abuse also affects animals, in spite of the existence of the totemism principle among the Shona.

In analysing Hove and Zimunya's representation of nature and rural landscape, I use what I refer to, after Dana Mount (2013: 21), as ecopostcolonialism or postcolonial ecocriticism. By definition, ecopostcolonialism 'is the study of the representation of nature and the environment in a dialogue with postcolonialism' (Mount 2013: 2). Ecopostcolonialism rejects the tendency of first-wave Euro-American ecocriticism to see environmental consciousness as the preserve of a Euro-American mindset and to construct the global South and its literatures as 'an exotic new arrival on the scene of environmental consciousness' (Mount 2013: 2–3). Contrary to this perception, environmental consciousness as always been an overlooked aspect of African literature and criticism.

However, ecopostcolonialism sees ecocriticism as postcolonialism 'not as antagonistic, but [as] dialogic' (Mount 2013: 5; see also Nixon 2005), where questions of ecology and the environment are tackled in relation to, or together with, questions of poverty, underdevelopment and exploitation (both human and environmental) (Iheka 2011; Huggan and Tiffin 2010). [...]

In other words, postcolonial ecocriticism is both ecologically and politically/socially committed, as it also engages with the politics of decolonisation, especially in an African context. This way, postcolonial ecocriticism avoids the pitfalls or parochialism of first-wave ecocriticism. In my analysis of Hove and Zimunya's poetry, I pay attention to both the environmental consciousness in the poetry and the poets' engagement with colonial injustices in Zimbabwe, formerly Rhodesia.

In their poetry, Hove and Zimunya make a mental journey to the lost world of their childhoods to shape memories of their rural lives and childhoods, and evoke the beauty of the rural landscape. Here the seasons, forests, and birds and their songs are all woven into the fabric of rural life, spirituality and belief systems of the people. But memories of rural beauty sit side by side with memories of the peasantry suffering due to inclement weather or prolonged drought—as nature is not always benevolent—and of painful poverty, as well as suffering, loosed upon the people by colonialism. For both authors, too, rural life and the beauty of the landscape are constantly vanishing owing to the ravages of colonial injustice. The land is being scarred by the bulldozer; hills and mountains are being denuded as the axe goes to work, tearing down trees; and sacred caves are desecrated by people from far-off lands—in short, home is fast becoming home no more. As Musiyiwa points out, colonialism and colonial experiences dislocated and overturned the Shona people's *mwana wevhu* (child of the soil) land philosophy as they were alienated and uprooted from the ancestral lands that formed the core of their existence. Later, however, independence did not bring the hoped-for transformation or change. Some of Hove's poems published in the late 1990s and in 2003 indicate, as I will show later, that independence did not bring freedom and happiness, as the people had expected, but more pain and suffering, as a result of the dictatorial tendencies of postcolonial leaders such as President Robert Mugabe.

From the foregoing, we notice that Hove and Zimunya are ecologically conscious poets who are nostalgic about rural life, the beauty of which was destroyed by the ravages of colonial rule in Zimbabwe. The two poets expose and lament the destruction of the land and the transitions taking place in the countryside, as well as the pain, suffering and dislocation of rural life, mainly occasioned by colonialism, which not only robbed the people of their much prized land, but also led to a spiritual death and exile, to the loss of culture and old ecological ways of seeing and imagining the world. Both poets also show a concern for nature—the seasons, the forest and its creatures—and acknowledge the beauty and revitalising nature of the rural world. However, memories of country life are not always beautiful or pleasant in the poetry. The poets are well aware of the challenges and suffering that rural life entails. They therefore reveal a broader vision of rural Zimbabwe, a vision that does not see rural societies only as idyllic and alluring, but as encompassing suffering as well. But beneath this vision of rural Zimbabwe perhaps lies 'the attitude of romanticising the past' that is observable in literature and other disciplines, an attitude 'which assumes that an eco-golden age existed at some point in the past' (Taringa 2006: 192).

REFERENCES

Huggan, Graham and Tiffin, Helen. *Postcolonial Ecocriticism: Literature, Animals, Environment.* Routledge, 2009

Iheka, Cajetan N. Postcolonial Ecocriticism and African Literature: The Nigeria Civil War Example. Thesis (M.A.)—Central Michigan University, 2011. vii, 109 leaves. Includes bibliographic references (leaves 101–109). oai:cdm15076.contentdm.oclc .org:p16010-01coll1/3443

Mount, Dana, C. 'Enduring nature: Everyday environmentalisms in postcolonial literature' PhD thesis, McMaster University, 2012

Taringa, Nisbert. 'How Environmental is African traditional religion?' Exchange 35, 2 (2006): 191–214

Chapter Thirty-Nine

WAITING FOR GAIA

Composing the Common World Through Art and Politics

BRUNO LATOUR

Let us ponder a minute what is meant by the notion of "anthropocene", this amazing lexical invention proposed by geologists to put a label on our present period. We realise that the sublime has evaporated as soon as we are no longer taken as those puny humans overpowered by "nature" but, on the contrary, as a collective *giant* that, in terms of terawatts, has scaled up so much that it has become the main geological force shaping the Earth.

What is so ironic with this anthropocene argument is that it comes just when vanguard philosophers were speaking of our time as that of the "posthuman"; and just at the time when other thinkers were proposing to call this same moment the "end of history". It seems that history as well as nature have more than one trick in their bag, since we are now witnessing the speeding up and scaling up of history not with a posthuman but rather with what should be called a *post-natural* twist! If it is true that the "*anthropos*" is able to *shape the Earth* literally (and not only metaphorically through its symbols), what we are now witnessing is anthropo*morphism* on steroids. [. . .]

What does it mean to be morally responsible in the time of the anthropocene, when the Earth is shaped by us, by our lack of morality—except there is no acceptably recognizable "we" to be burdened by the weight of such a responsibility—and that even the loop connecting our collective action to its consequence is thrown into doubt? [. . .]

It seems that, as in Lars von Triers's movie *Melancholia*, we might rather all be quietly enjoying the solitary spectacle of the planet crashing into our Earth from the derisory protection of a children's hut made out of a few branches by Aunt Steelbreaker. As if the West, just when the cultural activity of giving a shape to the Earth is finally taking a *literal* and not a symbolic meaning, resorted to a totally outmoded idea of magic as a way to forget the world entirely. In the amazing final scene of a most amazing film the hyper-rational people fall back onto what old primitive rituals are supposed to do—protecting childish minds against the impact of reality. Von Triers might have grasped just what happens after the sublime has disappeared. Did you think Doomsday would bring the dead to life? Not at all. When the trumpets of judgment resonate in your ear, you fall into melancholia! No new ritual will save you. Let's just sit in a magic hut, and keep denying, denying, denying, until the bitter end.

So what do we do when we are tackling a question that is simply too big for us? If not denial, then what? One of the solutions is to become attentive to the *techniques* through which scale is obtained and to the instruments that make *commensurability* possible. After all, the very notion of anthropocene implies such a common measure. If it is true that "man is a measure of all things" it could work also at this juncture.

It is a tenet of science studies and actor network theory that one should never suppose that differences of scale already exist but instead always look for how scale is produced. Fortunately, this tenet is ideally suited to ecological crisis: there is nothing about the Earth as Earth that we don't know through the disciplines, instruments, mediations, and expansion of scientific networks: its size, its composition, its long history and so on. Even farmers depend on the special knowledge of agronomists, soil scientists and others. And this is even truer of the global climate: the globe by definition is not global but is, quite literally, a *scale model* that is connected through reliably safe networks to stations where data points are collected and sent back to the modellers. This is not a relativist point that could throw doubt on such science but a *relationist* tenet that explains the sturdiness of the disciplines that are to *establish*, multiply and do the upkeep of those connections. [. . .]

The tricky notion of the anthropocene modifies both sides of what has to be bridged: the human side for sure, as we are deprived of the possibility of any longer feeling the sublime, but also the side of the geological forces to which we humans are now aligned and compared. At the same moment when humans have been changing the shape of the Earth without being used to their new Gargantuan clothes, the Earth has metamorphosed of late into something that James Lovelock has proposed to name Gaia. Gaia is the great Trickster of our present history. [. . .]

Gaia is not a synonym of Nature because it is highly and terribly *local*. During the period studied by Peter Sloterdijk as the time of the Globe, that is, from the 17th to the end of the 20th century, there was some continuity between all elements of what could be called the "universe" because it was indeed unified—but unified too fast. As Alexandre Koyré had said, we were supposed to have moved once and for all from a restricted *cosmos* to an infinite *universe*. Once we crossed the narrow boundary of the human polity, everything *else* was made of *same* material stuff: the land, the air, the moon, the planets, the Milky Way and all the way to the Big Bang. Such has been the revolution implied by the adjectives "Copernican" or "Galilean": no longer any difference between the sublunar and the supralunar world.

How surprising then to be told, quite suddenly, that there is after all a difference between the sublunar and the supralunar world. Also to be told that only robots and maybe a handful of cyborgian astronauts might go further and beyond but that the rest of the race, nine billion of us, will remain stuck down here in what has become once again, just as in the old cosmos, a "cesspool of corruption and decay", or at least, a crowded place of risk and unwanted consequences. No beyond. No away. No escape. As I said earlier, we can still feel the sublime, but only for what is left of nature *beyond* the Moon and only when we occupy the View from Nowhere. Down below, no longer any sublime. Here is a rough periodization: after the cosmos, the universe, but after the universe, the cosmos once again. We are not postmodern but, yes, we are postnatural.

[. . .] Gaia is not like Nature, indifferent to our plight. Not exactly that She "cares for us" like a Goddess or like Mother Nature of so much ecological New Age pamphlets; not even like the Pachacama of Inca mythology recently resurrected as a new object of Latin America politics. Although James Lovelock has often flirted with metaphors of the divine, I find his exploration of Gaia's indifference much more troubling: because She is at once extraordinarily *sensitive* to our action and at the same time She follows goals which *do not* aim for our well-being in the least. If Gaia is a goddess, She is one that we can easily put out of whack while She in turn may exact the strangest sort of "revenge" (to borrow from the title of Lovelock's most strident book) by getting rid of us, "shivering us" out of existence, so to speak. So in the end, She is too fragile to play the calming role of old nature, too unconcerned by our destiny to be a Mother, too unable to be propitiated by deals and sacrifices to be a Goddess.

Remember the energy spent in the past by so many scholars to weed out the difference between "nature" and "nurture"? What happens now when we turn to "nature" and realize that we are the ones that should be "nurturing" Her so as not to be reduced to irrelevance by Her sudden change of steady state. She will last. Don't worry about Her. We are the ones who are in trouble. Or rather with this enigma of the anthropocene there is some sort of Moebius strip at work here, as if we were simultaneously what encompasses her—since we are able to threaten Her—while She is encompassing us—since we have nowhere else to go. Quite a trickster, this Gaia. [. . .]

The third trait and probably the most important is that Gaia is a *scientific* concept. It would be of no interest if it were associated in your mind with some vague mystical entity such as Aywa, the networky Gaia of the planet Pandora in Cameron's *Avatar*. Even though Lovelock has long been a heterodox scientist and remains largely a maverick, the real interest of the concept he assembled from bits and pieces, is that *it is* assembled from bits and pieces, most of them coming from scientific disciplines—apart from the name suggested to him by William Golding. Developing a concept that was not made mainly of scientific content would be a waste of time since the requirement of our period is to pursue the anthropocene along lines dictated by its hybrid character. What we mean by spirituality has been too weakened by wrong ideas of science to offer any alternative. The supernatural, in that sense, is much worse than the natural from which it comes. So, in spite of the name, as far as we know from the comparative study of religion, Gaia does not really play the older role of a goddess. As far as I can figure, Gaia is just a set of contingent positive and negative cybernetic loops—as demonstrated in the wellknown "Daisy world" model. It just happens that those loops have had the completely unexpected effect, one after the other, of furthering the conditions for new positive and negative loops of ever more entangled complexity. There is no teleology, no Providence, in such an argument.

Of course, we should be careful with the label: when I say that Gaia is a "scientific" concept, I don't use the adjective in the *epistemological* sense of what introduces a radical and traceable difference between true and false, rational and irrational, natural and political. I take it in the new, and in a way much older sense of "scientific", as a cosmological (or rather a *cosmopolitical*) term designating the search for, as well as the domestication and accommodation of new entities that try to find their place in the collective *in addition* to those of humans, most often by displacing the latter. The great thing about Lovelock's Gaia is that it reacts, feels and might get rid of us, without being ontologically unified. It is not a superorganism endowed with any sort of unified agency.

It is actually this total lack of unity that makes Gaia *politically* interesting. She is not a sovereign power lording it over us. Actually, in keeping with what I see as a healthy anthropocene philosophy, She is no more unified an agency than is the human race that is supposed to occupy the other side of the bridge. The symmetry is perfect since we don't know more what *She* is made of than we know what *we* are made of. This is why Gaia-in-us or us-in-Gaia, that is, this strange Moebius strip, is so well suited to the task of composition. It has to be composed piece by piece, and so do we. What has disappeared from the universe—at least the sublunar portion of it—is continuity. Yes, She is the perfect trickster.

The fourth and last trick I want to review is of course quite depressing. The whole disconnect I have reviewed here is built upon the very idea of an immense threat to which we would be slow to react and unable to adjust. Such is the spring with which the trap has been set. Of course, confronted with such a threatening trap, the most reasonable of us react with the perfectly plausible argument that apocalyptic pronouncements are just as ancient as humans. And it is true, for instance, that my generation has lived through the nuclear holocaust threat, beautifully analysed by Gunther Anders in terms very similar to those used today by doomsday prophets— and yet we are still here. In the same way, historians of environment could argue that the warning against the dying Earth is as old as the so-called Industrial Revolution. Indeed, a further dose of healthy scepticism seems warranted when reading, for instance, that Durer, the great Durer himself, was simultaneously preparing his soul for the end of the world expected for the year 1500 while investing a bundle of hard money on printing his beautiful and expensive prints of the Apocalypse in the hope of a hefty profit. So with these comforting thoughts, we could reassure ourselves about the folly of prophesying Doomsday.

Yes, yes, yes. Unless, that is, it's just the other way around and that we are now witnessing another case of having cried wolf too long. What if we had shifted from a symbolic and metaphoric definition of human action to a *literal* one? After all, this is just what is meant by the anthropocene concept: everything that was symbolic is now to be taken literally. Cultures used to "shape the Earth" symbolically; now they do it for good. Furthermore, the very notion of culture went away along with that of nature. Post natural, yes, but also post cultural. [. . .]

I hope (ah, hope again!) to have shown why it might be important, even urgent, to bring together all the possible resources to close the gap between the size and scale of the problems we have to face and the set of emotional and cognitive states that we associate with the tasks of answering the call to responsibility without falling into melancholia or denial. It is largely for this reason that we have resurrected this rather out of fashion term of "political arts" for the new program we created in Sciences Po to train professional artists and scientists—social and natural—to the triple task of scientific, political and artistic representation.

The idea, at once daring and modest, is that we might convince Gaia that since we now weigh so much upon Her shoulders—and Her on ours—we might entertain some sort of a deal—or a ritual. Like the megabanks we too might have become "too big to fail". Our destinies are so connected that there might be an issue in the end as illustrated by this fascinating print by the Master of Messkirke in Basel where you see St. Christopher holding the young Christ himself embedded into a closed cosmos. St. Christopher seems to me a slightly more hopeful icon than that of the overburdened Atlas—only, that is, if hope could still be a blessing.

NOTE

I thank Michael Flower for many suggestions and for kindly correcting my English.

Chapter Forty

INTERVIEW WITH NEWTON HARRISON
Force Majeure

SNÆBJÖRNSDÓTTIR/WILSON

SNÆBJÖRNSDÓTTIR/WILSON: Newton, would you please give us an introduction to the concept of Force Majeure[, . . .] and what you see as the relationship between Force Majeure and the Anthropocene? As far as we understood it you were talking about the Anthropocene as being somehow a trace or something that happens 'after the event', whereas Force Majeure is something with which it is possible to work and for things to happen as consequence of that process.

NEWTON HARRISON: [. . .] In general terms, the Anthropocene is a way of describing the life webs response to what is happening to the energies available and the dramatic changes in the climate, but it does not account for the weakening of the life-web [caused] by our processes of extraction.

The Anthropocene makes a holistic claim but tends to act on single cause-and-effect phenomena such as the CO_2 effect. We think the *Force Majeure* is simply a more accurate way of describing what's happening.

SNÆBJÖRNSDÓTTIR/WILSON: Except that the Anthropocene could also be seen as a conceptual instrument, like an alarm—an instrument to alert people to the threat, so that they will pay attention?

NEWTON HARRISON: [. . .] The *Force Majeure* doesn't let anybody off the hook—the *Force Majeure* does not permit 'business as usual'. Anthropocene type thinkers say ' . . . well, it is going to be ok if we stop the carbon . . . 'Tell me—how are we going to de-acidify the ocean?' to ask a trivial question so

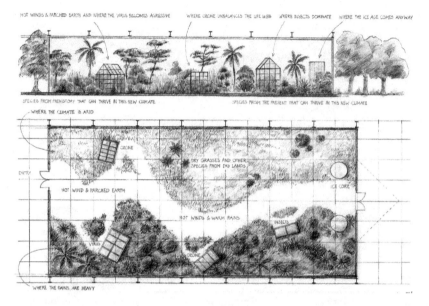

FIGURE 40.1. Helen and *The Garden of Hot Winds and Warm Rains*, drawing, 1994–95.
Source: Copyright the Harrisons.

to speak. The Anthropocene can't stand up to that kind of questioning. *Force Majeure* can.

SNÆBJÖRNSDÓTTIR/WILSON: One of the crucial dynamics of your practice has been to propose models for repair—by focusing in detail on the development of models and their specific relation to place, a sense of urgency is implied which is in itself arresting and commanding of attention. 'The Garden of Hot Winds and Warm Rains' (1994–5) for instance, appears as a proposal—was it ever realized in actuality? If so, it would be interesting to hear your reasons for representing this and so much of your work in proposal form as opposed to the documentation of work on site?

NEWTON HARRISON: What we wish to make evident is that the artist acting as creative generalist and totally unfearful of criticism, can take on these issues and truly they are not difficult. Even though actualization may look impossible or improbable in the now.

Our work has often been so many years ahead of its time that [at first], literally nobody would help us produce it or grant us monies to produce it. Although sufficient monies *were* available to think it and propose it, so we did the best we could with the resources available. No, the *Garden* was not constructed. However now 20 years later funds for 3 future garden ensembles on 2 continents at three very different altitudes are being initiated and in part, funded. I infer from your question that you may be thinking in 'art time' or 'museum time', which is always a few months to a year. We, on the other hand, doubted very much that the *Future Garden* would be made, but also believed we had a viable model and simply had to be patient as well as had to continue living.

SNÆBJÖRNSDÓTTIR/WILSON: Some things you propose are realizable and manageable as systemic models—others are speculative and in the scope of their ambition probably unrealizable—but there is an audacity implicit here—it's hard to call it absurd because of the plausibility afforded by the consistency in applied logic. What is interesting is that you are using the sciences to inform yourselves in respect of your own research, which then takes a lateral approach in focusing on linkage and bridging the ecological gaps and needs we find in our environment. Nevertheless, I'm still tempted to ask what part does play have in the construction and presentation of your work?

NEWTON HARRISON: For me, this is the fun of it, the high excitement of it, the ability to play with improvisation and indeterminacy. [And] let me tell you something about play. I am watching a pride of lions with their little cubs, all stuffed with food sitting in the sun in Africa. Ok? So I'm watching them and the two cubs are playing with each other and they are whacking each other around and one cub—the mother twitches her tail for some reason—one cub takes a look at that tail and you can see a light flashing in that little cub's head. The cub runs over to the tail, opens it's mouth and chomps down and bites the hell out of mum's tail. Mum leaps up and turns around to swat the cub—our cub has by this time figured out that mum's going to swat her (or him) so he watches for the swat and whichever way it is going he chooses the other direction and you can actually see him laughing. Or you could see the lion cub's amusement. Wherever I went I would see play, absurdity, and risk-taking, as part of everyday life. Now we take a look at what we want—we want sustainability. Sustainability is absurd—what you really need is continuity. One thing changes into another, you help it and are helped by it and you're part of that exchange. . . .

SNÆBJÖRNSDÓTTIR/WILSON: In what contexts do you believe your work to resonate most effectively—say, in terms of actual effect or its potential for effecting change . . . in human behaviour? I suppose we're asking here, who is your optimum audience?

NEWTON HARRISON: Hmmm [. . .] Let me say this—I have only once in my life addressed an audience or thought of 'art and audience'. I don't think of it. What we do is, we make a work. As that art goes out into the world it is a random moving force. Many of our earlier works are now being done by others . . .

SNÆBJÖRNSDÓTTIR/WILSON: This is your 'conversational drift . . .'

NEWTON HARRISON: Yes. But once, Helen and I broke this rule. We were in Holland. A guy from the Water Department came up to me and says 'you know we have this little problem—maybe you could do something about it. There is a place—about a 200sq km area of the Krimpenerwaard section of the Green Heart projecting out from the edge of Rotterdam and all these dairy farmers there they are demanding that we keep the water table low so they can get the best peat fertilizer for their cows grasses and we are sinking there more than a metre every hundred years. Now can you do a work of art for 12 people in our Water Department? [It's] political but cannot look political—because if your work looks political they will throw it out. And can this work of art convince these 12 people to set about convincing 300 farmers to go 'bye-bye' and then the land will stop sinking'. Well now, that's a really interesting thing for someone to ask us to do. So we said YES. We invented a new Dutch landscape by telling them to stop pumping water—if you stop pumping, the water-level will rise, the peat would stay level and not sink and you will end up with a 30–40 square kilometres lake, then this place would become more productive than it is now and we showed how that would happen. Five years later we get a letter from them telling us that it worked.

So you don't have to make things—you know there is such a temptation in our field to make things—but what you have to do, is to make things happen.

The only artefact we made was a glass column—in it was water and above the water, we had a patch of peat and it showed what happened if you let the water rise. And a few years later it is still there and the peat has not sunk. Of course not—it can't sink. So that would be addressing an audience. [. . .]

SNÆBJÖRNSDÓTTIR/WILSON: Can you explain your approach to the ethics of 'human collaboration with nature,' which I'm quoting from p.499 in the book, and the decision-making, which must be attendant on the human 'editing' and management of eco-systems? This question is made of course in the light of extirpation measures regarding, for instance, some 'introduced' species within specific environments, a consciousness regarding endangered species and possible extinctions and ultimately, the degree to which human need is seen as underpinning or being a critical factor in such interventions and adjustments. In short we can't help but make decisions which favour one species or one part of an ecosystem at the expense of another—but almost invariably, for reasons we discuss elsewhere here, we tend to underestimate the consequences of our actions in this respect because we are simply not capable of predicting those consequences as they play out in their networked intricacies . . .

NEWTON HARRISON: Ok the first understanding is very simple. For growing stuff and making decisions about what to plan, there is something called the 'feedback mechanism'. If you make a mistake that which you grow drops dead. So you don't want that to happen. What I find is that applies in all cases and forever. With every intervention, you cannot have the power of universal knowing. The only thing you can have is trust in your own ethical sense. You enter with no desire to hurt. The first few steps in—you enter there the best you can and the only thing that preserves you from doing damage is feedback. You have to be very fleet of foot when you do that because the minute there's a hint of negative feedback you have to change course. So that leaves you improvising along with everything else and therefore you have 'niched' into the life process of your improvisation—anything other than that, then you're trying to do what the insurance companies do—to predict and gain some certainty. I am no good at that.

SNÆBJÖRNSDÓTTIR/WILSON: For clarification, could you tell us a little more about the decision-making in testing—"the resilience ensemble"—in Sagehen? Which species did you select and why?

NEWTON HARRISON: We are entering our 2nd season in Sagehen. We will find out by species count what our survival rates are, then we will know how far we have gotten in determining the biotic content a resilience ensemble. 11 species were selected from the Sagehen watershed. They were selected, not because they were endangered or to protect them—so much other work around sets out to protect the status quo—rather, they were selected for their potential to continue living at various altitudes as the temperature rises as much as 5 degrees centigrade. That is to say, we are working with the idea of metaphorically driven design. The metaphor driving this design is *Every place is the story of its own becoming.* So we assume in our Sagehen watershed that the narrative or stories in its past will reveal how it will survive when temperatures rise. Perhaps in the Pliocene, similar species survived when temperatures were higher. With this thought in mind, we begin to propagate as best we could, to assist the migration of species simultaneously through time and through space. In so doing we pose the question, '. . . can we invent the framework for a replacement ecosystem to move into the space left by a retreating ecosystem (brought about) as a consequence of environmental stress?'

The interesting thing about this for me, is that so much of the (conservation) research is about helping things continue *in their present state*—they're worrying about how species are dying off and how they can help and they're worried about saving the weak—whereas what this approach does, it says, [ok] temperatures are going to rise by that much—who can live in it? And can we help species migrate through time and space? What are we doing? Again we're treating the whole situation as plastic and shapeable for the future, as opposed to something present that you respond to.

Chapter Forty-One

SEEDS = FUTURE

KEN RINALDO

How do animals, plants and insects develop relationships? These are questions which have been probed by philosophers since the beginning of time. In our cyber-enabled times, how do these relationships change and how are they asserted and co-evolve? One way is to allow them to intertwine over natural time, with natural time being the ideal instantiation of true co-evolution. Another way is by design, using the rapid speed of technological advancement to create systems we believe emulate those co-evolved relationships. This exhibition is about some of those experiments, within the realms of art and science all guided by probing and questioning the nature of natural systems and asking what are the lessons within.

My research into living systems set me on a path over thirty-five years ago, to emulate and create interactive objects and art installations that blur the boundaries between living and non-living entities. The evolution of my artwork involves the development of unique robotic interfaces for humans and other species, as well as constantly evolving approaches to looking at artificial-life systems and programming techniques and interactions within biological systems. In my works, integration of the organic and electro-mechanical elements assert a confluence and co-evolution between living and evolving technological material.

Philosophically, I believe it is imperative that technological systems acknowledge and model the evolved wisdom of natural living systems, so

FIGURE 41.1. Ken Rinaldo, *Prontay Seed*. Giclee print on paper produced at Centro Portuguese de Serigraphia, Lisbon Portugal 2013. Invited by Joao Prates.
Source: Copyright Ken Rinaldo.

they will inherently fuse, to permit an emergent and interdependent earth. I see humans now better understanding the structural and formal aspects of natural systems and now we are beginning to understand the natural processes themselves, that may also allow technological systems to act and behave in evolutive and process based ways.

The works produced for this exhibition are natural systems. The exhibition focuses on my continued work in using nature as model for designing the future and build on many previous works looking at natural systems as model. For this exhibition, I contrast colorful, imaginative artificial 3-D modeled seeds, looking at the evolved wisdom of plants and their ability to propagate based on exploiting wind, water and animal fur, to spread their genes. Seeds are the future of the plant and these works exist as models of future flowers, yet to bloom. The works are produced through research and study into the morphology of seeds and plant strategies. The incredible variety of plants and plant forms and the intriguing strategies they have come to utilize in spreading their genes are fascinating.

As plants are rooted in the ground and cannot travel, the seeds are an important evolutionary strategy for propagation and can be seen as the most precious of developments as they carry the next generation within.

In researching seeds and reading widely I think *The Bizarre and Incredible World of Plants*[1] captures it perfectly with:

> The seedlings would have to compete for space, light, water and nutrients with the parent plant and their siblings; and they would probably also encounter other unfavorable conditions and hazards such as predators and diseases, possibly already attracted by the parent plant. Traveling gives them the chance to colonize new sites, thus expanding the range of the species.
>
> In the end, the survival of not only the individual but of the entire species is dependent on the seed of reaching a suitable place of germination and establishment. Once ripe, a fruit has to somehow fulfill its true biological function, which is the dispersal of the seeds.
>
> The crucial role the fruits and seeds play in the life of a plant explains the great variety of dispersal strategies that plants have developed during the course of evolution. The strategies for dispersal—weather involving wind, water, animals and humans or an explosive force from the plant itself are reflected in a seemingly endless plethora of different colors, sizes and shapes.

The works within this exhibition are conflations of animal form, natural lessons and methods that would carry the potential seed rendered in hyper-realistic transgenic fashion. Bee seed for example is a look at the form of the bee, the hairs of the bee leg imagined with the coloring of the bee. Other works suggest seeds intermingling with the formal aspects of human form. As an artist, I am interested in seeds as a strategy—I am obsessed with the idea; that technology is also a seed. It is a seed of knowledge, idea and behavior actualized and sometimes propagated in culture. While it would be easy to, for example, look at all the negative technologies that have impacted our futures and who we are becoming, as an artist I have chosen to focus my energies, on creating real world solutions that plant ideas and real solutions to the future.

Technologies that promote urban agriculture for growing edible plants and vegetables to feed humans are one clear example of real world practical solutions. The project *Cascading GardensTM* uses the principles of biophilic design to create a more natural and calming environment. In this

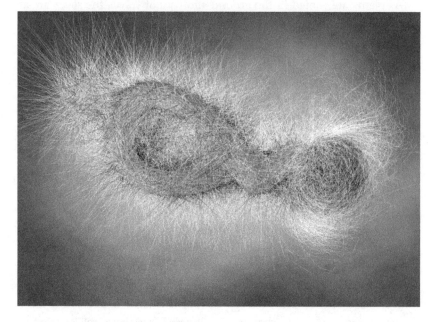

FIGURE 41.2. Ken Rinaldo, *Bee Seed*. Giclee print on paper produced at Centro Portuguese de Serigraphia, Lisbon Portugal 2013. Invited by Joao Prates.
Source: Copyright Ken Rinaldo.

living installation, built for the new Galeria Antonio Prates, houseplants provide oxygen to the indoor spaces and provide salubrious psychological effects, through the aesthetics of color. The water pumping system makes this garden almost self-sustainable and in winter evaporation from the planters adds moisture back into buildings. The color of the bags absorbs sunlight in winter months and radiates heat back into the room. In an outdoor version of *Cascading Gardens* you are able to grow your own edible vegetables while reprocessing green household food scraps with red wiggler worms.

Rainwater is collected from roofs and funneled into rain barrels and solar powered pumps lift the water to the top planters to cascade watering from planter to planter. Solar powered microprocessors with moisture sensors constantly monitor the moisture level of the roots, and when the roots are dry the watering pumps are activated. With gravity the rainwater drips from bag to bag cleansing the water and feeding the edible vegetables.

In the last bag of this garden, red wiggler worms eat the kitchen scraps, while bacteria, sow bugs, springtails and fungi further help to compost creating a natural fertilizer for the vegetables. Within these living systems, water drips from bag to bag, cleansing the water and feeding the plants nutrients, for long life.

This exhibition in both virtual and traditional material form, celebrates the full splendor of nature as inspiration, for artificial and the natural. Past works have also looked to creating seeds of idea and solution to the future and this exhibition, plants another cultural seed. Symbiotic intertwining between humans, their intelligent machines and their food systems are now upon us.

NOTE

1. Stuppy, Kesseler & Harley, *The Bizarre and Incredible World of Plants*, Papadakis Publisher, London, 2009.

PART IV

Emerging Ecologies

Chapter Forty-Two

INTERVIEW WITH KATHERINE McKITTRICK

Black Human Geographies

BETELHEM MAKONNEN

FIGURE 42.1. Katherine McKittrick, *Keep It Up (1)*, 2019

BETELHEM MAKONNEN: Black and anti-colonial studies, cultural geographies and gender studies that makes visible the links between epistemological narrative, liberation, and creative text—I am very curious as to the origins of your incredibly rich interdisciplinary practice, most especially the kinds of decisions and possibly errancy that led to your current line of transgressional philosophical inquiry?

KATHERINE MCKITTRICK: I am not sure there is an origin to my thinking—I would prefer to think of all these practices and narratives and geographies, that overlap and express differential struggles against liberation, as a way of black life or black livingness. So, for me the errancy is implicit across black studies and my work is one version or one iteration of that errancy. Interdisciplinarity opens up ways to think with, rather than solely *about* black worlds, which dislodges normative and typical approaches to studying blackness (where we, black people and our worlds, are the "objects" of study and are the "things" people do research "about"). This is moving toward a desire for expansive intellectual collaboration. I suppose, then, I would not theorize this kind of work as necessarily a philosophical inquiry, but perhaps our collective curious inquiries. For me, interdisciplinarity has dynamic and agentive underpinnings. I mean, this is how black people live—inventing and reinventing knowledge systems—and part of this work is learning and teaching and sharing that inventiveness and re-inventiveness. Learning and teaching and sharing is an expression of liberation. For me, engaging in this kind of intellectual work was not really an explicit decision, but instead a way I was already living that was evidenced in what I was reading and what I continue to read and listen to and see, as well as other forms of black livingness. To concretize this, there is always (still!) something exciting and new and familiar about Frantz Fanon's uses of multiple texts and ideas and stories and songs in his work; there is something meaningful about his intellectual rigor and his commitment to reading across black worlds to reimagine black worlds. The familiarity is breathtaking and the newness is jarring and I think this kind of methodology invites collaborative thinking and learning. In my work, I ask: what happens when we think about black ecologies, black placemaking, and black poetry as collaborative and tightly entwined texts that are not only critiquing white supremacy but totally rethinking the production of space? What kinds of clues and stories do black intellectuals and creatives offer that interrupt and remake our worlds? This is an invitation to wonder (and wander!) for me—an invitation to enter into wonder, curiosity, and intellectual rigor.

BETELHEM MAKONNEN: Could you please speak to Canadian Black history and its erasure as an influence on your fugitive geographical thinking?

KATHERINE MCKITTRICK: In my work I explore black Canada through the concept of "absented presence" (which is from, if I remember correctly, one of Dionne Brand's essays in *Bread Out of Stone*) as well as the concepts of surprise and wonder. These concepts have allowed me to theorize black Canadian communities and their geographies through the complicated paradoxes that are revealed when black folks inhabit a nation that denies their histories, geographies, and experiences. You see this on multiple levels: the refusal to acknowledge that slavery happened in Canada; the wilful razing of black communities across the nation; deportations; anti-black policing and violence, including the killing (and thus elimination) of black disabled folks, black women, black men, black queers. The erasure is sweeping and intense because it is, in practice, the removal of what-who are allegedly not here! It also impacts upon every aspect of black life and livingness: it is historic erasure, discursive erasure; it is murderous; it is subtle; it is explicit; it is urbicidal. In terms of geography, this—the removal of what is not here—opens up a way to think through and map blackness in Canada without assuming blackness has a stable absolutely knowable presence or origin story. In other words, if we are "here-not-here" we are *living place* differently and we are navigating our worlds across and against (rather than totally within) the empty logics of visual surplus that so often define and delimit black life (or, we are living place differently, and we are navigating our worlds, without being beholden to elimination, abandonment, erasure, displacement, deportation). Perhaps then, we can offer new or radical ways to imagine liberation. Perhaps we can offer spatial practices that do not seek to own and totally define place, but instead are capacious, opaque, and strongly committed to undoing-refusing the violence of colonial and plantocratic place-making practices. In *Demonic Grounds* I work with surprise and wonder—the latter is indebted to Sylvia Wynter and I still use it to think through black methodologies—to notice how the impossibility of black Canada invokes curiosity rather than a knowable set of bearings or cartographies. Geography, or at least colonial and plantocratic geographic practices, tend to be tied to authenticating practices (you find space, you take space, you own place and space and property, space [property] defines who and where you are and authenticates your owning-presence which is paired accumulation-as-dispossession [this is mine, not yours, get out]). Curiosity, wonder, reorient us, and situate black geographies, and black Canadian geographies, as sites of open inquiry.

BETELHEM MAKONNEN: How does the theory of "black human geographies" presented in your ground-breaking book *Demonic Grounds: Black Women and the Cartographies of Struggle* emerge and function as a discipline from what Sylvia Wynter's suggestion of "a third perspective," rather than an oppositionality tethered and in direct response to existing traditional geographical arrangements?

KATHERINE MCKITTRICK: The term "black human geographies" is intended to pair the discipline of human geography with black studies. It is an intervention into the assumption that human geography is, first and foremost, an academic and colonial way of knowing; it offers a somewhat clunky way (the term itself is cumbersome and imprecise to me) to centre and really contemplate these brilliant black geographic knowledges that circulate as acts of liberation and resistance. I am not abandoning geography, but instead illuminating different kinds of geographic practices that cannot be seen, or are rendered inadequate-problematic, within the context of white supremacy. I think it is important to also signal that the term is not meant to centre the human or the black human (in *Dear Science* I elaborate on the pitfalls of analytically centring "the human" in the work of Sylvia Wynter and more generally); it is, instead, an attempt to rethink and situate black geographies as robust and intricate and rebellious and creative sites of invention. I have tried to work this out through, and get some precision, in my theorization of "a black sense of place" which I position as an entangled discursive-material-imagined black methodology: a black sense of place draws attention to geographic processes that emerged from plantation slavery and its attendant racial violences yet cannot be contained by the logics of white supremacy; a black sense of place is not a standpoint or a situated knowledge (it is a location of difficult encounter and relationality); a black sense of place is not individualized knowledge—it is collaborative; a black sense of place assumes that our collective assertions of life are always in tandem with other ways of being; a black sense of place is a diasporic-plantocratic-black geography that reframes what we know by reorienting and honouring *where* we know from. For me, a black sense of place is where a third perspective can be and is engendered, because *where* is not conceptualized as insides or outsides (belonging/unbelonging inclusion/exclusion or even oppression/resistance) but is instead offering a set of conversations (not clear-cut instructions with

solutions) and rebellions and curiosities and creative works that are express-
ing black livingness through the production of space. This is, for me, where
invention and reinvention happen, and where geography, as we know it, is
totally undone.

BETELHEM MAKONNEN: What are the ways, in your opinion, that "imaginative-
real black human geographies" disrupts institutionalized Post-Humanism
discourses, and subsequently conceptions of the Anthropocene?

KATHERINE MCKITTRICK: I am not widely read on the posthuman or the
anthropocene so I can only speak to these ideas from a distance. It seems
both conceptualizations, at least in their etymological-theoretical foundations, rely on a temporal frame that cannot attend to black temporalities
and black livingness—and that would include imaginative and real black
geographies. Maybe that is a good thing! Even in their complexity, though,
the terms are weighed down by a kind of evolutionary script (we are moving
forward, we are moving away from one version of the human and toward
more complex (*subsequently* more complex) human, as a species we are
moving changing from this into that) that is grounded in scientific racism
(that future-toward is a teleological-evolutionary projection, time-stamped
with racial differentiation and punctuated by dehumanization). I realize
both these concepts are more complex that this—there are backward posthuman futures and the ecological disruptions caused by anthropocentric
violence are not lauded—but the weight of the linear temporality, which
structures each term so poignantly, is disquieting. It is sutured to a version of time that cannot actually bear blackness and black time (black time
is paused and forever and never and always and then waiting and quietly
torrent). I also find that some engagements with anthropocentric moments-
subjects, especially those that fold in black worlds, rely heavily on metaphor.
So, the preoccupation with the future or future-present, and ecology and
environmental catastrophes, gets absorbed into a framework that reduces
black life—that is our books, our ideas, our livingness, our poetry, our
sense of place—to a description. The engagement with black intellectual
life is not analytical; rather black ideas animate an otherwise unblack story.
There is a tendency to posit, for example, that vulnerable communities are
composed of "toxic bodies," with black people exemplifying the penulti-
mate environmental toxicity and thus providing an ideal analytical script
that proves, rather than questions, the brutality of environmental racism
(this is a rehearsal of what we already know: the tendency to conceptualize

non-white people and the land *together*, as one, is a crude and dehuman-izing expression of scientific racism). When race and environmental decline *conceptually* collide, scientific racism stays in place, and we read that passive black flesh is inscribed *by or represented as* ecology or that black bodies (not people) are the receptacles of noxious substances and thus *become*, through osmosis, toxic landscapes. Here, metaphor (black elements, black toxicity, black sedimentary rocks, black cenotes) prevails and cloaks black human-ity and black experience. We witness not an assertion of capacious black livingness that is in concert with non-black communities and extra-human processes and environments, but instead the argument that black bodies are like poison, black bodies are like geology, black bodies are waste, black bodies are toxic. The preoccupation with *describing* subjugated bodies is suffocating; both the environment and the racialized body become a sin-gular analytic site of degradation. Biological determinism (the evolutionary narrative) is normalized and spatialized and conversations (curiosities) that draw attention to relational and transnational resistances to eco-crises are foreclosed.

BETELHEM MAKONNEN: Thinking through Chapter 5 of the book, *Demonic Grounds: Sylvia Wynter*, in what ways does Sylvia Wynter's philosophical framework relate to the geography that you are making visible? What role did her work play in your confrontation with the discourses of "normalcy" that anchor the invention of Man, essentially the Human $^{\circledR\text{TM}}$ through which the world is spatialized?

KATHERINE MCKITTRICK: I read Sylvia Wynter as an anti-colonial scholar and as a black geographic thinker who has spent considerable time thinking through the production of space. When I first engaged her work—her essay "Beyond Miranda's Meanings"—I was struck by her ability to work through the complexities of black feminism in a way that theorized black femininity and black women's knowledge both through and beyond western feminist debates. Her thinking in this essay is really brilliant because she reorients black women not as excluded from or oppositional to feminist debate (e.g. left out of feminism, counter to feminism), but rather as agentive subjects whose intellectual displacement from normative western knowledge sys-tems provides the conditions for a completely *different* set of political prac-tices. She does not engage in a project that follows black women through exclusion-recovery-reclamation precisely because this kind of trajectory re-centres the infrastructures that make exclusion possible (and profit from the erasure of black thought). Instead, she formulates a totally different intellectual *place*—demonic ground. This different intellectual place is tethered to and cognizant of, but not beholden to, western discourses and literacies (what Wynter calls governing systems of meaning). This different intellectual place generates a perspective that—precisely because it is disavowed by the empowered—offers insight into the limitations of the discourses, literacies, governing systems of meaning that are underpinned by race thinking. When encountering this intricate pulling apart of feminism and black thought, I thought to myself, this is a brilliant spatial project! And I wondered: where are these demonic grounds located? From there, I studied Wynter as a geographic scholar and used her concept of demonic ground/demonic grounds to theorize the "where" of black geographies—not to pinpoint and demarcate them, but instead to work out how the production of space provides the conditions to generate the amazingly thoughtful writings, songs, places, and experiences of black intellectuals. I suppose, then, this has less to do with Man (and Man-as-human) and more to do with where black knowledge is and how, within the context of racial violence, black people understand their sense of place as one that is necessarily committed to anti-colonialism. I mean, this is one of the gifts of black studies for me—this a very nuanced thinking through of the *where* of black liberation that overturns the terms of abandonment by positioning black thought as an agentive and ongoing (rather than absent or oppositional) process.

Chapter Forty-Three

INTERVIEW WITH DOO-SUNG YOO

Organ-Machine Hybrids

JENNIFER PARKER-STARBUCK

I discovered Doo-Sung Yoo's work as I was continuing to develop my own ideas around the ever-present triangulation between humans, non-human animals, and technologies as understood through art and performance practices. Yoo's work not only reaches across human, animal and technological divides, but also exists at an interdisciplinary crossroads between art, performance, and science. This work is challenging; neither fully utopic nor dystopic, it stretches and permeates borders asking viewers to question what human-animal-techno futures might become.

Yoo's work immediately captivated me, first with his "Robotic Pig-Heart Jellyfish", part of his Organ-Machine Hybrid series that is just that, a hybrid figure that seemed a perfect example of what I was theorizing as "becoming-animate" a mode of reanimating the non-human animal within its human-technological relationship. [. . .] More recently I have been compelled by his piece "Lie," a series of wagging robotic cow tongues, which has helped me form an argument for technologized animalities as having potential to stage a Rancièrian "dissensus." What I was manifesting theoretically, Yoo was manifesting practically. When I initially reached out to him to ask a clarifying question for a paper I was giving, his detailed and considered response made me want to understand the impetus behind his work even more. [. . .] This interview has taken place over many months of email exchanges, and I feel it is only a beginning.

FIGURE 43.1. Doo Sung Yoo, *Vishtauroborg Version 3.1: Incompatibility* (2012). Performance: Wearable robotic devices and cow tongues.
Source: Photograph copyright 2012 Cameron Sharp and Doo Sung Yoo.

JENNIFER PARKER-STARBUCK: Although I am interested in your early experiments with media and human bodies, for this interview, I want to focus mainly on the work you've done with what I would consider 'animality', which I would describe as a consideration of animals for themselves, as they relate to humanity, and how they manifest as a condition in society. With this in mind, how and why did you become attracted to using animals in your work?

DOO-SUNG YOO: Instead of using animals as mere objects in my art, I materialize animals as ontological equivalents with humans and machines—they all become materials that balance with each other. Since I have been engrossed in calculating an equation of intersection between human body and technology in my early work, I have now added one more constant, 'the animal', to the equation. For me, like mathematics sets (such as a subset, complement set, and empty set), these three objects/subjects (human, machine, and animal) allow me to interpret their mutual relationship to my artistic practice to determine what artistic possibilities can be articulated or derived from these correlations.

Human beings always discover benefits from animals and from nature. My *Organ-machine Hybrid* series illustrates scientific trends, such as when medical science, for instance, utilizes pig bladders for regenerating human skin tissue or develops xenotransplants from animal to human, or robotic organ transplantation as well. I believe that the meaning of 'animality' has fluctuated in history and culture, and is subject to change when influenced by technological innovations. Involving animals in my artwork not only motivates me to reinterpret 'animality and humanity' in the technological environment but also allows me to interweave and find harmonies between the three. Many questions are ongoing in my art: what is shared, and importantly, what traits or values are not shared, at the intersections between 'human and animal', 'human and machine', 'machine and animal', and the three sets, 'human, machine, and animal'; how can we apply those constant values of the equations to artistic avenues and artistic interfaces. Respecting Donna Haraway's sense that we can look ourselves in the 'animal mirror', I would like to find humanity in the animal and other living non-human organisms. Simultaneously, I like to probe how technology can be a bridge between animality and humanity.

JENNIFER PARKER-STARBUCK: I became interested in your work initially through the Organ-Machine Hybrid series, beginning with the *Aqua001.co2: Robotic Pig Heart-Jellyfish* and have since also been writing about the piece *Lie: Robotic Cow Tongues*. What intrigues me is the hybridization of the actual animal part and a technological component to create a new hybrid 'species'. In response to my own discussions of your work (at conferences, for example), the use of animal parts is sometimes critiqued. How might you respond to questions of the use of animals to facilitate new affiliations between animals-humans-technologies? And to follow up, how important is the use of the actual animal in the work you develop?

DOO-SUNG YOO: Although I have used live animals, such as fish and leeches, in some of my work, I have mainly used parts of flesh and organs from edible and discarded parts of domestic animal bodies (mostly cows and hogs) that are easily purchased at butcher shops, groceries, and slaughterhouses. This application of 'animal' parts in my artwork differs slightly from other artists who might use the whole animal. The disembodied parts of animals—the meat and organs—are also in the context of food and the waste of animal industry. I am not an animal activist, but in comparing 'art animals' and 'industry animals', it is worth remembering that numerous animals are killed and trashed on machine belts, and the surplus from slaughterhouses is used for processing food and producing further commodities in clothing, cosmetics, ointments, and so on. These are equally disrespectable and disgusting practices behind the scenes of industries that most people are not aware of, or willing to pay attention to when thinking about food. My works remind people that we use animals in our everyday life and position them in art where they can be hybridized with humans and machines for further artistic and scientific benefits, not just traditional nutritional or industrial 'benefits'.

Although I do not agree with, for example, Tinkebell's self-justified killing of her cat to turn it into an art object in *My Dearest Cat Pinkeltje* (2004), and I would not like to drink or eat the human breast milk and cheese from Jess Dobkin's 'The Lactation Station' (2006) and Miriam Simun's 'The Lady Human Chees' (2011), I applaud the artists' challenges to think about a new vision: how can we do away with stereotypes in order to better understand consumable animals? How can human bodily substances become items for human consumption beyond the baby-momoligopoly or physical human-organ transplants? There are many things right in front of us that we do not notice, and we should rethink and reassess our understanding of these systems. Artists (including myself), scientists, engineers, and researchers are able to show these invisible opportunities and possibilities to ask: How can we view the increasingly multifaceted issues of using animals and then shift our relationships with them based on these new views? [. . .]

JENNIFER PARKER-STARBUCK: Based on your explanation about *Pig-bladder Clouds in Rainforest*, in the piece, if animals are hybridized and their body parts used and assembled as your performances imply, how is this beyond an animal dystopia? Is a techno-utopia one in which we hybridize animals, or is this actually a technodystopia?

DOO-SUNG YOO: Obviously, there is no such thing as a true or perfect utopia and dystopia. These notions are ideal states and cannot be achieved in the real world. (Actually, the etymology of utopia means "not" + "place" and this can be interpreted as synonymous with "fantasy" or "not real" which is how I use "utopia" in my work.) We have seen so many different attempts at utopia in our historical, political, economic, cultural, ethical, and religious circumstances that have caused much suffering. The real problem is that once we choose a system of thought for utopia, we act towards the achievement of the ideal and forget about the consequences of our actions. We have a delusional, self-righteous confidence that we are right and that we are helping others.

There are many instances how pursuing utopia has created a dystopia that coexisted in the cause and consequences. For example, John Gast's painting *American Progress* (1872) illustrates the idea of Manifest Destiny, in which constructing an American utopia stands on the other side of exterminating American bison and destroying the Native Americans' commissary and other life necessities, so as to provide food to construction workers on the Western railroad, and entertain hunting excursions.

I am using utopia and dystopia as metaphors and tropes to signal certain ways of thinking about relationships between humans, animals, and technology. I allow these ideas to play and dance in my performances. Then, audiences can think about how animals relate to humans and technology in a utopian or dystopian context. Humans and animals, for instance, can enhance each other through biological and genetic symbiosis, and machines can be powered by organic material and hybrids, such as biofuel (animal fats for biodiesel) and neurorobotics. We cannot fully escape our human condition to eat and use animals due to the human's intrinsic instinct to feed and kill its prey as a natural predator. Accepting this fundamental human trait, we can acknowledge that the animal-utopia is not possible within the human world.

Articulating my fantasy world is neither a true animal-utopia nor classical human-utopia, but it would be a sort of secular-driven proposition of utopia, an approximation or resemblance of a utopia in which the anthropocentric attitude for utilizing animals still inevitably exists at the level of survival and sustainability, but in a situation of minimized influence from humanity. My performances create a secular ritual mood, which tries not to disrespect animals, but rather to elevate them through the atmospherics of performance. This ritual does not need to be religious, but the devotional mood encourages respect in the audiences' feeling for the sacrificed animals, such as edible animals and laboratory animals, which in my work are technologized and genetically reincarnated into an artificial life. This simultaneous existence of ideal (imaginary) and real states in my performing contexts is "a kind of effectively enacted utopia" of Michel Foucault's notion of heterotopia, which is "simultaneously mythic and real". My techno-utopia would not be on either side of the argument—*for* or *against* animals, instead, my emerging techno-utopia involves binary oppositions with ambiguous boundaries: where forms are mixed and interlinked without traditional norms (like in Foucault's heterotopia); where whole things are interconnected and where we balance between nature and force as a perspective in Taoism; where we deconstruct classical utopian ideology of traditional humanism as a perspective of posthumanism. My techno-utopia stands on the point of ideal balance between utopias of anthropocentrism, ecocentrism, technocentrism, and others (heterotopia) rather than a single dominating utopia. All of those discourses question how "utopia" can be reinvented and reassessed without the binary opposition split. The 6th century philosopher and Zen master Seng-ts'an sums up my conceptual position, "If you want the truth to stand clear before you, never be for or against. The struggle between for and against is the mind's worst disease".

JENNIFER PARKER-STARBUCK: In your early interactive work you explored cyborgean concepts, for example, using the living performer to dance with an animated robotic heart in your 2002 performance in Seoul, *The Dynamic and Vital Media*. You describe this on your web site as illustrating 'the expanding humanization of media'. Do you feel media has been increasingly humanized or has it done the opposite—mediatizing humans? How has this early fascination with the cyborg developed as you've incorporated animality into your work?

DOO-SUNG YOO: Technology and humanity are like the two sides of a Mobius strip: while they are interconnected and actually part of the same thing, they are still separate. We control and are controlled by technology in a never-ending loop. Media (technology) has been increasingly humanized. The current Body Area Network (BAN) and Internet of Things (IoT), such as wearable and mobile technology on human bodies, are good examples that show how media has become an intimate interface for human use. When we return to the starting point on the strip, however, we are faced with the other side in which we are subordinated by technology. Technology is also a powerful interface to mediatize humans in politic, capitalistic, social, and cultural agendas.

I admire video artist Nam June Paik's standpoint toward humanizing technology, which suggests to us how we view technology's confrontation between 'control' and 'controlled'. In the globally broadcasted video, art via satellite, *Good Morning, Mr. Orwell* (1984), Paik denied George Orwell's dystopian vision that Big Brother's (telescreens) omniscient power dominates and mediatizes every citizen in a novel *Nineteen Eighty-Four* (1949). Rather, Paik celebrated that humans positively use media to interact with all global communities, which is now much more common in the current world of social media. Moreover, Paik has suggested we can intimately objectify media through humanistic approaches of using technology in his video sculpture series, including *TV Bra* (*TV Bra for Living Sculpture*, 1969), *TV Garden* (1974–2000), and *TV Bed* (1972–1991), which look like origins of current BAN and IoT. I agree with Paik's vision that technology's capability positively enables us to 'liberate people from the tyranny of TV' [which I would broaden to include the categories of media, technology, and power], although are we still in the Mobius strip when encountering different controversies about capitalistic, political media tyranny, such as Apple's iPhone Backdoor security and National Security Agency (NSA)'s global surveillance. Likewise, technology can be developed and applied for good or bad by humans' desires and greed in the endless strip; the duality of the strip reflects the duality of humanity. [. . .]

JENNIFER PARKER-STARBUCK: There has been a lot of discussion and debate over the term 'posthuman' from Katherine Hayles to Cary Wolfe to Rosi Braidotti, and each have their own ideas about what this term means and what its importance is. What do you mean when you use this term? What is its importance to you?

DOO-SUNG YOO: The concepts of my bio-art and robotic performance are mainly based on the notions of posthumanism. When I launched the organ-machine hybrids in 2007, my art concept began with the notion of transhumanism, which asserts that technology enables humans to radically exceed their biological and physical forms and capabilities beyond the conventional limitations. My early hybrids are mainly focused on visual metaphors of augmented bodies in electronic sculpturing forms. However, in adding more technical functions for human-machine interactions in future hybrid characters I needed to further research the philosophy of posthumanism to get out of my artistic rut, where I was stuck focusing on the prowess of technology and material forms. Through looking at the meaning of posthuman, I confronted the fundamental considerations and ontological questions of re-identifying new human roles and reassessing humanism *alongside* technology, beyond the mere physical transformation in nature, or as a posthuman being in the Anthropocene. Furthermore, as an artist, I have been considering what aesthetic points artists could derive from human evolution, such as becoming a posthuman entity and entering into new relationships with other species.

I support the fundamental change of concepts about humanism within posthumanism, which have been celebrated in my art. My human-animal-machine hybrid, *Vishtauroborg*, is based on the destruction of traditional humanity by disintegrating the binary boundaries between human and animal, and human and machine. In the *Vishtauroborg* performance, the human performer is not a privileged being in the artistic collaboration with the organ-machine. Sometimes, the performer's improvisatory choreography was controlled by the organ machines reactions, and sometimes vice-versa, which created harmonized motions in real time. This equivalent relationship illustrates Katherine Hayles' positive view of human's high consciousness and intelligent machine's partnership in our ongoing development of cognition environments. Cary Wolfe's cynical views on human superiority and Rosi Braidotti's feminist technological thinking alongside multiple-identities are also significant notions which I applied to *Vishtauroborg's* visual metaphors in hybridizing human/animal-parts/machine and human performers' androgynous characteristics. Humans are no longer standing atop a hierarchy in the theatrical mise-en-scène in order to destabilize hierarchical relationships between human/robot, human/animal, and male/female.

The notions of posthumanism will continually guide me in how I can view and understand humanity and humanism through the lens of technology. My artistic work will share Wolfe's wariness of the 'intensification of humanism', in which technology can only be used for human being's augmentation. In my work, I use technology for new paradigms of humanism outside of the anthropocentric stance. Following those posthumanists' concepts, I would like to continually probe what new human roles are, what new human responsibilities are, what new human life-forms are, and to discover new norms and standards in the coexistence of living entities and technology.

Chapter Forty-Four

INTERVIEW WITH KELLY JAZVAC

Plastiglomerate, the Anthropocene's New Stone

BEN VALENTINE

BEN VALENTINE: As an artist directly involved with research into the Anthropocene, [you are] uniquely equipped to bridge a discussion between the humanities and sciences. [. . . Your positioning of Plastiglomerates as artworks,
through found-object "sculptures" and photographs, captures the blurring of
"nature" and "culture" embodied in these stones (if there ever truly was such
a divergence). [. . .] How did you come to investigate these rocks?

KELLY JAZVAC: I went to a lecture on plastic pollution at the university where
I teach. The guest speaker was Charles Moore, an oceanographer and plastic
pollution activist. He spoke about seeing an unknown substance on a beach
in Hawaii that he thought was being formed by lava and plastic garbage mixing together. I was very interested in it, as it looked like both toxic waste and
sculpture. After the talk I sought out the person who invited Charles Moore,
geologist Patricia Corcoran. I suggested that if she ever wanted to collaborate
I'd be interested. She wanted to go to Hawaii to check out this unknown substance presented by Moore, but needed a partner to do the field work with,
and who would be willing to pay his or her own way. I happily volunteered.
She has been a remarkable collaborator ever since—knowledgeable, focused,
and open minded.

BEN VALENTINE: These Plastiglomerates are being used as evidence for our
being in a new geologic period, the Anthropocene. Do you think that term
is important or accurate?

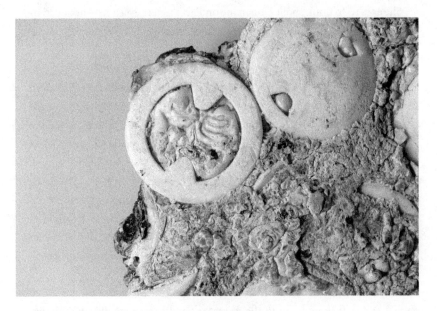

FIGURE 44.1. Kelly Jazvac, *Plastiglomerates*. Mixed media, 2013.
Source: Copyright Kelly Jazvac.

KELLY JAZVAC: I'm glad you asked this question. I think it's an important term but not a flawless one. It's important because it's clearly being used in many debates about human impact on the environment. For example, it's the word that the International Commission on Stratigraphy and the International Union of Geological Sciences are currently debating whether to officially use or not to describe our current geologic epoch (I'm not a geologist, but I'm guessing that hasn't happened before). It's also useful to have a word for a very expansive, amorphous phenomenon. It's much easier to talk about (and therefore potentially change) when it has a widely used name.

However, at the same time, I think it's important to fully assess and debate the term, especially as it comes into prominence. I think everyone who is interested in this subject should read the essay "Indigenizing the Anthropocene" by Zoe Todd, from the book *Art in the Anthropocene*. Todd argues for complicating the term from an indigenous perspective. For example, the word "Anthropocene" implies that all humans are now a geological force irreparably altering the earth, when in fact not all humans have equally contributed to, nor profited from, actions that have resulted in climate change.

She asks us to think about human life on Earth in terms of a network of complex relationships that include gender, race, colonization, geography, power, and capital.

BEN VALENTINE: Why are these stones important in this debate?

KELLY JAZVAC: Our 2013 paper on Plastiglomerate identifies its potential to act as a marker horizon in the future rock record. In other words, if a geologist takes a core sample a long time from now, there is the potential that she could see plastic in it. On Kamilo Beach in Hawaii, Patricia Corcoran and I saw large chunks of in situ Plastiglomerate buried in the sand. Once buried, the plastic will not be subject to erosion from wind and water, and thus has a greater potential to be preserved (unlike plastic floating around in the ocean that keeps breaking down into smaller pieces). Patricia is currently conducting experiments to determine the heat and pressure that Plastiglomerate can withstand. She's also working with graduate student Anika Ballent to determine the quantity of plastic at depth in Lake Ontario.

BEN VALENTINE: What role can art play in confronting climate change?

KELLY JAZVAC: In addition to the important and simple act of initiating discussion, art can help to visualize things that are very hard to visualize. Climate change is so large and all encompassing it's actually hard to "see" in its entirety. The visibility that artist Chris Jordan has given to the impact of plastic pollution on albatrosses comes to mind as an immediate example.

Furthermore, I think art can be adept at crossing disciplines, borders, and barriers in sophisticated and productive ways. It doesn't always play by the rules, and as such, it can be slippery and covert. Art can also make things uncomfortable, even if it's just for a moment, and ask us to confront our delusions and presumptions.

It's not a perfect system, of course, and there are lots of historical examples of really challenging art becoming nullified en route to the gift shop. However, I think there are truly remarkable instances of art's transgressive abilities in the pursuit of political and social change (because for me, climate change and political change go hand in hand). These instances include when artists have looked really closely at something in order to both analyze and mobilize. I'm thinking of projects like Forensic Architecture, Theaster Gates's work in Chicago, and Duane Linklater's sophisticated calling out of internet racism.

Chapter Forty-Five

A QUESTIONNAIRE ON MATERIALISMS

DAVID JESELIT CATHERINE LAMMERT-BEATTY,
AND HAL FOSTER WITH MEL Y. CHEN

Art history in the wake of poststructuralism has relied heavily on theories of subjectivity. Recent philosophical tendencies, characterized as "Actor-Network Theory," "Thing Theory," "Object-Oriented Ontology," "Speculative Realism," and "Vibrant Materialism," have profoundly challenged the centrality of subjectivity in the humanities and, arguably, the perspectives that theories of the subject from the psychoanalytic to the Foucauldian have afforded (on the operations of power, the production of difference, and the constitution of the social, for instance). At least four moves characterize these discourses:

- Attempting to think the reality of objects beyond human meanings and uses. This other reality is often rooted in "thingness" or an animate materiality.
- Asserting that humans and objects form networks or assemblages across which agency and even consciousness are distributed.
- Shifting from epistemology, in all of its relation to critique, to ontology, where the being of things is valued alongside that of persons.
- Situating modernity in geological time with the concept of the "Anthropocene," an era defined by the destructive ecological effects of human industry.

Many artists and curators, particularly in the UK, Germany, and the United States, appear deeply influenced by this shift. Is it possible, or desirable, to decenter the human in discourse on art in particular? What is gained in the attempt, and what—or who—disappears from view? Is human difference—gender, race, power of all kinds—elided? What are the risks in assigning agency to objects; does it absolve us of responsibility, or offer a new platform for politics?

We wonder if it is possible to reconcile the different positions we've outlined, many of which seem to contradict one another, in order to theorize a new materialism or objectivity. If it isn't, what is at stake in those irreconcilable differences? Which, if any, are the productive materialisms for making and thinking about art today? Please comment from the perspective of your own work on the significance and effects of these developments.

REPLY

Mel Y. Chen

A student I encountered a few years ago, in a thought experiment, noted that "sustainability in academia would be like reusing old ideas as much as possible." This statement ironizes the newness that sustainability performs, as a frequently corporatized discourse whose structural condescensions—dominant forms with powerful effects despite or perhaps due to their poor importation from other domains—opportunistically displace and discredit the resourceful strategies of oppressed or impoverished societies. I'd like this ironic thought to peck at scholarship's own recycling, or self-referential, strategies as well as to ask about competing approaches to matter. The implicit temporality of sustainability further suggests to reflect on the meaning of "old" and "new" in terms like the new materialisms. Here I meditate on "going cosmic"—a mode I identify in some social or scholarly gestures. By "going cosmic" I refer obliquely to experimental drug cultures of the sixties, in which drugs often enabled experiments of metaphysics. In an expanded reading, "going cosmic" suggests a (futuristically or relatively) "new materialism"—a cosmology whose material participants or collectivities are not as they seemed, and whose interrelations or relational potentials are experienced as novel. There is something necessarily experimental in scholarship that seeks to understand the life of matter from perspectives beyond those crystallized as conservatively "human"; I am deeply sympathetic to this experimentality.

My own consideration of materialism has been primarily in my exploration of animacy, a hierarchy of sentience, mobility, and personhood that effectively runs down and across orders of descent roughly from humans to animals to plants to minerals; as well as what it has further become in institutionalized and colonially conditioned settings: an obdurately racialized and sexualized and ableized set of coercive rules for favorable interactions between matter of different kinds. Strict coercivity can't help but leave gaps, enabling animacies that perform a kind of affective fibrillation. Decolonial and queer scholars, for instance, have recognized and theorized this kind of restive animacy under different terms, even if humanness may have remained an unnecessarily agentive core. The accountability I'm looking for refuses to accept that speciesism or human-centricity has ever worked the way that it seems to have. Difference-hierarchalizing systems of species and race, ability, sex, sexuality have been long working with and borrowing from one another, explicitly and latently mutually enabled by the non-coincidental overlap of colonialisms, imperialisms, Great Chains of Being, and capitalism. It is a form of whiteness, I think, that enables a thinker like Ian Bogost to claim that computers are "plastic and metal corpses with voodoo powers," without critically considering—or simply deeming irrelevant—the disabled racialized inhumanism of historical *and* contemporary zombies (not to mention his use of "voodoo"), or to claim that "environmental philosophy has argued that humankind is to ecology as man is to feminism or anglo saxonism is to race."

Gil Scott-Heron's famous song "Whitey on the Moon" ("Taxes takin' my whole damn check/The junkies make me a nervous wreck/The price of food is goin up/And if all that crap wasn't enough/A rat done bit my sister Nell/With Whitey on the moon/Her face and arms begin to swell/And Whitey's on the moon"), rather than simply rehearsing the Great Technological Divide, seems to suggest that at least one drive to go cosmic—the reach for the moon while his sister Nell can't afford to see the doctor— is identifiable as a feature of capitalism and empire. By the whiteness of going cosmic I refer to the set of patterns by which outer space becomes an empire of colonies, and by which even the "new" hippy dippy wonderment of things, some sustainability efforts included, risks calling on an exotified spiritual cosmopolitanism to embellish its own tainted garden.

To what extent then are new materialisms serving as structural condescensions, *themselves* new technologies engaged in acts of forgetting, in which lived differences such as race, class, sex and ability no longer serve as necessary considerations because fictions of scale mark them as irrelevant? Deracination is a profoundly political move from which novel materialisms cannot be taken as immune. Simultaneously, I commit to taking "old" materialisms as seriously as those heralded to be "new" ones, while resisting the easy categorization of either. In my ongoing dialogues with Julia Bryan-Wilson, we often discuss how art history, with its deep-seated considerations of materiality, seems to sit at an odd, partially forgotten location within the inevitably multidisciplinary exchange about matter. In multiple and overlapping genealogies of scholarship, questions abound as to the historical ownership of theories of matter, and they do not seem easily resolvable.

I continue to return to Noenoe Silva and Jonathan Goldberg's work on sharks and pigs' integral relevance for Native Hawaiian (Kanaka Maoli) sovereignty. At a talk on their work Silva commented, "For us the stone is alive; we don't have to *derive* it!" This counts as provocation only from the point of view of settler colonialist approaches to matter. To accept that a stone is simply living, not only under certain perspectival conditions, is to contest the habitual particularization and old-making of race or indigeneity. The authors rethink the political present using Kanaka Maoli transspecies and transanimate genealogies. This sets up an important exchange in which the statement "yes, one is related to a mountain," can be read as a direct rejoinder to colonially circulated reasoning about matter's identity, species, dynamism, and sexuality. To the extent that new materialisms seem to proffer cosmologies that function as somehow more potent than the old ones, and yet work to deracinate matter unequivocally, I would suggest that the new materialisms have the potential to enact structural condescensions of their own in spite of an aesthetics of equality; to function as a place of new racial or settler treachery, as sustainability discourses easily do.

Chapter Forty-Six

ART AS REMEMBRANCE AND TRACE IN POST-CONFLICT LATIN AMERICA

CYNTHIA E. MILTON

One of the foundational stories in the discipline of art history is that of the Corinthian Maid.[1] According to the tale, as told around 77 AD by the Roman natural philosopher Pliny the Elder, a Corinthian potter's daughter traced on the wall her lover's shadow, cast by candlelight. The soldier was about to leave for war and his future was uncertain. Moved by the sadness of his daughter upon the soldier's departure, the father made a sculpture of the young man, based on the drawing that she had done. In art, this technique is that of the trace or indexical sign of what once was present. In Latin America, after the decades of Cold War, civil wars, military incursions and dictatorships, this trace is known as the silhouette, the outline of a loved one disappeared, in most cases, by the state, which grew into the *siluetazo*, a movement to demand their return.[2] Yet, while similar in technique, the meaning of the act of tracing differs slightly. The Corinthian woman made a reproduction of her lover in anticipation of longing, and possibly in anticipation of the profound sorrow upon his loss. As art historian Lisa Saltzman notes, this story is of "a daughter who determines, with her anticipatory gesture of grief, the link between representation and remembrance" (Saltzman 2006: 3).

As an analogy or point of entry to discuss trauma, art and affect, this tale is not quite appropriate, for the Corinthian daughter made the art *before* the loss. Yet, much of the art produced in Latin America since the 1970s is *after* the loss: in Argentina, we find the silhouettes of loved ones who were disappeared that change from drawn outlines of figures into the grainy black and white identification photographs throughout Latin America that represent the dead and missing loved ones. These artforms and images are used to remember those who are no longer here, and for some it is the silhouette alone that remains, anchoring the memory of an individual—and in the case of Argentina, a generation—in the present.

Traces and silhouettes, and artistic and visual engagements with the past abound thus indicating what appears to be a near universal response to violence—art. In her seminal study, *The Body in Pain* (1985), Elaine Scarry posits that art in its many forms may express that which verbal language cannot.[3] This is a theme picked up by Jill Bennett (2005) in her notion of empathic vision, by Dominick LaCapra's (2001) concept of 'empathetic unsettlement' and Katherine Hite's reworking of the same (2012)—that art can express emotions otherwise left unspoken and elicit from the spectator an embodied response; Lisa Saltzman argues that art links us to non-verbal memories of the past through the trace or indexical sign of what once was.

Indeed, it is this ability of art to evoke for spectators other people's memories of a traumatic past that in part explains why art lends itself so well to memory studies. For as Marianne Hirsch has written, "it is this presence of embodied and affective experience in the process of transmission that is best described by the notion of memory as opposed to history. Memory signals an affective link to the past—a sense, precisely, of material 'living' connection—and it is powerfully mediated by technologies like literature, photography, and testimony" (2012: 33). I would add to her list of technologies visual representations and artistic practices more broadly.

That is, art offers a powerful means for recounting the past and for reaching a kind of understanding that otherwise remains beyond comprehension. The ability of art to speak about atrocity has been debated since Theodor Adorno famously remarked that to write poetry after Auschwitz was "barbaric" (Adorno 1981: 34). This remark has often been interpreted to mean that it is impossible, both actually and morally, to represent the Holocaust, and perhaps, more broadly, any atrocity, via art. Yet Adorno later in life acknowledged poetry as an important means of communication, for "perennial suffering has as much right to expression as a tortured man has to scream" (Koch, quoting Adorno, 1989: 15). Over the half century since the Holocaust, a plethora of artworks has emerged to broach the 'difficult'—in the meaning of both sensibility toward and comprehension of—thus allowing us, decades later, to move beyond the taboo of representing and giving expression to shameful and horrific pasts. Indeed, we should recognize the significant role art can play in making difficult pasts comprehensible, even if only in part. Thus, in a reworking of Adorno's famous words, the historian Steve Stern suggests that to *not* produce art in the aftermath of suffering would be to allow barbarity to reign unchecked (Milton 2014: 2).

Indeed, in Latin America, one of the intended aims of art in response to atrocity seems to be this: to contest the barbarity committed and to restore the humanity of citizens who have been harmed, the hundreds of thousands dead and disappeared since the 1970s and the millions of people affected and displaced. In the transition from state violence to democracy and the years following, issues of representation and memory have come to the forefront of political and cultural analyses and debates about conflict and repression in Latin America, especially since justice seems slow in coming, if at all. Protest art against authoritarian regimes and violence has made way for memorial art. In Argentina, *siluetazos*, which stood out as silent protests and evocations of missing citizens in the early and mid-80s, now adorn public state-sponsored memory sites dedicated to the *desaparecidos* (disappeared) (Bell 2014). Yet art may maintain continuity in its role regardless of regime type: whether under dictatorial or democratic rule, art *contests any totalizing vision of state power*. During dictatorships, to make art could be an act of resistance, as when Chilean women stitched picture appliqués (*arpilleras*) whose imagery denounced the Pinochet regime's human rights abuses (Agosín 2008). So, too, in post-conflict democracies, art reminds audiences of the ongoing tensions of the unresolved past in the present: for instance, post-civil war novels in Central America reference the violence of earlier decades in the context of today's insecurity (Moodie 2010); and the creativity of the *escraches* (happenings to denounce perpetrators) by Argentine and Chilean youth "remind us that while the dictatorships and even democratic regimes have tightly controlled our understanding of the real, cultural practices constantly subvert that discursive order" (Masiello 2001:7).

Art may help to achieve a fuller expression and better understanding of violent pasts. In a conversation between the historian Gonzalo Sánchez and the artist María Elvira Escallón, who made a photography exhibition after a fire in a nightclub in Bogota, called 'Desde Adentro', Sánchez reflects on the limits of written texts in recounting the Colombian violence: "a text can not say everything about the pain that covers our daily tragedies. We need to turn to images, and the multiple possibilities of artistic language" (Sánchez and Escallón 2007). Art may help not only those who have gone through traumatic events to put shape and give meaning to their experiences—to express something about the pain, to paraphrase Sánchez—but art may also help those who have not directly experienced such events to come closer to a sympathetic awareness of them. As Kyo Maclear has written in the context of post atomic bombings Japan, art can move viewers "emotionally and intellectually toward the unknown" (1999: 24). For some survivors, art came out of necessity and a desire to record what happened for future generations: "even now [thirty years later] I cannot erase the scene from my memory. Before my death I wanted to draw it and leave it for others", said Iwakichi Kobayashi, a seventy-year-old survivor of the atomic bombing of Hiroshima (Japanese Broadcasting Corporation 1977: 105). Thus, art also asks contemporary and future others to bear witness to the artists' acts of witnessing.

NOTES

1. This chapter draws extensively from the introduction to Milton (2014) and from my introductory comments as editor to the chapter of Jiménez's drawings (Jiménez 2014). I presented an earlier version of this paper at 'Surviving Genocide: On What Remains and the Possibility of Representation' conference at the International Max Planck Research School on Retaliation, Mediation and Punishment in Halle, Germany, December 2014, and at the ECPR Workshop 'Imagining Violence: the Politics of Narrative and Representation' in Pisa, Italy, April 2016. I thank Ralph Buchenhorst, Verena Erienbusch, Eliza Garnsey, Mihaela Mihai, and Fazil Moradi for their comments, as well as the Canada Research Chair Program, the Social Sciences and Humanities Research Council of Canada, the Alexander Von Humboldt Foundation, and the Fernand Braudel Fellowship Program of the European University Institute for funding support.

2. Siluetazo started as an artistic happening conceived by three Argentine artists in 1983: Julio Flores, Guillermo Kexel, and Rodolfo Aguerberry. The initial concept was to erect 30,000 silhouettes, which was the estimated number of people imprisoned and killed by the dictatorship between 1976 and 1983 in Argentina. The operation became a major popular event, and the silhouettes are a regular presence at subsequent rallies (Camnitzer 2007: 74).

3. See also Friedlander (1992: 5).

REFERENCES

Adorno, Theodor W. (1981): *Prisms*. Translated by Samuel and Shierry Weber. Cambridge, Mass.: MIT Press.

Agosín, Marjorie (2008): *Tapestries of Hope, Threads of Love: The Arpillera Movement in Chile*. Lanham, MD: Rowman & Littlefield.

Bell, Vikki (2014): *The Art of Post-Dictatorship: Ethics and Aesthetics in Transitional Argentina*. Abingdon & New York: Routledge.

Bennett, Jill (2005): *Empathic Vision: Affect, Trauma, and Contemporary Art*. Stanford: Stanford University Press.

Camnitzer, Luis (2007): *Conceptualism in Latin American Art: Didactics of Liberation*. Austin: University of Texas Press.

Friedlander, Saul (ed.) (1992): *Probing the Limits of Representation: Nazism and the "Final Solution."* Cambridge: Harvard University Press.

Hirsch, Marianne (2012): *The Generation of Post-Memory: Writing and Visual Culture after the Holocaust*. New York: Columbia University Press.

Hite, Katherine (2012): *Politics and the Art of Commemoration: Memorials to Struggle in Latin America and Spain*. London: Routledge.

Japanese Broadcasting Corporation (NHK) (1977): *Unforgettable Fire: Pictures Drawn by Atomic Bomb Survivors*. New York: Pantheon Books.

Jiménez Quispe, Edilberto (2014): 'Chungui: Ethnographic Drawings of Violence and Traces of Memory'. In: Milton, Cynthia E. (ed.): *Art from a Fractured Past: Memory and Truth-telling in Post-Shining Path Peru*. Durham, NC: Duke University Press, pp. 75–102.

Koch, Gertrud (1989): 'The Aesthetic Transformation of the Image of the Unimaginable: Notes on Claude Lanzmann's Shoah'. *October* 48, pp. 15–24.

LaCapra, Dominick (2001): *Writing History, Writing Trauma*. Baltimore: Johns Hopkins University Press.

Maclear, Kyo (1999): *Beclouded Visions: Hiroshima-Nagasaki and the Art of Witness*. Albany: State University of New York Press.

Masiello, Francine (2001): *The Art of Transition: Latin American Culture and Neoliberal Crises*. Durham, N.C.: Duke University Press.

Milton, Cynthia E. (ed.) (2014a): *Art from a Fractured Past: Memory and Truth-telling in Post-Shining Path Peru*. Durham, NC: Duke University Press.

Moodie, Ellen (2010): *El Salvador in the Aftermath of Peace: Crime, Uncertainty and the Transition to Democracy*. Philadelphia: University of Pennsylvania Press.

Saltzman, Lisa (2006): *Making Memory Matter: Strategies of Remembrance in Contemporary Art*. Chicago: University of Chicago Press.

Sánchez, Gonzalo/Escallón, María Elvira (2007): 'Memoria, imagen y duelo: Conversaciones entre una artista y un historiador'. In: *Análisis Político* 20, 60, pp. 60–90.

Scarry, Elaine (1985): *The Body in Pain: The Making and Unmaking of the World*. New York: Oxford University Press.

Chapter Forty-Seven

INTERVIEW WITH MANUELA ROSSINI

Critical Posthumanisms

DAVID DE KAM, KATRIEN VAN RIET, AND HANS VERHEES

MANUELA ROSSINI: As a preliminary point, I would like to say a few words about my understanding of the terms 'posthumanism,' 'posthuman,' and 'posthumanist.' Very broadly speaking, 'posthumanism,' is a world-view as well as a paradigm, mode of interpretation or epistemological frame to reflect on humanism and its aftermath. It also refers, like any other '–ism,' to an ethical and political standpoint. Of course there is not only one posthumanism, like the other '—isms,' it has different forms and ideological colours. The 'posthuman' would relate more to the subject as figured in narratives and images in literature and culture at large. And, finally, we [Rossini speaks of herself and the general editors of the Rodopi monograph series "Critical Posthumanisms"] mainly use 'posthumanist' to denote a critical practice, a theoretical approach and attitude that is, arguably, next in line after post-structuralism and postmodernism. For the readers of *Frame* it is perhaps interesting to mention that posthumanism as a critical and cultural theory has mainly been developed by scholars of English and American Studies in the USA from the 1960's onwards. [. . .]

DAVID DE KAM, KATRIEN VAN RIET AND HANS VERHEES: Still, if critical posthumanism is to constitute a new ethics of difference, subverting human-ist ethics, would you agree that the persistence of hierarchical structures is contradictory to that effort?

MANUELA ROSSINI: That depends on what we do with that hierarchy. Some dogs in the pack are quite happy in a passive position. Every being has the potential to be happy. This is the Deleuzian notion of potential according to which everyone should be able to live a good life. You should form structures in such a way that you can contribute even if you are in an inferior position to the overall project. I noticed that in my team at work. I focus on their strong points and not their weaknesses, because it takes too much energy to say: "you'll have to learn how to do that." I rather form a team in which everyone has a place and meaning in the system, and where the system has more agency than its individual parts. This understanding fosters an ethics that is mutually sustaining: we should sustain the potential—what a body can do—of everyone. Globally, we should recognize that we depend on one another, depend on other countries. Countries like Switzerland, my home country, should be aware that the privileges currently enjoyed by its natives are sooner (rather than later) over—what with the economic and ecological crises also effecting our way of life. Hence, we should move towards a global ethics and global justice—now! I agree with you, however, that the current hierarchical structures impede the realisation of such a posthumanist ethics of difference.

DAVID DE KAM, KATRIEN VAN RIET AND HANS VERHEES: Hearing you talk of the need to recognise everyone's worth and to construct structures that attempt to facilitate the potential to live a good life for all people, this global ethics of difference sounds like a very idealistic, almost romantic notion.

MANUELA ROSSINI: I believe that as a general attitude one should always try to be a 'good' host, unconditionally welcoming the other/Other. But in this sense, critical posthumanism is an ideal, a utopia in which we do not accept the world as it is today. We need to strive for a sustaining ethics of difference, an ethics more related to caring, empathy and solidarity on the grounds of our shared mortality.

DAVID DE KAM, KATRIEN VAN RIET AND HANS VERHEES: Are you hopeful that we are currently moving towards a posthuman ethics of difference?

MANUELA ROSSINI: Yes, I think we are forced somehow. Recent global ecological disasters attest to an entanglement of humanity and the material world. Such disasters will automatically force us to find solutions and cooperate more. We have to determine, as a society, where we want to go in the recognition that there are no islands. Because of the fact that the actions of one country will affect other countries, one cannot distance oneself from these other countries. Critical posthumanism is aware of the agency of matter; it takes into account the posthuman condition of entanglement. We should not have the illusion we humans are in control. These global crises, say pandemics, will, sadly, bring the necessity of a global ethics of difference to the fore.

DAVID DE KAM, KATRIEN VAN RIET AND HANS VERHEES: When the validity for a global ethics of difference is based on the fact that we are threatened by the same things, does that not render this ethics fragile? Are we really embracing difference or do we, rather, recognize that one's survival is aided by this cooperation in which one postpones difference, if you will?

MANUELA ROSSINI: Perhaps that is the compromise? Fragility is indeed a good term: these relationships are very precarious and we will need to work continuously at engaging in relationships beyond difference as hierarchy and the legitimation of oppression and murder. As Donna Haraway also points out: we cannot completely refrain from instrumentalising each other or machines and animals. Haraway insists that relationships are, to different degrees, always instrumental and asymmetrical, but we should be closely aware of this and think about ways to improve the situation. I should be constantly aware of how I exclude others, how I suppress others, how I use others, but using each other is part of being in the world. Again, it is quite idealistic, but I believe that we should all reflect upon our own behaviour and act upon it in the interest of sustaining all that matters.

Chapter Forty-Eight

AFRICAN AFRO-FUTURISM
Allegories and Speculations

GAVIN STEINGO

Afro-futurism developed largely as a response to the condition of forced diaspora—of transatlantic slavery. Such is already evident in Mark Dery's 'Black to the Future,' a text widely recognized as the movement's seminal theoretical statement. Dery begins his text by observing that only a handful of African-American novelists 'have chosen to write within the genre conventions of science fictions,' something he finds

> especially perplexing in light of the fact that African Americans, in a very real sense, are the descendants of alien abductees; they inhabit a sci-fi nightmare in which unseen but not less impassable force fields of intolerance frustrate their movements; official histories undo what has been done; and technology is too often brought to bear on black bodies (branding, forced sterilization, the Tuskegee experiment, and tasers come readily to mind).
> (DERY 1994, 180)

The focus on forced diaspora as a kind of 'alien abduction' laid the terrain for much of the theoretical and creative work to follow. Of course, Dery was only reflecting on decades of music, literature, and art that had explored this theme: Sun Run's 'intergalactic research,' Jimi Hendrix's 'Astro Man,' Octavia Butler's *Parable of the Sower*, and Anthony Braxton's 'Trillium R,' to name just a few. But what, precisely, does 'alien' designate in Afro-futurist production? Although Eshun is partly correct that Afrofuturism 'adopts a cruel, despotic, amoral attitude towards the human species' (1998, 00[-005), it is important to also note the opposing tendency to domesticate and re-humanize aliens.

Many argue, in fact, that Afro-futurism derives its affective and political force by allegorizing conditions of slavery through the *metaphor* of the alien. The allegorical nature of Afro-futurism is articulated in the pithy title of Alondra Nelson's 2001 article, 'Aliens Who Are Of Course Ourselves.' In Nelson's reading of artist Laylay Ali's representations of an alien community called the Greenheads, the key point of the images is that they 'reflect contradictions of the *human* condition' (2001, 99; my emphasis). 'Alienness' is on this view a metaphor for 'human connection and detachment' (100–101), or as Nelson notes, the alienness we project onto each other—and particularly the alien foreignness of black subjects in an inhospitable world.

Ken McLeod makes a similar argument in an extended discussion of 'alien and futuristic imagery in popular culture' (2003, 337). He argues that the important Afro-futurist musician George Clinton 'assumed the alter ego of an alien named Starchild who was sent down from the mother-ship to bring Funk to earthlings. Starchild was an *allegorical representation of freedom and positive energy*—an attempt to represent an empowering and socially activist image of African-American society during the 1970s' (2003, 343; my emphasis).

And indeed, a similar line of argumentation guides the interpretation of other non-human forms within Afro-futurist discourse. Discussing the issue of technology and the cyborg, Tricia Rose interprets Afrika Bambaataa's use of android metaphors as 'an understanding of themselves as *already having been robots*. Adopting 'the robot' reflected a response to an existing condition: namely, that they were labour for capitalism, that they had very little value as people in this society' (in Dery 1994, 213–4; original emphasis). For Rose, the cyborgic confusion of human with technology only throws humanity into sharper relief. The human 'robot' can never be an affirmative figure for Rose—it can only ever represent the dehumanization and reification of certain humans through racial capitalism.

As suggested by the above examples, Afro-futurist theorization often trades on constitutive paradoxes to the effect of: 'ruminating on alien life is really about human life'; 'explorations of technology are really about human capabilities'; 'visions of the future are really about the present.' These paradoxes can be formalized as 'X is actually about non-X.' Or perhaps a more pertinent formalization would be: 'non-X is really about X'—since in each case 'X' is really what matters.

Even Kodwo Eshun, who has long taken a strong anti-humanist position, advocates the allegorical position in a text published five years after his magnum opus. 'The conventions of science fiction,' he writes, 'marginalized within literature yet central to modern thought, *can function as allegories* for the systemic experience of post-slavery black subjects in the twentieth century' (Eshun 2003, 299; my emphasis). Here again, science fiction scenarios ('non-X') are really about the here and now ('X'). For Samuel R. Delany, similarly—at least in as Eshun's reading of him—Afrofuturism is less concerned with the future than with providing 'a significant distortion of the present' (Delany, quoted in Eshun 2003, 290). Writing about the future, in this rendering, is really a matter of distorting the here and now.

What one witnesses in much Afro-futurist interpretation, then, is a kind of crypto-humanism. This is a humanism rerouted through metaphors of the alien and the cyborg. Rather than becoming something other than human, 'aliens' and 'cyborgs' are understood as metaphors for those humans who are denied humanity, for those humans who are not valued as such. In almost every case, what first appears to be the creation of something completely other (extraterrestrials, androids) turns out to be what is most familiar. There is seemingly no thought beyond what is already known—every thought of the outside is 'in fact' about us. As Nelson tells us, the aliens are of course ourselves.

Without diminishing the potency of this mode of interpretation,[1] I want to ask if it may be possible to think about Afro-futurism outside the rubric of allegory. I will be asking, that is, what Afro-futurism might look and sound like if we think about it in terms of a speculative exploration of the unknown—an exploration of the unknown *qua* unknown, rather than as a metaphor of the Same. A step in this direction is already suggested in a famous scene from the film *Space is the Place*. When Sun Ra teleports into a youth center in Oakland, California, and announces his imminent departure into space, a young African-American man asks him: 'Are there any whiteys up there?' To this, Sun Ra responds: 'They're walking there today. They take frequent trips to the moon. I notice none of you have been invited.' In his response, Sun Ra makes a clear political point about the exclusion of African Americans from U.S. society and technological development. But it is also relevant to view the exchange in terms of what George Clinton (2016) has recently characterized as a 'futurist standpoint' that came 'from an era when we were contemplating space travel.' In the second half of the twentieth century, metaphors of space became indissociable from actual space navigation and exploration. In a similar vein, speculation about life on other planets, conspiracy theories about alien contact, and advances in space exploration technology form an uneasy relationship. Discourses about extraterrestrial space—alien life included—are not necessarily or exclusively metaphorical. Outer space is not *merely* a metaphor for Earth.

If certain African-American products push interpretation in this direction, it seems to me that African-based Afro-futurism moves even further away from allegory. This move is due, in part, to the fact that African musicians and artists are not compelled to deal directly with the condition of diaspora. And because of this, references to 'outer space' and 'aliens' have less obvious metaphorical resonance.

In general, African-based practitioners of Afro-futurism opt for a more speculative vision of 'the outside.'[2] Whereas allegory reveals a hidden meaning about how things are, speculation is a form of thought or action about how things are not. Allegory implies a vector of return—a reflection of or a detour through the other back to a (reconstituted) self. As such, allegory is ultimately about the here and now. Speculation, by contrast, is directed outwards towards the unknown and the unanticipated.

NOTES

1. Indeed, there are good arguments for a non-naïve, 'reparative humanism' (see Gilroy 2011).

2. I use this term roughly in Ochoa Gautier's sense (2014, 61). Ochoa Gautier borrows the term from Seeger (1987). I do however acknowledge that allegory forms the interpretive matrix for much science fiction (if not exactly Afro-futurist) production in Africa as well. For example, white South African author Lauren Beukes frequently refers to her South Africa-based sci-fi novels *Moxyland* (2008) and *Zoo City* (2010) as 'allegories' or 'allegorical apartheids' (Beukes 2013). And to provide one additional, completely banal example, consider Roger Ebert's (2009) review of South African sci-fi film *District 9*, which he calls 'a harsh parable . . . about the alienation and treatment of refugees.'

REFERENCES

Beukes, Lauren. 2013. Interview with The Geeks Guide to the Galaxy. *Lightspeed*. September (40). http://www.lightspeedmagazine.com/nonfiction/interview-lauren-beukes.

Bryant, Levi, Nick Srnicek, and Graham Harman, eds. 2011. *The Speculative Turn: Continental Materialism and Realism*. Melbourne: re:press.

Chidester, David. 2005. *Authentic Fakes: Religion and American Popular Culture*. Berkeley: University of California Press.

Clinton, George. 2016. 'George Clinton Talks Sun Ra, Kendrick, Prince, Jimi Hendrix and More.' *Nuvo*, May 2, 2017. http://www.nuvo.net/ACulturalManifesto/archives /2016/05/02/george-clinton-talks-sun-ra-kendrick-prince-jimi-hendrix-andmore.

Coplan, David, and Bennetta Jules-Rosette. 2005. 'Nkosi Sikelel' iAfrika and the Liberation of the Spirit of South Africa.' *African Studies* 64 (2): 285–308.

de Lange, Deon. 2012. 'Dana: We Should All Speak Swahili.' *Cape Times* [Cape Town]. January 18, 2012. http://www.iol.co.za/news/politics/dana-we-should-all-speak-swahili -1215244.

Dery, Mark, ed. 1994. 'Black to the Future: Interviews with Samuel R. Delany, Greg Tate, and Tricia Rose.' In *Flame Wars: The Discourse of Cyberculture*, 179–222. Durham, NC: Duke University Press.

Ebert, Roger. 2009. Review of *District 9*. August 12, 2009. http://www.rogerebert.com /reviews/district-9-2009.

Eshun, Kodwo. 1998. *More Brilliant Than The Sun: Adventures in Sonic Fiction*. London: Quartet.

——. 2003. 'Further Considerations of Afrofuturism.' *CR: The New Centennial Review* 3 (2): 287–302.

Golumbia, David. 2016. "Correlationism': The Dogma That Never Was.' *boundary 2* 43 (2): 1–25.

Griaule, Marcel, and Germaine Dieterlen. 1965. *Le Renard Pâle*. Paris: l'Institut d'Ethnologie.

Lewis, Tyson, and Richard Kahn. 2005. 'The Reptoid Hypothesis: Utopian and Dystopian Representational Motifs in David Icke's Alien Conspiracy Theory.' *Utopian Studies* 16 (1): 45–74.

McLeod, Ken. 2003. 'Space Oddities: Aliens, Futurism and Meaning in Popular Music.' *Popular Music* 22 (3): 337–355.

Mutwa, Vusamazulu Credo. 1966. *Indaba, My Children*. London: Kahn & Averill. Orig pub. 1964.

Nelson, Alondra. 2001. 'Aliens Who Are Of Course Ourselves.' *Art Journal* 60 (3): 99–101.

Ochoa Gautier, Ana María. 2014. *Aurality: Listening and Knowledge in Nineteenth Century Colombia*. Durham, NC: Duke University Press.

Seeger, Anthony. 1987. *Why Suyá Sing: A Musical Anthropology of an Amazonian People*. Cambridge: Cambridge University Press.

Simbao, Ruth Kerkham. 2007. 'Credo Mutwa: Time Unraveller.' *Art South Africa* 5 (4): 43–46.

Steingo, Gavin. 2016. *Kwaito's Promise: Music and the Aesthetics of Freedom in South Africa*. Chicago: University of Chicago Press.

Szendy, Peter. 2013. *Kant in the Land of the Extraterrestrial: Cosmopolitical Philosofic-tions.* Translated by Will Bishop. New York: Fordham. Orig. pub. 2011.

Uncertain Commons. 2013. *Speculate This!* Durham, NC: Duke University Press.

Young, Hershini Bhana. 2016. 'She's Lost Control Again': Representations of (Dis)ability in Contemporary Performances of *Spoek Mathambo* and *Die Antwoord.' African and Black Diaspora: An International Journal* 9 (1): 109–124.

Chapter Forty-Nine

WHOSE ANTHROPOCENE? A RESPONSE

DIPESH CHAKRABARTY

BIOGEOLOGICAL ASPECTS OF CLIMATE CHANGE

I fundamentally agree with Boggs that one can no longer separate the biological agency of humans from their geological agency in the way in which I appeared to do in my essay "The Climate of History," though the separation continues to mark much of the policy literature. One generally finds two approaches to the problem of climate change. One dominant approach is to look on the phenomenon simply as a one-dimensional challenge: How do humans achieve a reduction in their emissions of greenhouse gases (GHGs) in the coming few decades? The climate problem is seen in this approach as a challenge of how to source the energy needed for the human pursuit of some universally accepted ends of economic development, so that billions of humans are pulled out of poverty. The main solution proposed here is for humanity to make a transition to renewable energy as quickly as technology and market signals permit. The accompanying issues of justice concern relations between poor and rich nations and between present and future generations: What would be a fair distribution of the "right to emit GHGs"—since GHGs are seen as scarce resources—between nations in the process of this transition to renewables? Should not the less developed and more populous countries (like China and India) have a greater right to pollute, while the developed nations take on more responsibility to make deep cuts in their emissions? The question of how much sacrifice the living should make as they curb emissions, to ensure that unborn humans inherit a world that enables a better quality of life than the present generation, remains a more intractable one, and its political force is reduced by the fact that the unborn are not here to argue about their share of the atmospheric commons.

Within this broad description of the first approach, however, are nested many disagreements. Most imagine the problem to be mainly one of replacing fossil fuel-based energy sources by renewables; many also assume that the same mode of production and consumption of goods will continue. These latter analysts imagine a future in which the world is more technologically advanced and connected than now, but with the critical difference that a consumerist paradise will be within the reach of most, if not all, humans. Some others—on the left—would agree that a turn to renewables is in order, but argue that because it is capitalism's constant urge to "accumulate" that has precipitated the climate crisis, the crisis itself provides yet another opportunity to renew and reinvigorate Marx's critique of capital. I am not sure about the kind of economy that these latter scholars visualize as replacing the global capitalist regime, but there is clearly an assumption that a globalized, crowded (nine to ten billion people), and technologically connected post-capitalist world can somehow come into being and avoid the pitfalls of the drive to accumulate. And then there are those who think of not just transitioning to renewable sources of energy but of actually scaling back the economy, de-growing it, and thus reducing the ecological footprint of humans while desiring a world marked by equality and social justice for all. Still others think—in a scenario called "the convergence scenario"—of reaching a state of economic equilibrium globally whereby all humans live at more or less the same standard of living. And then, of course, there are those who think of the most desirable future as capitalist or market-based growth with sustainability.

Against all this, there is another way to view climate change: as part of a complex family of interconnected problems, all adding up to the larger issue of a growing human footprint on the planet that has, over the last couple of centuries and especially since the end of the Second World War, seen a definite ecological overshoot on the part of humanity. This overshoot, of course, has a long history but one that has picked up pace in more recent times. The Israeli historian Yuval Noah Harari explains the issue well in his book, *Sapiens: A Brief History of Humankind*. "One of the most common uses of early stone tools," writes Harari, "was to crack open bones in order to get to the marrow. Some researchers believe that this was our original niche." Why? Because, Harari explains, "genus *Homo*'s position in the food chain was, until quite recently, solidly in the middle."[1] Humans could eat dead animals only after lions, hyenas, and foxes had had their shares and cleaned the bones off all the flesh sticking to them! It is only "in the last 100,000 years," says Harari, "that man jumped to the top of the food chain."[2] This has not been an evolutionary change. As Harari explains:

> Other animals at the top of the pyramid, such as lions and sharks, evolved into that position very gradually, over millions of years. This enables the ecosystem to develop checks and balances that prevent lions and sharks from wreaking too much havoc. As the lions became deadlier, so gazelles evolved to run faster, hyenas to cooperate better, and rhinoceroses to be more bad-tempered. In contrast, humankind ascended to the top so quickly that the ecosystem was not given time to adjust.[3]

The problem of humans' ecological footprint, we can say, was ratcheted up over the last 500 years with European expansion and colonization of faraway lands inhabited by other peoples, and the subsequent rise of industrial civilization. But a further ratcheting up by several significant notches happened after the end of the Second World War when human numbers and consumption rose exponentially, thanks to the widespread use of fossil fuels, not only in the transport sector but also in agriculture and medicine. GHG emissions gave humans the capacity to interfere in Earth systems processes that regulate the climate of the whole planet, in short yielding the geological agency that I wrote about in my essay under discussion. This planet-wide geological agency of humans, however, cannot be separated—as Boggs and Ziolkowski usefully remind us—from the way humans interfere in the distribution of natural life on the planet. Not only have marine creatures not had the evolutionary time to adjust to our new-found capacity to hunt them out of existence through deep-sea fishing technology, but our GHG emissions now also acidify the oceans, threatening the biodiversity of the great seas, and thus endangering the very same food chain that feeds us. Ziolkowski is thus absolutely right to point out that it is the human record left in the rocks of this planet as fossils and other forms of evidence—such as terraforming of the ocean bed—that will constitute the long-term record of the Anthropocene, perhaps more so than the excess GHGs in the atmosphere. If human-driven extinction of other species results—say, in the next few centuries—in a Great Extinction event, then (my geologist friends tell me), even the epoch-level name of the Anthropocene may be too low in the hierarchy of geological periods.[4]

Viewed thus, climate change indeed points to what Boggs calls a "biogeological force of humanity." Boggs, Ziolkowski, and Richter remind us that the climate change problem is not a problem to be studied in isolation from the general complex of ecological problems that humans now face on various scales—from the local to the planetary—creating new conflicts and exacerbating old ones between and inside nations. There is no single silver bullet that solves all the problems at once; nothing that works like the mantra of transition to renewables to avoid an average rise of 2°C in the surface temperature of the planet. What we face does indeed look like a wicked problem, one that we may diagnose but not be able to "solve" once and for all.[5]

ANTHROPOCENE AND THE INEQUITIES OF CAPITALISM

Here let me address some critical questions raised by McAfee that have also been raised by others in additional contexts. I am a little surprised that she finds my position to be the same as E. O. Wilson's, who recommends that we think of ourselves as a species and act as a rational species. Let me put aside for the moment the questions I actually raised about our not having ontological access to our being-a-species, which makes the question of acting like a "rational species" very problematic. I thought I had also argued for a double position (in the "Four Theses" essay): of both acknowledging the role of (scientific) reason in defining and adapting to climate change—for without scientific research and verification, there is no problem called "global warming"—but also of maintaining a postcolonial vigilance against "universals" that actually hide particular interests. I also cautioned that human politics—even leftist politics—could never be about rationality alone. This is the reason that I struggled somewhat towards the conclusion of that essay with Adorno's idea of a negative universal. I tend to share her criticisms of ecomodernists who plan for a "good Anthropocene" and I am sympathetic towards Clive Hamilton's critique of the "good Anthropocene" thesis. But surely the findings of science do more than simply reflect relations of power (which they also do)? I would repeat something I have said in that essay and elsewhere: that climate change would only accentuate the inequities of the global capitalist order as the impact of climate change—*for now and in the immediate future*—falls more heavily on poorer nations and on the poor of the rich nations.

I say "for now and the immediate future" for a good reason. For there is a more basic misunderstanding at work when I get criticized for saying that there is one respect in which the crisis of climate change is different from the crises of capitalism: in the case of the crisis posed by climate change, I said: "There are no lifeboats for the rich," meaning that the rich could not escape this crisis. Andreas Malm and Alf Hornborg took me to task for saying this and others have too. Now McAfee, citing them, repeats the charge: "Contra Chakrabarty, the rich may face the same storms and they *do* have lifeboats." Barnes is also in strong agreement with McAfee and others on this point. I give examples of Australian or Californian fires, but she remains incredulous: "I am not fully convinced by this argument. As a large body of scholarship within environmental justice and political ecology has demonstrated, the burden of environmental risks, whether climate change-related or not, falls unevenly on different social groups, mediated by class, race, gender, and ethnicity. Fires in wealthy neighborhoods may be devastating, but are probably less devastating to households that have home insurance, have invested in fire safety measures, or own cars to flee in response to warnings."

I find it ironic that some scholars on the left should speak with a similar assumption to that made by members of the rich who do not necessarily deny climate change but believe that, whatever the extent of the warming and destabilization of the climate, they will always be able to buy their way out of the problem! This is understandable coming from economics textbooks that envision capitalism as an economic system that will always face periodic crises and overcome them, but never face a crisis of such proportions that it could upset all capitalist calculations. It is easy to think within that logic that climate change was just another of those business cycle-type challenges that the rich had to ride out from time to time. Why would scholars on the left write from the same assumptions? Climate change is not a standard business cycle crisis. Nor is it a standard "environmental crisis" amenable to risk-management strategies. The danger of a climate tipping point is unpredictable but real.

Left unmitigated, climate change affects us all, rich and poor. They are not affected in the same way, but they are all affected. A runaway global warming leading to a Great Extinction event will not serve the rich very well. A massive collapse of human population caused by climate dislocation— were it to happen—would no doubt hurt the poor much more than the rich. But would it not also rob global capitalism of its reserve army of "cheap" labor on which it has so far depended? A world with freakish weather, more storms, floods, droughts, and frequent extreme weather events cannot be beneficial to the rich who live today or to their descendants who will have to live on a much more unfriendly planet. Remember that the American scientist James Hansen's book, *Storms for My Grandchildren*, spoke of the perils that future generations of Americans will face. Hansen's book was about his own grandchildren, not the grandchildren of friends Hansen may have in India or China. Besides, if the rich could simply buy their way out of this crisis and only the poor suffered, why would the rich nations do anything about global warming unless the poor of the world were powerful enough to force them to be altruistic? Rich nations were never known for their altruism!

McAfee recommends a politics of solidarity of the poor: "Today reality calls for a politics that identifies and forges links among the multiple fractions of humanity who comprise the *majority* of us and who are impoverished, materially and otherwise, by the effects of global warming and other ongoing consequences of capitalism and colonialism." I wish her well with that project, but I do not know that politics will ever correspond to any one, single reading of "reality." A better case for rich nations and classes to act on climate change is couched in terms of their enlightened self-interest. The science of global warming allows us to do so by precisely making the point that for all its differential impact, it is a crisis for the rich and their descendants as well—as Hansen's popular book amply makes clear. So yes, a politics of even broader solidarity is called for.

POLITICS IN/OF THE ANTHROPOCENE

Meyer and Barnes are both sensitive to social justice questions, and are concerned to ensure that there is no "climate reductionism" in operation in our discussions, occluding from view issues of human inequality and oppression. But they do not reduce the climate problem to human injustice alone. While the point of their cautionary words is well taken, I find myself in broad agreement with them.

The more difficult question to ponder is whether or not the climate crisis—as symptomatic of humanity's ecological overshoot—also signals the first glimpse we might have of a possible limit to our very human-centered thinking about justice, and thus to our political thought as well. Global warming accentuates the planetary tendency towards human-driven extinction of many other species, with some scientists suggesting that the planet may have already entered the beginnings of a long (in human terms) Great Extinction event.[6] Anthropogenic climate change thus produces a crisis in the distribution of natural reproductive life on the planet. But our political and justice-related thinking remains very human-focused. We still do not know how to think conceptually—politically or in accordance with theories of justice—about justice towards nonhuman forms of life, not to speak of the inanimate world. Thinkers of animal rights have extended questions of justice towards some animals, but their theories are limited by strict requirements relating to the threshold of sentience in animals. Besides, some philosophers also argue that, whatever the practical value of a category such as life in biology, "life as such" cannot be a strict philosophical category. Yet we cannot think "extinction" without using the category "life," however difficult it may be to define it. The really difficult issue that arises when scholars write about humans being stewards of the planet is what our relationship, conceptually, would be to bacteria and viruses, given that many of them are not friendly to the human form of life (while many are). Yet it is undeniable that the natural history of species life on this planet involves the histories and activities of bacteria and viruses.

So while I agree that politics as we know it continues and will continue into the Anthropocene, and that there is no politics of the Anthropocene as such (but much politics about the label "Anthropocene," as we know!), a deepening of the climate crisis and of the ecological overshoot of which it is a symptom may indeed lead us to rethink the European tradition of political thought that has, since the seventeenth century and thanks to European expansion, become everybody's inheritance today.

SPECIES THINKING

Now to the question of whether or not we should think of humans through the biological category of "species," alongside other historical categories such as "capitalism," as we think through this crisis. I find Sideris's words of caution valuable. And I have never subscribed to the idea of "consilience" of the sciences, though some big names in the subfield of Big History recommend it. Nor have I ever invested our species with any particular moral significance that could work as a telos for human history. Let this not be a debate about E. O. Wilson. He is a serious and respected thinker, but there can be legitimate disagreements over his work. The question is not about him but rather about human beings as a biological species, and how we might make room for that natural history in our accounts: Can the story of ecological overshoot by humans be thought of not simply as the story of modernization and its inherent inequalities but also as the story of a particular species—Homo sapiens—coming to dominate the biosphere to such an extent that its own existence was challenged? Think of the story as Harari tells it. Today with their consumption, numbers, technology and so on, humans—yes, all humans, rich and poor—put pressure on the biosphere (the rich and poor do it in different ways and for different reasons) and disturb what I called above the distribution of life on the planet. Harari puts the point well: "Humankind ascended to the top [of the food chain] so quickly that the ecosystem was not given time to adjust. Moreover, humans themselves failed to adjust. Most top predators of the planet are majestic creatures. Millions of years of domination have filled them with self-confidence. Sapiens by contrast is more like a banana republic dictator. Having so recently been one of the underdogs of the savannah, we are full of fears and anxieties over our position. . . ." He concludes: "Many historical calamities, from deadly wars to ecological catastrophes, have resulted from this over-hasty jump."[7]

If one could imagine someone watching the development of life on this planet on an evolutionary scale, they would have a story to tell about Homo sapiens rising to the top of the food chain within a very, very short period in that history. The more involved story of rich-poor differences would be a matter of finer resolution in that story. As I have said elsewhere, the ecological overshoot of humanity requires us to both zoom into the details of intra-human injustice—otherwise we do not see the suffering of many humans—and to zoom out of that history, or else we do not see the suffering of other species and, in a manner of speaking, of the planet.[8] Zooming in and zooming out are about shuttling between different scales, perspectives, and different levels of abstraction. One level of abstraction does not cancel out the other or render it invalid. But my point is that the human story can no longer be told from the perspective of the 500 years (at most) of capitalism alone.

Humans remain a species in spite of all our differentiation. Suppose all the radical arguments about the rich always having lifeboats and therefore being able to buy their way out of all calamities including a Great Extinction event are true; and imagine a world in which some very large-scale species extinction has happened and that the survivors among humans are only those who happened to be privileged and belonged to the richer classes. Would not their survival also constitute a survival of the species eventually (even if the survivors quickly differentiated themselves into, as seems to be the human wont, dominant and subordinate groups)?

STORIES WE TELL, AND QUESTIONS OF HOPE

Faced with the problem of the ecological over-reach of humans, what kind of stories do we now tell about ourselves, and how? Many scholars have challenged, both in writing and in conversation, my proposition that because we do not have any ontological access to our "being species" we cannot experience being a species, and have suggested that creative and imaginative work of fiction, films, music, and painting, may indeed enable us to have such access. Here I must say that my statement was intended as a provocation to both thought and action, though I stand by the philosophical claim that I was making. But I am a deep believer in the role of the arts and imaginative work in this crisis, and have no problems accepting the general points made by Richter, Weik von Mossner, and others. Even angry, anti-capitalist narratives blaming the rich for all the ills of humanity may have a positive political role to play in this crisis.

One point I would make in response to Richter's proposition about the need for a Virgilian "Georgic" narrative, however, is that the scholarship collected here already documents the multiple and sometimes contradictory narratives that we produce to explain our situation to ourselves. Hee documents the story of the business sector optimistically embracing a sustainability narrative, though she herself points out the need, ultimately, for a change in our consumerist lifestyle, a point that many sections of business may not yet agree with. They would rather combine sustainability with consumerism in their pursuit of an Edenic story of profits and plenty. Watt, on the other hand, shows in her extremely thoughtful statement how difficult it is for us in our comfortable everyday lives to let go of some of the luxuries (such as a 24-hour supply of hot water) that we have come to consider basic—not just to our sense of hygiene and cleanliness but to our deepest sense of ourselves as well! And LeCain ends his powerful opening neomaterialist essay on a note that is far from the Georgic one that Richter is looking for. He writes: "It is difficult to predict what the history of the 'nonhuman human'—the human who is as much coal, oil, and other things as culture and idea—might look like. But I think it is safe to say that phenomena like justice and freedom, as well as their opposites, will increasingly be understood not solely as human ideas or creations, but as products of the powerful material things we partner with." LeCain gives agency to an entangled entity—humans partnering somewhat blindly with other materials as they seek to make themselves at home in a planet that was not necessarily designed to see humans as the culminating point of its history! Yet this partnership is all we have, and the stories we tell about it will change and become richer in their diversity as the ecological crisis unfolds. All I can say at this stage is that if there is one source of hope, it lies in human creativity and resilience. Its expression will take multiple narratives and forms. A crisis is indeed a time for renewed creativity.

NOTES

1. Yuval noah harari, *Sapiens: A Brief History of Humankind* (New York: Harper Collins, 2015), 9.
2. Ibid.
3. Ibid., 11–12.
4. "If global warming and a sixth extinction take place in the next couple of centuries, then an epoch will seem too low a category in the hierarchy [of the geological timetable]." Personal communication with Professor Jan Zalasiewicz, 30 September 2015.
5. See the detailed and excellent discussion in Frank P. Incropera, *Climate Change: A Wicked Problem—Complexity and Uncertainty at the Intersection of Science, Economics, Politics, and Human Behavior* (New York: Cambridge University Press, 2016).
6. Gerardo Ceballos et al., "Accelerated Modern Human-Induced Species Losses: Entering the Sixth Mass Extinction," *Science Advances* 1, no. 5 (2015): 1–5.
7. Harari, *Sapiens*, 11–12.
8. Dipesh Chakrabarty, "The Human Significance of the Anthropocene," in *Modernity Reset*, ed. Bruno Latour (Cambridge, MA: MIT Press, forthcoming).

Chapter Fifty

UNRULY EDGES

Mushrooms as Companion Species

ANNA TSING

Wandering and love of mushrooms engender each other. Walking is the speed of bodily pleasure and contemplation; it is also just the speed to look for mushrooms. After the rains, the air smells fresh with ozone, sap, and leaf litter, and my senses are alive with curiosity. What better than to encounter the orange folds of chanterelles pushing through the dark wet or the warm muffins of king boletes popping up through crumbly earth. The excitement of color, fragrance, and design—not to speak of pride to be the first to find them—well up. But of these delights the best, I think, are two: first, the undeserved bounty of the gift; and second, the offer of a *place* that will guide my future walks. These mushrooms are not the product of my labor, and because I have not toiled and worried over them, they jump into my hands with all the pleasures of the unasked for and the unexpected. For a moment, my tired load of guilt is absolved, and, like a lottery winner, I am alight with the sweetness of life itself. *Bismillah irachman irachim.*[1]

Delight makes an impression: an impression of place. The very excitement of my senses commits to memory the suite of colors and scents, the angle of the light, the scratching briars, the solid placement of this tree, and the rise of the hill before me. Many times, wandering, I have suddenly remembered every stump and hollow of the spot on which I stood—through the mushrooms I once encountered there. Conscious decision can also take me to a spot of past encounters, for the best way to find mushrooms is

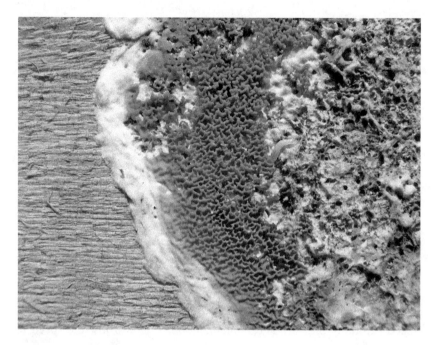

FIGURE 50.1. Artist Unknown, *Serpula Lacrimans*.
Source: Public domain, CC BY-SA 3.0.

always to return to the places you found them before. In many cases, the growing body (mycelium) that gives rise to mushrooms as its fruits lasts from season to season; besides, some mushroom growing bodies are life-long companions to particular trees. If you want to find chanterelles in central California, you must look under oaks—but not just any oak: You must look for *the* oak that lives with chanterelle mycelium, and you'll know it because you have seen the mushrooms there before. You visit the spot enough, and you know its seasonal flowers and its animal disturbances; you have made a familiar *place* in the landscape. Familiar places are the beginning of appreciation for multi-species interactions.

Foraging worked just this way for most of human history. To find a useful plant, animal, or fungus, foragers learned familiar places and returned to them again and again. High-powered rifles and fish-overstocking make it possible to succeed in killing something in a random pass through the countryside; but sportsmen still do better with a local guide. Through their familiar places, foragers learn not just about ecological relations in general, but also about the stochastic natural histories through which particular species and species associations happened to flourish in particular spots. The familiar places of foraging do not require territorial exclusivity; other beings—human and otherwise—learn them too. Their expansive and over-lapping geographies resist common models, which divide the world into "your space" and "mine." Furthermore, foragers nurture *landscapes*—with their multiple residents and visitors—rather than single species. Familiar places engender forms of identification and companionship that contrast to hyper-domestication and private property as we know it. You who search for a world of mutually-flourishing companions, consider mushrooms.

Mushrooms are well known as companions. The concept of "symbio-sis"—mutually beneficial interspecies living—was invented for the lichen, an association of a fungus and an alga or cyanobacteria. The non-fungal partner fuels lichen metabolism through photosynthesis; the fungus makes it possible for the lichen to live in extreme conditions. Repeated cycles of wetting and drying do not faze the lichen, because the fungal partner can reorganize its membranes as soon as water appears, allowing photosyn-thesis to resume.[2] Lichen may be found in frozen tundra and on parched desert rocks.

For mushroom lovers, the most intriguing interspecies companionship is that between fungi and plant roots. In *mycorrhiza*, the threads of the fun-gal body enter or sheathe the roots of plants. Indian pipes and other plants without chlorophyll are supported entirely from the nutrients they gain from fungi in their roots; many orchids cannot even germinate without fungalassistance.[3] More generally, the fungus obtains sustenance from the plant while offering it minerals from the surrounding soil. Fungi can even bore into rocks, making their mineral elements available for plant growth. In the long history of the earth, fungi are responsible for enriching soil thus allowing plants to evolve; fungi channel minerals from rocks to plants.[4] Trees are able to grow on poor soils because of the fungi that bring their roots phosphorus, magnesium, calcium, and more. In the area I live, forest-ers inoculate the roots of the Douglas fir seedlings they plant with *Suillus* (slippery jack) to aid reforestation. Meanwhile, many of the most favored mushrooms of cuisine are mycorrhizal. In France, truffle farmers inocu-late tree seedlings in fenced plots.[5] But, of course, the fungi are perfectly capable of doing this work themselves—but with a more open geography.

And so we mushroom-lovers wander, seeking the companionship of trees as well as mushrooms.

Fungi are not always benign in their interspecies associations.[6] Fungi are dauntingly omnivorous in their carbon conversion habits. Various fungi subsist on live as well as dead animals and plants. Some are ferocious pathogens. (*Cryptococcus neoformans* kills many AIDS patients.[7]) Some are irritating parasites. (Think of ringworm or athlete's foot.) Some slide through their hosts' intestines innocuously waiting to arrive in a pat of dung in which to flourish. Some fungi find totally unexpected substrates: *Cladosporium resinae*, originally found in tree resins, has found a taste for airplane fuel, causing blocked fuel lines.[8] Some hurt one host while living happily with another: *Puccina graminis* bonds with the barberry bush and feeds flies with its nectar to produce the spores that will kill as they grow on wheat.[9] Fungal appetites are always ambivalent in their benevolence, depending on your point of view. The ability of fungi to degrade the cellulose and lignin of dead wood, so feared in protecting wooden houses, is also fungi's greatest gift to forest regeneration. Otherwise, the forest would be stacked with dead wood, and other organisms would have a smaller and smaller nutrient base. Meanwhile, the role of fungi in ecosystem renewal makes it more than obvious that fungi are always companions to other species. Species interdependence is a well-known fact—except when it comes to humans.

Human exceptionalism blinds us. Science has inherited stories about human mastery from the great monotheistic religions. These stories fuel assumptions about human autonomy, and they direct questions to the human *control* of nature, on the one hand, or human *impact* on nature, on the other, rather than to species interdependence.[10] One of the many limitations of this heritage is that it has directed us to imagine human species being, that is, the practices of being a species, as autonomously self-maintaining—and therefore constant across culture and history. The idea of *human nature* has been given over to social conservatives and sociobiologists, who use assumptions of human constancy and autonomy to endorse the most autocratic and militaristic ideologies. What if we imagined a human nature that shifted historically together with varied webs of interspecies dependence? *Human nature is an interspecies relationship.* Far from challenging genetics, an interspecies frame for our species opens possibilities for biological as well as cultural research trajectories. We might understand more, for example, about the various webs of domestication in which we humans have entangled ourselves.

Domestication is ordinarily understood as human control over other species. That such relations might also change humans is generally ignored.[11] Moreover, domestication tends to be imagined as a hard line: You are either in the human fold or you are out in the wild. Because this dichotomization stems from an ideological commitment to human mastery, it supports the most outrageous fantasies of domestic control, on the one hand, and wild species self-making, on the other. Through such fantasies, domestics are condemned to life imprisonment and genetic standardization, while wild species are "preserved" in gene banks while their multi-species landscapes are destroyed. Yet despite these extreme efforts, most species on both sides of the line—including humans—live in complex relations of dependency and interdependence. Attention to this diversity can be the beginning of an appreciation of interspecies species being.

Fungi are indicator species for the human condition. Few fungi have found their way into human domestication schemes, and only a few of those—such as fungi used for industrial enzyme production—have had their genomes badly tampered with. (Supermarket button mushrooms are the same *Agaricus bisporus* as those growing in meadows.) Yet fungi are ubiquitous, and they follow all our human experiments and follies. Consider *Serpula lacrymans*, the dry rot fungus, once found only in the Himalayas.[12] Through their South Asian conquests, the British navy incorporated it into their ships. *S. lacrymans* flourished in the unseasoned woods often used in ships for naval campaigns, and thus it traveled around the world. By the early 19th century, the decay of wood in British naval ships was called a "national calamity," and panic ensued until the introduction of ironclad war ships in the 1860s.[13] Dry rot, however, just kept spreading, as the fungus found new homes in the damp basement beams and railroad ties of British-sponsored civilization. British expansion and dry rot moved together. As in this example, the presence of fungi often tell us of the changing practices of being human.

NOTES

1. In the name of God, the most bountiful and the most merciful.
2. D.H. Jennings and G. Lysek, *Fungal Biology*, second edition. Oxford: Bios Scientific Publishers, 1999, p. 75. Recent studies of interspecies mutualisms emphasize the active and strategic work of all involved species. For example, studies of

nitrogen-fixing bacteria in the root nodules of soybeans show that soybeans discourage bacterial strains that deliver less nitrogen—by limiting their oxygen (E. Toby Kiers, Robert Rousseau, Stuart West, R. Ford Denison, 2003. "Host Sanctions and the Legume-Rhizobium Mutualism," *Nature* 425(4 September): 78–81).

3. Orchids were a fashion in 19th century botany; mycorrhizae were first appreciated by Western scientists when it was found that many orchids depend on fungal partners. G.C. Ainsworth, *Introduction to the History of Mycology*, Cambridge: Cambridge University Press, 1976, p. 102–4. Indian pipes: Clyde M. Christensen. 1965. *The Molds and Man*. Minneapolis: University of Minnesota Press, p. 50.

4. Nicholas Money, *Mr. Bloomfield's Orchard*. Oxford: Oxford University Press, 2002, p. 60.

5. Ibid, p. 85.

6. The term fungi refers to a larger biological classification (a kingdom contrasted with plants and animals among others) of which mushrooms form one part. All mushrooms are fungi; not all fungi bear mushrooms.

7. Money, p. 25.

8. Jennings and Lysek, p. 67, 138.

9. Money, p. 172–79.

10. An important exception to this generalization is the medical and ecological literature on human diseases and parasites, in which the co-existence of species is of central concern. Yet this exception underlines the problem. As long as the relevant other species are found—at least sometimes—inside the human body, we can study them in relations of co-habitation and dependency. If the other species is outside the human body, that is, part of the "environment" for humans, analysis suddenly switches to a discourse of human impact, management, and control.

11. Haraway's work on dogs is of course a key interruption (op. cit.).

12. Jennings and Lysek, p. 138.

13. Ainsworth, p. 90–93.

Chapter Fifty-One

THE RISE OF CHEAP NATURE

JASON W. MOORE

ANTHROPOCENE QUESTIONS, CAPITALOCENE ANSWERS

The dominant Anthropocene argument therefore poses a question that it cannot answer: *How* have humans become a "geological force"? (Were we not *already* a geological force?) Anthropocene advocates do of course respond to the question. But they are responses, not explanations in any reasonable sense. Most of these responses focus on demography and technology, though additional factors are often recognized—consumerism, trade liberalization, investment flows, and so forth. These imply, but do not engage, questions of power, work and capital. The identification of multiple "trajectories" of the Anthropocene describes a lot, and explains very little.

The Anthropocene argument cannot explain *how* the present crisis is unfolding for a basic reason: it is captive to the very thought-structures that created the present crisis. At the core of these thought-structures is Cartesian dualism. The term is one of my possible shorthands. This dualism owes its name to René Descartes' famous argument about the separation of mind and body. Descartes surely does not deserve all blame. He personified a much broader scientific and especially philosophical movement that encouraged:

a strict and total division not only between mental and bodily activity, but between mind and nature and between human and animal. As mind becomes pure thought—pure *res cogitans* or thinking substance, mental, incorporeal, without location, bodiless—body as its dualised other becomes pure matter, pure *res extensa*, materiality as lack. As mind and nature become substances utterly different in kind and mutually exclusive, the dualist division of realms is accomplished and the possibility of continuity is destroyed from both ends. The intentional, psychological level of description is thus stripped from the body and strictly isolated in a separate mechanism of the mind. The body, deprived of such a level of description and hence of any capacity for agency, becomes an empty mechanism which has no agency or intentionality within itself, but is driven from outside by the mind. The body and nature become the dualised other of the mind (Plumwood, 1993: 115).

To be sure, humans had long recognized a difference between "first" and "second" natures, and between body and spirit (Cicero, 1937). *However*, capitalism was the first civilization to organize on this basis. For early modern materialism, the point was not only to interpret the world but to control it: "to make ourselves as it were the masters and possessors of nature" (Descartes, 2006: 51). This sensibility was a key organizing principle for an emergent capitalist civilization.

Thus Cartesian dualism is a problem not merely because it is philosophically problematic, but because it is *practically* bound up with a way of thinking the world—ontologically (what is?) and epistemologically (how do we know?)—that took shape between the 15th and 18th centuries.

These centuries saw the rise of capitalism. Most people—and most scholars—still think about capitalism as matter of "economics." Markets, prices, money, and all that—not necessarily the most exciting thing to think about. What if, instead of thinking capitalism = economics, we asked if "capitalism" was about something much more profound? One alternative is to think about the rise of capitalism as a new way of organizing nature, and therefore a new way of organizing the relations between work, reproduction, and the conditions of life. Markets, prices, and money are still important in this frame. But the alternative allows us to start looking at how every market, every price, and every movement and accumulation of money was bundled with extra-human nature.

Instead of capitalism as world-economy, then, we would start to look at capitalism as *world-ecology*. From this angle of vision, three entwined historical processes were fundamental. One was what Marx called primitive accumulation (1977: Part VIII). This entailed a range of processes that made humans dependent on the cash nexus for their survival. Social scientists call this "proletarianization," and it assumed the widest range of forms. It was nearly always partial ("semi-proletarianization"). It is about the transformation of human activity in labor-power, something to be "exchanged" in the commodity system—sometimes called "the labor market." Even if one thinks that human activity is somehow independent of nature, there is no avoiding one fact: proletarianization was rooted in the governance of nature and the replacement of custom and common by the dictatorship of the commodity. Sometimes peasants were forced off the land and found their way to the towns; but sometimes peasants were kept on the land, reduced to cottagers and forced into agricultural wage work—or neo-serfdom as in Poland—to provide what small plots could not. And sometimes proletarians did not look *proletarian* at all—African slaves in Brazilian and Caribbean sugar plantations were a good example (Mintz, 1978). Like workers in seventeenth-century England or Peru, they depended upon the cash nexus to survive.

Proletarianization was never principally *economic*; it was a product of the new forms of territorial power that emerged after 1450. Here is our second process. The old territorial power—the overlapping jurisdictions and personalized authority of medieval Europe—had crumbled in the long feudal crisis (c. 1315–1453). West-central Europe's ruling classes had tried to restore feudal labor systems—and failed. The most dynamic of the new states owed their dynamism to an alliance with merchant capitalists who were far more than merchants. It was the alliance of the Iberian crowns with Genoese capital that, quite literally, made the space that made capitalism possible. In its early centuries, capitalism was trans-Atlantic or it was nothing (Moore, 2003a, 2003b, 2007). The new empires—but also the internal transformations of the Low Countries and England—were made possible by power of a new type. At its core was the generalization of private property. For a new *praxis* of modern private property emerged in these centuries. Its "strategic goal" was the separation of the peasantry from non-market access to land: arable and grazing land, forests, wetlands, and all the rest (Sevilla-Buitrago, 2015). This was the fundamental condition of proletarianization, and like proletarianization, these enclosures and dispossessions were enormously varied. So too were the states and empires that pursued this strategic goal. Their "central function" was "the

internal maintenance and external defence of a private property regime"
(Teschke, 2006: 51; also Parenti,). And may we add that these states and
empires were equally central to the *expanded, globalising, reproduction* of
that regime?

Our third great historical process turned on new ways of knowing the world. These were symbolic, but they were far more than symbolic. The ongoing condition of turning human activity into labor-power
and land into property was a symbolic-knowledge regime premised on
separation—*on alienation*. Let us think of the new knowledge regime as
a series of "scientific revolutions" in the broadest sense of the term. This
regime made it possible to launch and sustain a process that now threatens
us all today: putting the whole of nature to work for capital. The job of "science" was to make nature legible to capital accumulation—transforming it
into units of Nature and counterpoised to the forces of capital and empire.
The job of "the economy" was to channel this alienation through the cash
nexus. The job of "the state" was to enforce that cash nexus. To be sure,
that "separation from nature" was illusory: humans could never escape
nature. But the terms of the relation *did* change. And those changing
terms of humanity/nature—a complex and protracted process—bundled
the symbolic and material. It was a *world-praxis* of remaking the world in
the image of capital.

To say *praxis* is to invoke an ongoing process of capital's self-reflection
and capacity for innovation—symbolically and materially. For no civilization has been so adept at overcoming its limits. The new knowledge regime
prized dualism, separation, mathematization, the aggregation of units. Its
innovations, clustered into scientific revolutions, were at once producers
and products of the previous two transformations—of labor (proletarianization) and land (property). At the core of the new thought-structures was
a mode of distinction that presumed separation. The most fundamental of
these separations was Humanity/Nature. Some people became Humans,
who were members of something called Civilization, or Society, or both—
as in Adam Smith's "civilised society" (1937: 14). From the beginning, most
humans were either excluded from Humanity—indigenous Americans, for
example—or were designated as *only partly* Human, as were virtually all
European women. As with property, the symbolic boundaries between who
was—and who was not—part of Nature (or Society) tended to shift and
vary; they were often blurry; and they were flexible. But a boundary there

was, and much of the early history of modern race and gender turns on the struggles over that line. (Is it so different today?)

That boundary—the Nature/Society divide that the Anthropocene affirms and that many of us now question—was fundamental to the rise of capitalism. For it allowed nature to become Nature—environments without Humans. But note the uppercase 'H': Nature was full of humans treated as Nature. And what did this mean? It meant that the web of life could be reduced to a series of external objects—mapped, explored, surveyed, calculated for what Nature could do for the accumulation of capital. And the substance of that value? Human labor productivity—but not all *humanly productive work*—measured without regard for its cultural, biophysical, and cooperative dimensions. Human work as abstracted, averaged, deprived of all meaning but for one: value as the average labor-time making the average commodity. For this to occur, not only did new conceptions of nature—as external Nature—take shape, but new conceptions of time and space. For good reason, Mumford tells us that the "key machine" of modernity is not the steam engine but the mechanical clock, the physical expression of an earth-shaking idea: linear time (1934: 14). The clock, Marx underlines, was the "first automatic machine applied to practical purposes" (1979: 68). Nor did this early modern revolution of abstraction stop with labor and time. Successive cartographic revolutions, beginning in the 15th century, made possible an extraordinary new apprehension of geography. In the new cartography, geography was cleansed of its troubling particularities and meanings. It became "space as pure quantity" (Biggs, 1999: 377). It became abstract space—and therefore, abstract Nature.

Here we can begin to see the thought-structures of modernity as more than "superstructures." To turn work into labor-power and land into private property was to transform nature into Nature—and to treat Society as something outside of Nature, the better that Society could turn Nature into a set of discrete units, into a repertoire of calculable objects and factors of production. Marx tells us, famously, that the relations of capital and labor "drip with blood and dirt" (1977: 926). Does not also the dualism of Society and Nature? We do well to grasp Society and Nature not merely as false, but also as *real* abstractions with real force in the world. In highlighting Cartesian dualism as a key source of the problem—unconsciously embraced by the Anthropocene argument—we are seeking to make sense of three great thought-procedures that have shaped the modern world: 1) the imposition of "an ontological status upon entities (substance) as opposed to relation-ships (that is to say energy, matter, people, ideas and so on became things)"; 2) the centrality of "a logic of either/or (rather than both/and)"; and 3) the "idea of a purposive control over nature through applied science" (Watts, 2005: 150–51; Glacken, 1967: 427).

These thought-procedures dominate Anthropocene thinking in all sorts of ways—not least in their embrace of technical fixes such as geo-engineering. The point I wish to emphasize, however, concerns the fun-damentally substantialist and arithmetic character of the Anthropocene perspective. Anthropocene thinking remains firmly rooted in a model that "*aggregate[s]* socio-economic and Earth system trends" (Steffen, et al., 2015: 8). The model is descriptively powerful, yielding powerful visual represen-tations of the "Great Acceleration" (New Scientist, 2008). Descriptively powerful, perhaps—but analytically anemic. Nature and Society are taken as non-problematic; the concepts are confused for actually existing histori-cal processes, in which capitalism is actively shaped by the web of life—and vice-versa. In sum, the perspective *integrates* factors but does not synthe-size them. Absent is the actual whole of power, capital, and nature entwined in modern world history. More problematic still: the adding-up of Nature and Society makes claims for wholeness that undermine efforts to forge a new, post-Cartesian synthesis of humanity-in-nature.

REFERENCES

Biggs, Michael (1999). "Putting the state on the map," *Comparative studies in society and history* 41(2), 374–405.

Cicero (1933). *Cicero in Twenty-Eight Volumes*. H. Rackham, trans. Cambridge: Harvard Univ. Press.

Descartes, René (2006). *A Discourse on the Method of Correctly Conducting One's Rea-son and Seeking Truth in the Sciences*. Ian Maclean, ed. Oxford: Oxford Univ. Press.

Gimbutas, Marija (1999). *The Living Goddesses*. Miriam Robbins Dexter, ed. Berkeley: Univ. of California Press.

Glacken, Clarence J. (1967). *Traces on the Rhodian Shore*. Berkeley: Univ. of California Press.

Marx, Karl (1977). *Capital*, Vol. I. Ben Fowkes, trans. New York: Vintage.

Marx, Karl (1979). *The Letters of Karl Marx*. S.K. Padover, trans. Englewood Cliffs, NJ: Prentice-Hall.

Mintz, Sidney W. (1978). "Was the plantation slave a proletarian?" *Review*, 2(1), 81–98.

Moore, Jason W. (2003a). "Nature and the Transition from Feudalism to Capitalism," *Review* 26, 2, 97–172.

Moore, Jason W. (2003b). "*The Modern World-System* as Environmental History? Ecology and the Rise of Capitalism," *Theory & Society* 32, 3, 307–377.

Moore, Jason W. (2007). *Ecology and the Rise of Capitalism*. PhD dissertation. Department of Geography, Univ. of California, Berkeley.

Mumford, Lewis (1934). *Technics and Civilization*. London: Routledge and Kegan Paul.

New Scientist (2008). "The facts about overconsumption," *New Scientist* (15 October), http://www.newscientist.com/article/dn14950-special-report-the-facts-aboutover -consumption#.VWKSGvlVhBd.

Plumwood, Val (1993). *Feminism and the Mastery of Nature*. New York: Routledge.

Sevilla-Buitrago, Alvaro (2015). "Capitalist Formations of Enclosure," *Antipode*, 47(4), 999–1020.

Smith, Adam (1937). *An Inquiry into the Nature and Causes of The Wealth of Nations*. New York: Modern Library.

Steffen, Will, et al. (2015). "The trajectory of the Anthropocene," *Anthropocene Review*, 2(1), 81–98.

Teschke, Benno (2006), "The metamorphoses of European territoriality," in Michael Burgess and Hans Vollaard, eds., *State, territoriality and European integration*. London: Routledge, 37–67.

Watts, Michael J. (2005), "Nature:Culture," in P. Cloke and R. Johnston, eds., *Spaces of Geographical Thought*. London, Sage, 142–174.

Chapter Fifty-Two

FROM FORENSIC ARCHITECTURE

Notes from Fields and Forums

EYAL WEIZMAN

FIGURE 52.1. Forensic Architecture located photographs and videos within a 3D model to tell the story of one of the heaviest days of bombardment in the 2014 Israel-Gaza war. The Image-Complex, Rafah: Black Friday, Forensic Architecture, 2015.

The pyramids of Gaza, so a Forensic Architect once told me, proliferate throughout the Strip, but are most commonly seen in the camps and neighborhoods that ring Gaza City and along the short border to Egypt. They are the result, he said, of an encounter between two familiar elements in the area—a three-story residential building, of the kind that provides a home for refugees, and an armored Caterpillar D9 bulldozer. While the bulldozer circles the building, its short shovel can reach and topple only the peripheral columns. The internal columns are left intact, forming the peak of the pyramid. The floor slabs break at their approximate center, around the crest, then fold down and outward to form the faces of the structure. The geometry of the pyramids of Gaza is less ideal than that of the Pyramids of Giza. Their irregularities register differences in the process of construction—the uneven spread of concrete, for example—or in the process of destruction—the inability (or reluctance) of the bulldozer operator to go completely around the building. Sometimes, the irregularity is a result of a previous firefight or a tank shell, shot at a corner of the building to hasten the departure of its inhabitants. Near the border, one can sometimes see a fallen pyramid that has sunk into a collapsed tunnel. Partially exposed under the fine sands of Rafah, the scene resembles that of a colonial-era archaeological expedition. [. . .]

Within the field of war-crime investigation, a methodological shift has recently led to a certain blurring. The primacy accorded to the witness and to the subjective and linguistic dimension of testimony, trauma, and memory—a primacy that has had such an enormous cultural, aesthetic, and political influence that it has reframed the end of the twentieth century as "the era of the witness"—is gradually being supplemented (not to say bypassed) by an emergent forensic sensibility, an object-oriented juridical culture immersed in matter and materialities, in code and form, and in the presentation of scientific investigations by experts. [. . .]

In the wake of the war-crime investigations following Israel's 2008/9 attack on Gaza, one of the world's foremost Forensic Architects, assembling evidence against the military, was suspended when it was publicly revealed—to great media fanfare—that he was a collector of Nazi-era fetish items, and thus allegedly unsuited to investigating the Israeli military impartially. I thought that, if true, the fact that he had such a collection should, to the contrary, increase his credibility (or shall we say his probability?).

If fetishism is the attribution of an inherent power and a certain agency to inanimate objects, then what do we expect those experts who speak to buildings and cities (and expecting them to speak back) to be? [. . .]

If fetishes are to be destroyed by their modern enemies, what fate should be reserved for a fetish that is already a ruin? How to destroy the destruction?

In the spring of 2009, the Gaza-based and Hamas-run Ministry of Public Works and Housing compiled an astounding archive containing thousands of entries, each documenting a single building that was completely or partially destroyed, from cracked walls to houses reduced to rubble. Each entry in this book of destruction included a single, frontal-view photograph displaying a catalogue number spray-painted onto the ruin itself.

Each file also recorded how the damage to the building was inflicted: "destroyed by armored D9 bulldozers," "bombed from the air," "shelled from the ground," "directly targeted," "indirectly struck," or subject to "controlled demolition by explosives"; the state of the building: "reduced to rubble," "partially destroyed," or "still standing but dangerous and requiring demolition." In reconstructing histories of violence from the trash and rubble left behind, this archive is another instance of Forensic Architecture. Both practical and political, its forensics escapes, however, the limited frame of international law.

The destruction of refugee camps is often understood as "the destruction of destruction"—the destruction of the destruction of Palestine. The camp is not a home; it is a temporary arrangement. Its rubble is the last iteration in an ongoing process of destruction that connects the destroyed village of 1948 to the destroyed camp of 2009, but the destruction of the latter is also interpreted as possessing a restorative potential.

What could the forensics of the "destruction of destruction" be?

The twelfth-century Andalusian scholar ibn-Rushd (Averroes) penned a treatise of this very name—*Tahafut al-Tahafut*—in which he refuted the refutation of classical philosophy proposed by Sufi ascetic Ghazali in his eleventh century *Tahafut al-Falasifa.*

So is it the refutation of the displacement, a proto-Hegelian *negation of the negation,* here applied to the realm of political domesticity? Should we be packing up for return, when all we can do is to clear up the mess and rubble, destroy the fetish of the pyramids, recycle their components, and start rebuilding the camp all over again, and better this time?

Rebuilding the camp does not stand in contradiction to return; rather, it is its precondition.[1]

NOTE

1. Sandi Hilal, Alessandro Petti, and Eyal Weizman, *Book of Return,* Decolonizing Architecture Art Residency, September 2009, www.decolonizing.ps (accessed October 2011).

Chapter Fifty-Three

LETTERS TO DEAR CLIMATE

LOUIS BURY

10/23/17

Dear Climate,

In the middle of the artist's book published in conjunction with her gnomic and unsettling Queens Museum exhibition, *The Wandering Lake, 2009–2017*, Patty Chang offers a stunning meditation on the role of art in the Anthropocene. Contemplating the practice of Japanese Ama divers, who descend as much as sixty feet underwater without breathing equipment, Chang cites mid-century scientist Pierre Dejours on the four stages of underwater breath holding: the "easy-going phase"; the "gasping point"; the "struggle phase"; and the "breaking point." According to Dejours, the struggle phase begins with involuntary gasps for air and ends, if the diver cannot get back above water in time, with loss of consciousness and, shortly thereafter, death.

Chang has long been aesthetically interested in situations of bodily discomfort and duress. Dejour's respiratory schema pinpoints the hard-to-measure "moment before a trauma." In realms of endeavor beyond diving, Changs asks, what are the "signs of a struggle phase"? Her ecologically-inflected answer: "Art making as a grieving of living as opposed to a fight against it. Is it a sign of acceptance or giving in?" The proposition–presented first as a statement, then, more tentative, as a rhetorical question–is literally and figuratively breathtaking. We like to believe that contemporary ecological art engages in a struggle for positive cultural change, but Chang entertains the possibility that such work is actually engaged in a struggle with its own fatalistic and disempowered sense of grief over the culture's impending demise.

As a sometime professional poker player, I have long understood, at least in the intellectual abstract, the importance of accepting those aspects of fortune that you cannot control. But I only understood acceptance in a fuller, embodied sense when I began to practice yoga. In yoga, origami sequences of movement and breath fold your thoughts in upon themselves until they take a shape near-coincident with that of your body. Such careful attention to the body's angle and measure requires neither willpower nor surrender. Instead, the practice facilitates a meditative state of focused distraction, a narrowing of concentration to the immediate physical moment that is the obverse side of illness and pain.

Climate, dear abstraction, my species' struggle to know you with greater immediacy is our way of preparing for traumas we sense are on verge of arrival. "Prepare" not in the sense of pre-planning for action but in the sense of readying to cope. Letters like this one, artworks like Chang's, are the needles and yarn we bring to the oncologist's office for distraction. Their soft clacks spook and sooth as we await the dread prognosis.

Climate, in the fabled past, artworks addressed themselves to a human future understood as ongoing and indefinite, even if uncertain. But today the present understands its anxious tumult as the species's death rattle. Focusing our attention on the pain, here at its acute onset, helps us grieve a future incapable of grieving for us.

Artfully yours,

Lou

10/27/17

Dear Climate,

Each of the half-dozen podcasts in Marina Zurkow's and Una Chaudhuri's multimedia conceptual project, Dear Climate, focus the listener's attention with introductory and concluding chimes. Like the vibratory yogic mantra Om, the sonorous chimes, lasting for about ten seconds each, sonically demarcate the beginning and end of a period of heightened receptivity.

The podcast scripts, recited with hypnotic equanimity by the alternating voices of a man and a woman, also have a meditative bent. "May all beings be happy + free," begins "Laguardia," as the sound of an airplane taking off whirs in the background, "May all beings be protected from outer + inner harm."

Created in collaboration with artists and intellectuals Fritz Ertl, Oliver Kellhammer, and Sarah Rothberg, the project, which includes separate visual and written components (in the form of posters and letters), moves beyond quietistic plea by virtue of its knowing humor. "Laguardia," for example, entreaties not simply for the stereotypical objects of ecological concern ("May all earthworms be happy + free") but also for overlooked or underappreciated humans ("May all coffee, bagel, magazine and gadget concession works be happy + free"), as well as for harmful, unwanted, or threatening non-human entities ("May all free radicals be happy + free").

Climate, I used to practice with a yoga teacher who was fond of instructing us, in the middle of difficult poses, to "turn up the corners of your mouth." The principle behind the instruction is that if you lead with the body, the mind will follow: performed willingly, a simulated smile has a way of becoming an actual one. It felt corny doing it, but the trick always worked.

Climate, I'm writing to seek your and Zurkow's and Chaudhuri's help in leading with my body. I want to learn, from your example, how to smile with contentment even as I grieve. I want you to teach me how to welcome death as a way of life. *Shavasana*, they call it in yoga, from the Sanskrit, for "corpse pose." It's the pose I practice, each morning, at my desk, as a writer. Breathlessly yours,
Lou

10/30/17
Dear Climate,
The problem with writing or talking about yoga is that yoga enacts a species of knowledge—embodied, preconscious—resistant to articulation. Hence the reliance, in popular yogi speak, on shopworn mantras and New Age clichés: hollow linguistic forms that don't pretend to be anything more than placeholders for experiences they can't adequately describe.

Zurkow's and Chaudhuri's *Dear Climate* project evidences a sophisticated understanding of this linguistic predicament. In a series of seventy downloadable posters, they use dark, almost fatalistic, humor to deform stock expressions. "CLIMATE CHANGE," asks one such poster, "WILL IT MAKE ME LOOK FAT?" "DON'T KNOW/ YOUR PLACE," reads another, with an image of a hurricane-addled house occupying the space of the line break. The posters' impish wordplay adopts a tone far different from the grave admonitions of much ecological discourse.

Like a mouth turned up at the corners beckoning the mind to follow, the posters' jokey embrace of disaster begets the podcasts' reassuring equanimity. Where the posters confront stale language by reinvigorating cliché, the podcasts accept language's inadequacies and limitations by using it in a simple, ostensive way. "Puddles. Springs. Sources," begins "The Hydrosphere Incantation," as water drips rhythmically in the background, "Phytotelmata. Oases. Cienegas." The catalogue form here, with its steady splash of syllables, emphasizes the words' sounds over their sense. "Seeps. Boils. Geysers. Headwaters. Channels. Brooks. Licks," the poem continues, content to let language point, unadorned.

This state of meditative content receives its fullest expression in the chimes that begin and end each podcast. More than just calls to attention or temporal boundary markers, the chimes are sounds that, similar to an *Om* chant, convey a para-linguistic sense of felt presence. Like a shot of whiskey on a winter night, the sound spreads from the torso to the extremities in ripples of concentric warmth. It's a sensation of acceptance—self-sufficient and vibratory—that develops from the inside out.
Warmly,
Lou

11/2/17
Dear Climate,
Chanting *Om* feels a bit like swallowing your own tongue. You close your eyes, clasp your hands in prayer at your heart, and try to speak the word that would obliterate speech.
as ever, faithfully yours, etc.,
Lou

11/3/17
Dear Climate,
The curious thing about Patty Chang's designation of my species' ecological angst as a "struggle phase" is that, for her, this struggle is less a sign of

resistance than of giving in. Like a gong shivering at the memory of the mallet, the climate noises we're making sound out the shape of our acceptance.
Mum's the word,
Lou

11/4/17
Dear Climate,
I wish I could better know the ways in which you and I know each other, wish I could hear you on my tongue and feel you in my thoughts. Absent this unattainable awareness, I trust in art's ability to frame your intimations.
Happily + freely,
Lou

11/6/17
Dear Climate,
The increasing brevity of these letters resembles the point in an *Om* chant when the reserves of breath are near-depleted and the held *mmm* sound dissipates to a ticklish strain in the lungs.

Climate, the real correspondence will begin when we know each other well enough not to fuss over hellos and goodbyes, questions and answers, diagnoses and cures. Meantime, if you need me, I'll be listening for the sound of your smile.

FIGURE 53.1. Marina Zurkow, Una Chaudhuri, Oliver Kellhammer, Frits Ertl and Sarah Rothberg, *Dear Climate* selection of posters, 2014, CC-BY-3.0.

FIGURE 53.2. Marina Zurkow, Una Chaudhuri, Oliver Kellhammer, Frits Ertl and Sarah Rothberg, *Dear Climate* selection of posters, 2014, CC-BY-3.0

FIGURE 53.3. Marina Zurkow, Una Chaudhuri, Oliver Kellhammer, Frits Ertl and Sarah Rothberg, *Dear Climate* selection of posters, 2014, CC-BY-3.0

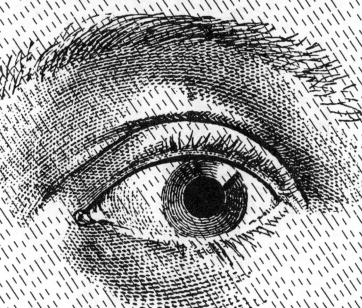

THE CLIMATE DOESN'T CARE ABOUT ME.

FIGURE 53.4. Marina Zurkow, Una Chaudhuri, Oliver Kellhammer, Frits Ertl and Sarah Rothberg, *Dear Climate* selection of posters, 2014, CC-BY-3.0

FIGURE 53.5. Marina Zurkow, Una Chaudhuri, Oliver Kellhammer, Frits Ertl and Sarah Rothberg, *Dear Climate* selection of posters, 2014, CC-BY-3.0

FIGURE 53.6. Marina Zurkow, Una Chaudhuri, Oliver Kellhammer, Frits Ertl and Sarah Rothberg, *Dear Climate* selection of posters, 2014, CC-BY-3.0

CODA

Reflections on Art and Posthumanism

CARY WOLFE

As one of the editors of this volume, Giovanni Aloi, noted in an interview we did together a few years ago, of all the things I've written about art, one of the more controversial was a chapter on the work of Sue Coe and Eduardo Kac in my book *What Is Posthumanism?* In that book, I try to walk us through several substantially different art forms (Coe's illustrations of animals in factory farms, Kac's bioart, Lars von Trier's film *Dancer in the Dark*, architectural projects by Rem Koolhaas and Bruce Mau and by Diller+Scofidio, Brian Eno and David Byrne's landmark record *My Life in the Bush of Ghosts*, and the poetry of Wallace Stevens). My aim in doing so was to show how the posthumanist theoretical position I had been developing since the early 1990s—built increasingly out of the cross-conjugation of systems theory (social and biological) and deconstruction—could open up our understanding of art and its relationship to philosophical and ethical questions in new and unexpected ways.

Part of what I was interested in in that book in bringing posthumanist thinking to bear upon art was to put a good deal of pressure on what struck me then (and strikes me now) as a rather facile understanding of the relationship between art and posthumanism: the idea, for example, that because Sue Coe's work promotes an anti-anthropocentric commitment to taking seriously the ethical treatment of farm animals, her work is somehow more or less automatically posthumanist. Against this assumption,

FIGURE CON.1. Eduardo Kac, *GFP Bunny*, 2000, copyright Eduardo Kac.

I insisted that what matters—in art, and in theory and philosophy—is not one question but two: not just what the ostensible content of the work is (let's say, questioning anthropocentrism, to stay with the current example), but *how* the work tries to make good on that commitment. The issue is not just *what* you're doing (which is usually the easy and obvious part) but *how* you're doing it. And this is a matter—in philosophy and in art—of the articulation of form and content, even though philosophy and art have different resources for performing that articulation (which is precisely why they can learn a lot from each other—not a new, much less posthumanist, theme in the history of philosophy, of course).

In fact, one of the main thrusts of *What Is Posthumanism?* was to insist that the "post-" of posthumanism is not about "transcending" or "surpassing" humanism: the "new" and "next" cool thing versus the old-fashioned and benighted fuddy duddies of yore. That understanding of posthumanism is in fact, I think, a quintessentially humanist fantasy of our ability to make transparent to master and make transparent to ourselves our deep, intractable cultural and philosophical inheritances. Rather, posthumanism, at least in part, is about how the many admirable aspects of the humanist legacy that we might want to hold onto—the insistence, for example, in stalwarts of humanist philosophy such as Kant and Bentham, that cruelty

FIGURE CON.2. Sue Coe, *El hombre modern seguido por los fantasmas de su carne*, 2013, illustration. Copyright Sue Coe.

toward animals is a bad thing—are actually undercut by the philosophical frameworks that try to justify them.

In chapter six of *What Is Posthumanism?*, I staged this question as a bit of a provocation, and framed it that way rhetorically: specifically, what is the relationship (if indeed there is a systematic one) between speciesism in philosophy and representationalism in art? Now you'd be well within your rights to ask, why would this question arise in the first place? Well, because it would seem reasonable to ask whether the decentering of the sensorium of *homo sapiens* under posthumanist theory is more compellingly expressed in art practices that don't take for granted, in their representational practice, a human orientation toward what is being represented—works that indeed must presume such an orientation for a representation to function *as* a representation in the first place. And what are the technologies and techniques (in the broadest sense of those terms) that are bound up with that particular rendition of world or *umwelt* presumed and reproduced by the work of art (to use Jakob von Uexküll's wonderful term, which got taken up by Heidegger in his thoughts on humans versus "animals" versus stones, only later to be the focus of Derrida's long-running hand-to-hand combat with Heidegger on this question in a whole series of texts, culminating, for me, in *The Animal that Therefore I Am* and the second set of seminars on *The Beast and the Sovereign*).

Some time later, I realized that I was liable to being misunderstood in this gambit I had staged in *What Is Posthumanism?*: as if I were against *all* representational art, in general. Representational art: bad. Non-representational art: good. But that was never my point. As I said to Giovanni in that same interview, when I was in Amsterdam a couple of years ago I had an intense experience of what one might call the "animality" or "ahumanism" of Rembrandt's use of paint as a medium, particularly in some of the later self-portraits. These are, to be sure, representational works of art, but you see a kind of dynamic decomposition of the representational visual field that begins to "steal the show," as it were, as the "molecular" level of the work overtakes the "molar" (to use the language of Deleuze and Guattari) in Rembrandt's use of paint, light, etc.

So the question—to put it another way—is not whether a work of art "is" or "is not" representational; the question is whether the formal and material features of the work set up a recursive system of "restraints" (to use Gregory Bateson's phrase) that invite you, even compel you, to have a non-representationalist account of what you're experiencing in the work, and why it matters. That is, after all, what is so compelling about these works: not that they are "a self-portrait of a face," but that something deep and maybe unprecedented in the history of art is going on in the transaction between paint as a medium for art and the decomposition of what Foucault called "something on the order of a subject" under the force of extreme artistic scrutiny. There are those who will say (and have said, as you'll see if you go to the Rembrandt house in Amsterdam) that that decomposition in the paintings is an index of what was going on in Rembrandt's personal life: that he is getting older, has lost yet *another* fortune, and so on. Is that a "humanist" or "posthumanist" reading of the situation, and what are the stakes of the difference? That is exactly the kind of question, I think, that posthumanism suggests we should be asking when it comes to works of art. Is Rembrandt a "posthumanist" painter, or did he become one? Can we see him as part of a genealogy of posthumanist art that isn't at all about a sheer chronology, but is rather (as Foucault suggested in his framing of the difference between genealogy and historicism) about an ongoing reinvention of the past in relation to the present?

In some of my writing on art since *What Is Posthumanism?*, I have moved on to questions of biopolitics, extinction, what it means to do environmental art, and so on. But within the domain of biopolitical thought, the problem essentially remains the same. The question is *how* you think the problem of the "bio-" of biopolitics (or bioart). How do you think the question of "life"? Here again, we find very large stakes, I think, in the differences between, say, Agamben and Foucault: differences that cash out, as they say, when you try to think the biopolitical dimensions of industrialized exploitation of animals in contemporary society and what that has to do with the plight of human populations of varying demographics under biopolitical regimes.

As I argue in *Before the Law*, it matters whether you have a humanist or posthumanist approach to the question of the "bio-" of biopolitics and the thinking of "life" in relation to political formations; it allows you (or prevents you) from thinking the treatment of non-human beings as part of a *political* and not just ethical problematic that is continuous with the plight of some human beings as well, part of the same biopolitical fabric. And this provides a framework, in turn, to look at the differences between contemporary art practices that focus our attention on the thick, empirically instantiated instances of the "living" under biopolitical apparatuses (and how those same apparatuses link humans and non-humans in a common biopolitical plight for which species distinctions are not fundamental), and those that continue to work within a more familiar humanist concept of "Life" (a theological concept, finally, I would argue) that connects human beings to the rest of existence in a very different way. It's not a question of "representation," but rather, you might say, a question of "strategy" and "practice." Don't get me wrong: I love beautiful works of art. But all the beauty in the world won't show us why art is vital to our existence in a way that can be distinguished from therapy or entertainment, and how posthumanism can help us bring that difference into focus.

CONTRIBUTOR BIOS

Susan McHugh, Professor of English at the University of New England, researches and teaches literary, visual, and scientific narratives. Her monographs include *Animal Stories: Narrating across Species Lines* (2011) in the *Posthumanities* series, and *Love in a Time of Slaughters: Human-Animal Stories Against Genocide and Extinction* (2019) in the *Anthroposcene* series. She is co-editor of the volumes *Human-animal Studies* (2018), *Indigenous Creatures, Native Knowledges, and the Arts: Animal Studies in Modern Worlds* (2017), and *The Routledge Handbook of Human-Animal Studies* (2014), as well as of the book series *Palgrave Studies in Animals and Literature*. She serves as Managing Editor of the Humanities for *Society & Animals*.

Giovanni Aloi is an author, educator, and curator specializing in environmental subjects and the representation of nature in art. He has published with Columbia University Press, Phaidon, Laurence King, and Prestel and is co-editor of the University of Minnesota Press series 'Art after Nature'. Since 2006, Aloi has been the Editor in Chief of *Antennae: The Journal of Nature in Visual Culture*. He is the author of *Art & Animals* (2011), *Speculative Taxidermy: Natural History, Animal Surfaces, and Art in the*

Anthropocene (2018), *Why Look at Plants? The Botanical Emergence in Contemporary Art* (edited and co-authored, 2018—winner of the 2019 Choice Outstanding Academic Title Award), *Botanical Speculations* (edited, 2018), *Animal: Exploring the Zoological World* (co-author and edited, 2018), and *Lucian Freud Herbarium* (2019—listed among the best art history books of 2019 by four general and specialist publications). He is a regular public speaker at the Art Institute of Chicago, a BBC radio contributor, and has curated exhibitions in the USA and abroad. Aloi has worked at Whitechapel Art Gallery and Tate Galleries in London, and currently lectures on modern and contemporary art at the School of the Art Institute of Chicago and Sotheby's Institute of Art in New York.

Karen Barad is Professor of Feminist Studies, Philosophy, and History of Consciousness at the University of California at Santa Cruz. Barad is also affiliated with the Critical Race and Ethnic Studies Program. Barad is a founding member of the Science & Justice Research Center and has served as the Director and the Co-Director of the Science & Justice Graduate Training Program. Barad's PhD is in theoretical particle physics. Barad held a tenured appointment in a physics department before moving into more interdisciplinary spaces. Barad is the author of *Meeting the Universe Halfway: Quantum Physics and the Entanglement of Matter and Meaning* (Duke University Press, 2007) and numerous articles in the fields of physics, philosophy, science studies, poststructuralist theory, and feminist theory. Barad's research has been supported by the National Science Foundation, the Ford Foundation, the Hughes Foundation, the Irvine Foundation, the Mellon Foundation, and the National Endowment for the Humanities.

Jane Bennett is an Andrew W. Mellon Professor of the Humanities at Johns Hopkins University. She often finds herself amazed by the shapes and powers of ordinary things—by a leaf of grass or of tea or of a book. She writes about ecology, philosophy, art, and politics. She is the author of *Vibrant Matter: A Political Ecology of Things* (Duke, 2010) and of a forthcoming book called *Influx & Efflux: Writing up With Walt Whitman* (Duke 2020). That new book explores Whitman's image of a "cosmic" self, and an "I" fuelled by and collaborating with the many different people, places, and things it encounters.

Rosi Braidotti is Distinguished University Professor at Utrecht University. Braidotti's philosophical project investigates how to think difference positively, which means moving beyond the dialectics that both opposes it and thus links it by negation to the notion of sameness. She has published dozens of monographs and volumes, including *Posthuman Knowledge* (2019), *Posthuman Ecologies* (with Simone Bignall, 2019), *A Feminist Companion to the Posthumanities* (with Cecilia Åsberg, 2018), *The Posthuman* (2013), and *Nomadic Subjects: Embodiment and Difference in Contemporary Feminist Theory* (1994, 2011). Throughout her work, Braidotti asserts and demonstrates the importance of combining theoretical concerns with a serious commitment to producing socially and politically relevant scholarship that contributes to making a difference in the world. Her work has been translated in more than twenty languages, and all of her main books have been published in at least three languages other than English.

Ron Broglio has just completed desert dwelling experiments with the art/design group FoAM including an acoustic ecology album. His books include *Beasts of Burden: Biopolitics, Labor, and Animal Life* (2017), *Surface Encounters: Thinking with Animals and Art* (2011), and the co-edited collection *The Edinburgh Companion to Animal Studies* (2018). Currently he is writing an artistic and theoretical treatise titled *Animal Revolution: Events to Come*, and engaged in a number of long-term thinking-making experiments in the deserts of the American Southwest. Broglio is Director of Desert Humanities and Co-Director of the Institute for Humanities Research at Arizona State University.

Louis Bury is the author of *Exercises in Criticism* (2015), which uses self-imposed rules and procedures to write poetic and autobiographical criticism about literary constraint. "Dear Climate" comes from a book-in-progress about climate change and anticipatory grief. He writes regularly about climate change and visual art for *Hyperallergic* and *BOMB* magazines, and his other creative and critical work has appeared in *Bookforum*, the *Brooklyn Rail*, the *Los Angeles Review of Books*, *Boston Review*, and the *Believer*. He is Assistant Professor of Hostos Community College, City University of New York.

Cassils is a visual artist working in live performance, film, sound, sculpture and photography. Cassils has achieved international recognition for a rigorous engagement with the body as a form of social sculpture. Drawing on conceptualism, feminism, body art, and gay male aesthetics, Cassils forges a series of powerfully trained bodies for performative purposes. It is with sweat, blood, and sinew that Cassils constructs visual critique around ideologies and histories. Cassils is the recipient of the USA Artist Fellowship, Guggenheim Fellowship, ANTI Festival International Prize for Live Art, Creative Capital Award, and Visual Artist Fellowship from Canada Council of the Arts.

Artists and researchers, **Oron Catts** and **Ionat Zurr** formed the internationally renowned Tissue Culture & Art Project in 1996. Often working in collaboration with other artists and scientists, they have developed a body of work that addresses needs for new cultural articulations of evolving concepts of life. Catts is the Co-Founder and Director of SymbioticA: the Centre of Excellence in Biological Arts, School of Human Sciences at the University of Western Australia (UWA). Dr. Zurr is the Chair of Fine Arts at UWA's School of Design as well as SymbioticA's academic coordinator. Their wide-reaching work has proven influential to developments in textiles, design, architecture, ethics, fiction, and food science. They are considered pioneers in the field of Biological Arts; they publish widely and exhibit internationally. Their work was exhibited and collected by museums such as Pompidou Centre in Paris, MoMA NY, Mori art Museum, NGV, GoMA, Yerba Buena Center for the Arts, San Francisco, Ars Electronica, National Art Museum of China, and more.

Zane Cerpina is an Oslo based artist, curator, organizer, and publisher working within experimental new media and electronic arts. Zane currently works as creative manager and editor at PNEK (Production Network for Electronic Art, Norway), project manager and curator at TEKS (Trond-heim Electronic Arts Centre), and editor and manager at EE: Experimental Emerging Art. Her extensive body of works include curating and produc-ing FAEN - Female Artistic Experiments Norway, a three-week exhibition and symposium program at Atelier Nord (2019); The Dangerous Futures Conference (2018); Oslo Flaneur Festival (2016); and The Anthropocene Cookbook event series (2016 -). She is one of the curators of The Tempo-rary Library of Norwegian Media Art. Her writing and editorial work also includes the ongoing publication series, The PNEK FILES (2015-).

Dipesh Chakrabarty holds a BSc (physics honors) degree from Presidency College, University of Calcutta, a postgraduate Diploma in management (considered equivalent to MBA) from the Indian Institute of Management, Calcutta, and a PhD (history) from the Australian National University. He is currently the Lawrence A. Kimpton Distinguished Service Professor in History, South Asian Languages and Civilizations, and the College. He is the Faculty Director, University of Chicago Center in Delhi, a faculty fellow of the Chicago Center for Contemporary Theory, an associate of the Depart-ment of English, and by courtesy, a faculty member in the Law School.

Mel Y. Chen is Associate Professor of Gender & Women's Studies at U.C. Berkeley and Director of the Center for the Study of Sexual Culture. Their research and teaching interests include queer and gender theory, animal studies, critical race theory and Asian American studies, disability studies, science studies, and critical linguistics come together in their award-win-ning book *Animacies: Biopolitics, Racial Mattering, and Queer Affect* (2012). With Jasbir K. Puar, Chen coedits a book series entitled *Anima*, highlight-ing scholarship in critical race and disability post/in/humanisms at Duke University Press. Chen's short film, *Local Grown Corn* (2007), explores interweavings of immigration, childhood, illness, and friendship, and has been screened at both Asian and queer film festivals.

DEAR CLIMATE is an ongoing creative-research project that was collab-oratively founded in 2012 to seek a new way to talk about the weather, one that explores a more personal relationship to the geo-political forces of climate change. Its many incarnations include posters, guided meditations, installations, and workshops. Currently active members include eco-theater pioneer Una Chaudhuri, who is Director of XE: Experimental Humanities & Social Engagement, Collegiate Professor, and Professor of English, Drama, and Environmental Studies at New York University as well as a founding member of the Climate Lens theater collective; Canadian land artist, permaculture teacher, writer, and activist Oliver Kellhammer, whose botanical interventions and public art projects demonstrate nature's surprising abilitiy to recover from damage; and media and participatory practice artist Marina Zirkow, a faculty member of NYU's Interactive Technology Program, who builds animations and participatory environments that focus on human relations with animals, plants, and the weather. DEAR CLIMATE has been featured in exhibitions in Ireland, the Netherlands, and the United States.

James Elkins is Chair of the Department of Art History, Theory, and Criticism at the School of the Art Institute of Chicago, as well as Chair of the Department of Art History at University College Cork in Ireland. His writing focuses on the history and theory of images in art, science, and nature. His many books range from focusing exclusively on fine art, such as *What Painting Is* (1998) to considering natural history, scientific, and non-art images, including *The Domain of Images* (1999) and *How to Use Your Eyes* (2000). Recent titles include the experimental nonfiction *What Photography Is* (2012) and revised editions of *Artists with PhDs* (2009, 2014) and *Art Critiques: A Guide* (2011, 2012). Impelled by the lack of experimental writing in art history, he presently is writing a novel with images.

Francesca Ferrando teaches Philosophy at NYU-Liberal Studies, New York University. A leading voice in the field of Posthuman Studies and founder of the NY Posthuman Research Group, she has been the recipient of numerous honors and recognitions, including the Sainati prize with the Acknowledgment of the President of Italy. She has published extensively on these topics, and her latest book is *Philosophical Posthumanism*

(Bloomsbury 2019). In the history of TED talks, she was the first speaker to give a talk on the topic of the posthuman. US magazine *Origins* named her among the 100 people making change in the world. More info is available at www.theposthuman.org.

Professor Foster teaches and publishes in the areas of modernist and contemporary art, architecture, and theory. He is a member of the School of Architecture and an associate member of the Department of German; in addition, he co-directs the Program in Media & Modernity and sits on the executive committees of the Interdisciplinary Doctoral Program in the Humanities and the Gauss Seminars in Criticism. A member of the American Academy of Arts and Sciences, Foster was a founding editor of Zone Magazine and Books, and he writes regularly for October (which he coedits), Artforum, and The London Review of Books. He is the recipient of the Frank Jewett Mather Award for Art Criticism in College Art Association (2012) and the Clark Prize for Excellence in Arts Writing (2010), and he has been the Siemens Fellow at the American Academy in Berlin and the Paul Mellon Senior Fellow at the National Gallery of Art in Washington. Foster will deliver the Mellon Lectures at the National Gallery in spring 2018.

Amy Ge works and lives in Toronto, ON. She is currently a JD/MBA candidate at Osgoode Hall Law School and Schulich School of Business at York University. Ge is a tech startup entrepreneur, writer, and activist.

Lucian Gomoll is an Andrew W. Mellon Postdoctoral Fellow and Visiting Assistant Professor at Wesleyan University's Center for the Humanities. He resists a common presentism and rhetoric of "the new" in discussions of performance, interactivity, and experience in museums, connecting recent trends to ways that bodies have been displayed and collected since the early nineteenth century. He served as Director of Museum and Curatorial Studies at the University of California, Santa Cruz, from 2009–2012, hosting lectures by distinguished scholars such as Griselda Pollock, Amelia Jones, and Irit Rogoff. In 2010, he organized with Lissette Olivares the international conference *The Task of the Curator: Translation, Intervention and Innovation in Exhibitionary Practice.*

Graham Harman is Distinguished Professor of Philosophy at SCI-Arc in Los Angeles. His work on the metaphysics of objects led to the development of object-oriented ontology, a driving force in the speculative realism trend in contemporary philosophy. His insistence that everything is an object allows for distinctions between real and sensual (or intentional) objects, which sets his philosophy apart from flat ontology. He is the author of many books, including *Weird Realism: Lovecraft and Philosophy* (2012), *Immaterialsim: Objects and Social Theory* (2016), and *Object-Oriented Ontology: A New Theory of Everything* (2018). He edits the book series *Speculative Realism* and serves as editor-in-chief of the journal *Open Philosophy.*

Peter Gratton is Professor of Philosophy at Southeastern Louisiana University. He has published numerous articles in political, continental, and intercultural philosophy and is the author of *The State of Sovereignty: Lessons from the Political Fictions of Modernity* (2012). He serves as co-editor of *Society and Space (Environmental Planning D)*, executive board member of the International Association for Philosophy and Literature, and books editor of *Derrida Today*. He co-edited *Traversing the Imaginary* (2007) and *Jean-Luc Nancy and Plural Thinking: Expositions of World, Politics, Art, and Sense* (2012).

Donna Haraway is Distinguished Professor Emerita in the History of Consciousness Departments at the University of California, Santa Cruz. Attending to the intersections of biology with culture and politics, her work explores the web of science fact, science fiction, speculative feminism, speculative fabulation, science and technology studies, and the more-than-human world. She engages deeply with artists who work for multispecies environmental justice and care. Her books include *Staying with the Trouble* (2016); *When Species Meet* (2008); *Modest_Witness@Second_Millennium* (1997, 2018); and *Primate Visions* (1989). With Adele Clarke, she co-edited *Making Kin Not*

Population (2018). A feature-length film made by Fabrizio Terravova, *Donna Haraway: Story Telling for Earthly Survival* (2016), is available on DVD.

Newton and **Helen Mayer Harrison** are among the earliest and the best-known social and environmental artists. They produced multimedia work in collaboration with biologists, ecologists, historians, activists, architects, urban planners, and fellow artists to initiate dialogues and create works exploring biodiversity and community development. Both are Professors Emeriti at University of California, Santa Cruz, and University of California, San Diego. They have had numerous international solo exhibitions and their work is in the collections of public institutions including the Pompidou Center, MoMA, and the Chicago Museum of Contemporary Art. *The Helen and Newton Harrison Papers*, an extensive archive that documents their life and work with a significant amount of audiovisual material and born-digital files, has been acquired by Stanford University Library.

Heide Hatry is a visual artist and curator. She grew up in Germany, where she studied art at various art schools and art history at the University of Heidelberg. Since moving to NYC in 2003 she has curated several exhibitions in Germany, Spain, and the USA, notably *Skin* at the Goethe Institute in New York, the Heidelberger Kunstverein and Galeria Tribeca in Madrid, Spain; *Out of the Box* at Elga Wimmer PCC in NYC; *Carolee Schneemann, Early and Recent Work, A Survey* at Pierre Menard Gallery in Cambridge, MA; and *Meat After Meat Joy* at Daneyal Mahmood Gallery, NYC. She has shown her own work at museums and galleries in those countries as well and edited more than a dozen books and art catalogues. Kehrer Verlag published her book *Skin* in 2005.

N. Katherine Hayles is the Distinguished Research Professor at the University of California, Los Angeles, and the James B. Duke Professor Emerita from Duke University. Her 11 print books include *Unthought: The Power of the Cognitive Nonconscious* (2017), *How We Think: Digital Media and Contemporary Technogenesis* (2015), and *How We Became Posthuman: Virtual Bodies in Cybernetics, Literature and Informatics* (1999), in addition to over

100 peer-reviewed articles. Her books have won several prizes, and she has been recognized by many fellowships and awards, including two honorary degrees. She is a member of the American Academy of Arts and Sciences. She is currently at work on *Cyber-bio-symbiosis: A General Ecology of Cognitive Assemblages*.

Kathy High is an internationally renowned interdisciplinary artist working in the areas of technology, science, speculative fiction, and art. She produces videos and installations posing queer and feminist inquiries into areas of medicine/bio-science, and animal/interspecies collaborations that have been exhibited across North America, Europe, Asia, and Australia. High is Professor of Video and New Media in the Department of Arts, Rensselaer Polytechnic Institute in Troy, NY. She is a supporter of community DIY science and ecological art practices. Among many honors, she is the recipient of fellowships and awards from the National Endowment for the Arts, and the Guggenheim Foundation.

Myra J. Hird is Professor, Queen's National Scholar, and Fellow of the Royal Society of Canada in the School of Environmental Studies, Queen's University, Canada (www.myrahird.com). Professor Hird is Director of *Waste Flow*, an interdisciplinary research project focused on waste as a global scientific-technical and socio-ethical issue (www.wasteflow.ca). Hird has published nine books and over seventy articles and book chapters on a diversity of topics relating to science studies. Hird's forthcoming book is entitled *Canada's Waste Flows* and will be published by McGill-Queen's University Press.

Tim Ingold is Emeritus Professor of Social Anthropology at the University of Aberdeen. He has carried out fieldwork among Saami and Finnish people in Lapland, and his wide-ranging research interests include human-animal relations, evolutionary theory, language, technology and skilled practice, environmental perception, art and architecture, creativity, and anthropologies of line and surface. His recent books include *The Perception of the Environment* (2000), *Lines* (2007), *Being Alive* (2011), *Making* (2013), *The Life of Lines* (2015), *Anthropology and/as Education* (2017), and *Anthropology: Why* *it Matters* (2018). Ingold's current projects include remapping the interfaces of anthropology, archaeology, art, and architecture on the level of practice, as mutually enhancing ways of engaging with our surroundings.

Zakiyyah Iman Jackson is Assistant Professor of English at the University of Southern California. Her work has appeared in Feminist Studies, Gay and Lesbian Quarterly, Qui Parle: Critical Humanities and Social Sciences, South Atlantic Quarterly, and Catalyst: Feminism, Theory, and Technoscience. She is the author of *Becoming Human: Matter and Meaning in an Antiblack World* (2020).

Brian M. John is an artist and freelance photographer based in Los Angeles, California. His work focuses on the myriad personal, political, and environmental complexities of the Southwest, and manipulates sound, light, color, and space in order to subvert the intended uses of mediating technologies. He has taught art at the University of Illinois at Chicago and at the School of the Arts Institute of Chicago.

David Joselit began his career as a curator at The ICA in Boston from 1983 to 1989. After receiving his PhD from Harvard in 1995, he has taught at the University of California, Irvine, and Yale University where he was Department Chair from 2006-09, and most recently at the CUNY Graduate Center. Joselit is author of Infinite Regress: Marcel Duchamp 1910-1941 (MIT, 1998), American Art Since 1945 (Thames and Hudson, 2003), Feedback: Television Against Democracy (MIT, 2007), and After Art (Princeton University Press, 2012). He co-organized the exhibition, "Painting 2.0: Expression in the Information Age," which opened at the Brandhorst Museum in Munich in 2015. Joselit is an editor of the journal OCTOBER and writes regularly on contemporary art and culture. His most recent book is *Heritage and Debt: Art in Globalization* (forthcoming as an October Book from MIT Press in Spring 2020).

Edward King and **Joanna Page** co-authored *Posthumanism and the Graphic Novel in Latin America* (2017). King is Lecturer in Portuguese at the University of Bristol and the author of *Science Fiction and Digital Technologies in Argentine and Brazilian Culture* (2013) and *Virtual Orientalism in Brazilian Culture* (2015). Page is Senior Lecturer in Latin American Cultural Studies at the University of Cambridge and the author of *Crisis and Capitalism in Contemporary Argentine Cinema* (2009), *Creativity and Science in Contemporary Argentine Literature* (2014), and *Science Fiction in Argentina: Technologies of the Text in a Material Multiverse* (2016).

Carrie Lambert-Beatty is Professor in the Department of History of Art and Architecture and the Department of Visual and Environmental Studies at Harvard University. An art historian with a focus on art from the 1960s to the present, she is currently at work on an art history of the post-truth turn.

Angela Last is Lecturer in Human Geography at the University of Leicester. Her research interests have moved from art and design into geography through a growing concern for the environmental, cultural. and labor conditions of the creative industries. In addition to co-editing *Routledge International Handbook of Interdisciplinary Methods* (2018), she has published several articles in academic journals and collections such as *Postcolonial Transitions after Political Ontology and Posthumanism* (2017), *Feminist Review* (2018), and *Decolonising the University: Context and Practice* (2018). Since 2007, she has been writing the interdisciplinary blog *Mutable Matter*.

Bruno Latour is Professor Emeritus and former Director of the Médialab at Sciences Po Paris. His focus on the complex, heterogeneous relationships shared by human and nonhuman agents has been influential to the development of actor-network theory. Latour's many books include *We Have Never Been Modern* (1991; English translation, 1993), an anthropology of science that questions modernity's nature-science duality, and *Paris: Ville Invisible* (1998), a photographic inquiry into social theory. He has curated and co-curated several major international art exhibitions, including *Critical Zones* at Zentrum fur Media Kunst, Karlsruhe (2020) and the Taipei Biennale of Art (2020).

Betelhem Makonnen was born in Ethiopia. She received her MFA from the Art Institute of Chicago and completed graduate coursework in painting, time-based media, and modern and contemporary art history at the School of Visual Arts of Parque Lage in Rio de Janerio. Makonnen received her B.A. in History and Literature of the African Diaspora from UT Austin. Her recent exhibitions and projects include *Natural 20* and *Video Art From Africa* in Los Angeles, CA; Staycation Tresholds, SoundSpace: *Word/Play*, UNESCO Media Arts Exhibition at SXSW; *constant escape* in Austin; and *Intersections* in San Antonio.

Erin Manning is a professor in the Faculty of Fine Arts at Concordia University, a cultural theorist and political philosopher, as well as a practicing artist in the areas of dance, fabric design, and interactive installation. She is also the founder of *SenseLab*, a laboratory that explores the intersections between art practice and philosophy through the matrix of the sensing body in movement. Her exhibitions include the Sydney and Moscow Biennales, Vancouver Art Museum, House of World Cultures (Berlin), and Galateca Gallery (Bucarest). She has published several books including *The Minor Gesture* (2016), *Always More Than One: Individuation's Dance* (2013), *Relationscapes: Movement, Art, Philosophy* (2009), and, with Brian Massumi, *Thought in the Act: Passages in the Ecology of Experience* (2014). Current art projects are focused around the concept of minor gestures in relation to color and movement.

Michael Marder is IKERBASQUE Research Professor in the Department of Philosophy, at the University of the Basque Country, Vitoria-Gasteiz. Much of his philosophical work has focused on building philosophies that take into account plants as beings with their own form of subjectivity. His many books include *Plant-Thinking: A Philosophy of Vegetal Life* (2013), *The Chernobyl Herbarium: Fragments of an Exploded Consciousness* (2016), and, with Luce Irigaray, *Through Vegetal Being: Two Philosophical Perspectives* (2016). He is an editor of three book series: *Political Theory and Contemporary Philosophy*; *Critical Plant Studies*; and *Future Perfect: Images of the Time to Come in Philosophy, Politics, and Cultural Studies*. His blog, *The Philosopher's Plant*, is hosted by the *LA Review of Books*, where he also directs *The Philosophical Salon*.

Chus Martínez is a renowned curator and head of the Art Institute at the FNHW Academy of Arts and Design in Basel, Switzerland. Her unique curatorial practice researches how thinking emerges through the substance of art. She was the head of the department of artistic direction and a member of the core agent group for dOCUMENTA(13), for which she edited, with Bettina Funcke, the series *100 Notes–100 Thoughts*. Martínez has organized numerous exhibitions and publications with contemporary artists in Europe as well as North and South America. Martínez has also served as curatorial advisor for exhibitions including the 2015 Istanbul Biennial, the 29th São Paulo Art Biennial in 2010, and for the 2008 Carnegie International. She is currently leading a research project on the role of education enhancing women's equality in the arts.

Garry Marvin is a social anthropologist and Professor of Human-Animal Studies at the University of Roehampton, London. His explorations of human-animal relationships began with his doctoral research into the bullfight in Spanish culture. Since then he has conducted ethnographic research, and published, on cockfighting; zoos; English foxhunting; the motivations and experiences of big game hunters; hunting photographs, trophies, and taxidermy; and relations between humans and wolves. His books include *Bullfight* (1994) and *Wolf* (2012), and with Bob Mullan *Zoo Culture* (1998). With Susan McHugh, he co-edited *The Handbook of Human-Animal Studies* (2014) and the four-volume series, *Human-Animal Studies* (2018). With Rebecca Cassidy, he co-edits the book series *MultiSpecies Anthropology: New Ethnographies*.

Katherine McKittrick researches in the areas of black studies, anti-colonial studies, cultural geographies, and gender studies. Her research is interdisciplinary and attends to the links between epistemological narrative, liberation, and creative text. McKittrick also researches the writings of Sylvia Wynter. She is a member of the Royal Society of Canada (College) and the American Academy of Arts and Science and former editor of Antipode: A Radical Journal of Geography.

Cynthia E. Milton is a Pierre Elliott Trudeau Fellow, Past President of the College of New Scholars of the Royal Society of Canada, and Canada Research Chair in Latin American History at the Université de Montréal. Her interdisciplinary research studies truth commissions, human rights, and cultural interventions in the constructions of historical narratives after state violence. Her book projects include *The Art of Truth-Telling about Authoritarian Rule* (2005), *Art from a Fractured Past: Memory and Truth-Telling in Post-Shining Path Peru* (2014), *Curating Difficult Knowledge: Violent Pasts in Public Places* (2011), and most recently *Conflicted Memory: Military Cultural Interventions and the Human Rights Era in Peru* (2018).

Born in Swaziland, **Nandipha Mntambo** is an artist based in Johannesburg, South Africa, who experiments with sculptures, videos, and photography. One of her favorite materials to use in her pieces is cowhide, often also used as a covering for human bodies—boneless sculptures—in ways that subvert expectations about corporeal presence, femininity, sexuality, and vulnerability. *Material Value*, a solo exhibition of her work, was shown at Zeitz Museum of Contemporary Art Africa (2017). Mntambo won the Standard Bank Young Artist Award for Visual Art in 2011, for which she produced the national travelling exhibition *Faena*. She has had seven solo shows at Stevenson Cape Town and Johannesburg (2007–17) and two at Andréhn-Schiptjenko, Stockholm (2013–15).

Jason W. Moore is an environmental historian and historical geographer at Binghamton University, where he is Professor of Sociology. He is author or editor, most recently, of *Capitalism in the Web of Life* (2015), *Anthropocene or Captialocene? Nature, History, and the Crisis of Capitalism* (2016), and, with Raj Patel, *A History of the World in Seven Cheap Things* (2017). His books and articles on environmental history, capitalism, and social theory have been recognized as widely influential. He also coordinates the World-Ecology Research Network, a community of artists, scholars, and activists committed to planetary justice and the study of historical change—including the history of the present—as if nature matters.

Timothy Morton is Rita Shea Guffey Chair in English at Rice University. He has collaborated with Björk, Laurie Anderson, Jennifer Walshe, Jeff Bridges, Sabrina Scott, Olafur Eliasson, and Pharrell Williams. He is the author of *Being Ecological* (2018), *Humankind: Solidarity with Nonhuman People* (2017), *Dark Ecology: For a Logic of Future Coexistence* (2016), and *Hyperobjects: Philosophy and Ecology after the End of the World* (2013). Along with many other books, he has published two hundred essays on philosophy, ecology, literature, music, art, architecture, design, and food. His work has been translated into 10 languages. He co-wrote and appears in *Living in the Future's Past*, a 2018 film about global warming.

Syned Mthatiwa was born on 28th August 1976 in one of the remote villages of Malawi. He holds BA and MA degrees from the University of Malawi, and a PhD from the University of the Witwatersrand, Johannesburg, South Africa. Mthatiwa's research interest is in ecocriticism or ecophilosophy more generally, postcolonial literary and cultural studies, oral literature, popular literature, poetry, and the novel. He has published journal articles on literature both within and outside Africa. He teaches literature at Chancellor College, a constituent College of the University of Malawi.

Pauline Oliveros was a world-renowned composer and performer known for conceiving a unique, meditative, improvisatory approach to music. Early works shaped through meditative improvisation were collectively called *Sonic Meditations* (1971), and laid the foundation for her development of the titular concept of *Deep Listening Pieces* (1990), a series of some three dozen works devised to teach students to merge the involuntary, unfiltered act of hearing with listening—a voluntary act involving selective inclusion and exclusion of sounds from the auditory experience. She also published several influential books, including *The Roots of the Moment:*

Collected Writings 1980–1996 (1998) and *Deep Listening: A Composer's Sound Practice* (2005).

Jennifer Parker-Starbuck is the author of Cyborg Theatre (2011), co-author of Performance and Media (2015), and co-editor of Performing Animality (2015). She is a Contributing Editor to Antennae and other journals, and was Editor of Theatre Journal (2015–19). She is the Head of School, Performing and Digital Arts, at Royal Holloway, University of London.

Jay Prosser is Reader in Humanities in the School of English at the University of Leeds. His initial research interests in transsexual representation led to studies of the interweaving of photography and narrative, including autobiography in the works of Nan Goldin and Gillian Wearing. His books include *Second Skins: The Body Narratives of Transsexuality* (1998), *Light in the Dark Room: Photography and Loss* (2004), and the co-edited collection *Picturing Atrocity: Photography in Crisis* (2012), published in support of the work of Amnesty International. He presently is publishing a family memoir, which is also cultural history, centering on how the Baghdadi Jewish diaspora came to include intermarriage with Chinese people in Southeast Asia.

Joshi Radin is an artist who investigates questions concerning nature, cosmology, and expanded landscape using photo/video, print media, and writing. Drawing on childhood experiences living within a utopian back-to-the-land community, she traces historical and genealogical roots of utopianism and nature through imagery and processes as spaces of knowledge production. She questions what previous utopianists sought: what might forms of resistance to globalized capitalist modernity look like? Radin has published essays and presented work in artist-run spaces, galleries, and museums.

Yvonne Rainer, former Distinguished Professor of Studio Art at the University of California, Irvine, is a pioneering avant-garde choreographer and filmmaker. Her seminal work, Trio A (1965), is still performed by both dancers and non-dancers in theatre and museum settings. After making seven experimental feature films, including *Lives of Performers* (1972) and *MURDER and murder*

(1996), she returned to dance. Retrospective exhibitions of her work have been presented at Kunsthaus Bregenz and Museum Ludwig, Cologne (2012), the Getty Research Institute, Los Angeles (2014), and Raven Row, London (2014). Her awards include two Guggenheim Fellowships, a MacArthur Fellowship, a USA Fellowship, and the Yoko Ono Courage Award. Her autobiography, *Feelings Are Facts: A Life*, was published by MIT Press and the documentary film, *Feelings Are Facts: The Life of Yvonne Rainer* (2015), is available on DVD.

Ken Rinaldo creates interactive art installations that develop hybrid ecologies with humans, machines, plants, and animals by constructing idealized social, biological, and machine symbionts. His work interrogates fuzzy boundaries and posits that, as new machinic and algorithmic species arise, we need to understand the complex constructive and destructive ecologies that a semi-living species may shape. Trans-species communication enhanced by machine learning will empower animal agency along with insect, bacterial, and emergent machine intelligences, while expanding understanding of others as us. Rinaldo's works have traveled to 30 countries, receiving an Award of Distinction at Ars Electronica, First prize at Vida 3.0 for Autopoiesis, a United Nations Green Leaf Award, and commissions from Nuit Blanche, Vancouver Olympics, and Te Papa and Kiasma Museums.

Manuela Rossini works as Executive Manager/ Head of Administration for the Department of Comparative Language Science at the University of Zurich. She also acts as Executive Director of the European Society for Literature, Science and the Arts, and continues to pursue matters of concern as an independent scholar and General Editor of the Critical Posthumanism Network as well as the book series *Experimental Practices* (Brill) and *Entanglements* (MDPI). She has authored numerous essays on posthumanism in literature and culture. Among several other joint ventures, Rossini co-edited *European Posthumanisms* (2014); *The Cambridge Companion to Literature and the Posthuman* (2016); and a special issue of *New Formations* titled *Posthuman Temporalities* (2017).

Nicole Shukin is an Associate Professor of English at the University of Victoria. Her work explores questions of animal life and death within lethal landscapes of late capitalism, including lands and lives in Fukushima rendered radioactive when the earthquake and tsunami struck Japan in 2011, damaging two nuclear plants. Interested in theories of biopower, posthumanism, and interspecies affect, her work continuously reveals the material conditions and costs of seemingly magical or immaterial technologies of communication, from early cinema to cell phones. She is the author of *Animal Capital: Rendering Life in Biopolitical Times* (2009), which develops the double entendre of "rendering" to implicate a range of symbolic economies in the carnal business of boiling down animal remains for glue or gelatin. In other work, she extends feminist critiques of reproductive labor to the affective labors of nonhuman animals, traces biopolitical shifts from cruelty to kindness in human-animal relationships, and asks about the hard lessons decolonial thought holds for those working in the fields of posthumanism or animal studies.

Born in Kahnawake Mohawk Territory, **Skawennati** holds a BFA from Concordia University in Montreal, where she is based. She is Co-Director, with Jason E. Lewis, of Aboriginal Territories in Cyberspace (AbTeC), a research network of artists, academics, and technologists investigating, creating, and critiquing Indigenous virtual environments. She also co-directs their workshops in Aboriginal Storytelling and Digital Media. Skins, This year, AbTeC launched IIF, the Initiative for Indigenous Futures; Skawennati is its Partnership Coordinator.

Snæbjörnsdóttir/ Wilson are a collaborative art partnership. Their 20-year interdisciplinary art practice is research-based, exploring issues of history, culture, and environment in relation to locus, humans, and non-human species. Working very often in close consultation in the field with experts including professionals and amateurs, they use their work to test cultural constructs and tropes, and human behavior in respect of ecologies, extinction, conservation, and the environment. With a particular focus in the north, their projects and artworks have been commissioned, generated and exhibited internationally, in Europe, Australia, and the USA. Frequent speakers at conferences worldwide, their works have been widely discussed in texts across many disciplinary fields. Their artwork is installation-based using a variety of media including photography, video, text, drawing, objects, and sound. Mark Wilson is Professor of Fine Art at the Institute of the Arts, University of Cumbria, UK, and Bryndís Snæbjörnsdóttir is Professor of Fine Art at the Iceland University of the Arts, Reykjavík, Iceland.

Gavin Steingo is Assistant Professor of Music at Princeton University. He seeks to understand globally circulating musical practices from the perspective of the geopolitical South by examining music and value, infrastructures and audio technologies, sound and race, and the politics of world music circulation. He is the author of the award-winning *Kwaito's Promise: Music and the Aesthetics of Freedom in South Africa* (2016), and co-editor of the book series *Critical Conjectures in Music and Sound*. Performance forms an important part of his research process, and he regularly records in a variety of styles and genres, for example, on an album by the Venda singer Jininka Nkanyane. In 2017, he curated "The Social Life of the Universe," a daylong event at the Akademie Schloss Solitude in Germany featuring artists Bill Dietz, Dima Hourani, Janine Jembere, Kapwani Kiwanga, and Antoni Rayzhekov.

Beth Stephens and **Annie Sprinkle** have been life partners and 50/50 collaborators on multimedia art projects 18 years. Currently they do art/life experiments imagining the "Earth as lover," and aim to make the environmental movement more sexy, fun, and diverse. Their *Ecosex Manifesto* launched an international ecosex movement. Their latest film, which premiered at documenta 14 and screened at NY MOMA, *Water Makes Us Wet*, can be viewed on Amazon Prime. Stephens is Director of E.A.R.T.H. Lab at the University of California, Santa Cruz, where she is Chair of the Art Department and Professor. Stephens has a PhD in Performance Studies, and Sprinkle has a PhD in Human Sexuality.

Kim TallBear is an Associate Professor, Faculty of Native Studies and Canada Research Chair in Indigenous Peoples, Technoscience & Environment, University of Alberta. She is a graduate of the University of California, Santa Cruz, and of the Massachusetts Institute of Technology. Professor TallBear is the author of one monograph, *Native American DNA: Tribal*

Belonging and the False Promise of Genetic Science (2013), which won the Native American and Indigenous Studies Association First Book Prize. She is the co-editor of a collection of essays published by the Oak Lake Writers, a Dakota and Lakota tribal writers' society in the USA. Professor TallBear has written nearly two-dozen academic articles and chapters published in the United States, Canada, Australia, and Sweden. She also writes for the popular press and has published in venues such as *BuzzFeed, Indian Country Today,* and *GeneWatch.* She is a frequent blogger on issues related to Indigenous peoples, science, and technology. Professor TallBear is a frequent commentator in the media on issues related to Indigenous peoples and genomics including interviews in *New Scientist, New York Times, Native America Calling, National Geographic, Scientific American, The Atlantic,* and on *NPR, CBC News,* and *BBC World Service.*

Sunaura Taylor is an artist, writer, and activist. Taylor's artworks have been exhibited at venues across the country, including the CUE Art Foundation, the Smithsonian Institution, and the Berkeley Art Museum. Her written work has been printed in various edited collections as well as in publications such as the *Monthly Review, Yes! Magazine, American Quarterly, and Qui Parle.* Taylor worked with philosopher Judith Butler on Astra Taylor's film *Examined Life* (2008). Taylor holds an MFA in art practice from the University of California, Berkeley. Her book *Beasts of Burden,* which explores the intersections of animal ethics and disability studies, is forthcoming from the Feminist Press. She is currently a PhD student in American Studies in the Department of Social and Cultural Analysis at NYU.

Linda Tegg works with photography, video, performance, and installation to reconfigure viewership experiences. Animals enter gallery spaces; nature documentaries don't play out as expected; thousands of plants are assembled in cultural institutions. Within a culture of mediation these works seek moments of instability where categorical shifts can occur. Tegg has received major commissions from the Australian Centre for Contemporary Art (Tortoise, Melbourne, 2013), the Samstag Museum of Art (Tortoise, Adelaide, 2016), and the Melbourne International Arts Festival (Grasslands, 2014). Her practice is also characterized by significant interdisciplinary collaborations, most recently with Baracco + Wright Architects as Creative Directors of the Australian Pavilion at the Venice Architecture Biennale, 2018.

Anna Tsing is a professor of anthropology at the University of California, Santa Cruz. Between 2013 and 2018, she was a Niels Bohr Professor in the Department of Culture and Society at Aarhus University in Denmark, where she directed the Aarhus University Research on the Anthropocene (AURA) Project to study the kinds of lives that are made and the futures that become possible in the ruined, re-wilded, and unintended landscapes of the current era. Her books include *In the Realm of the Diamond Queen* (1993), *Friction* (2005), and *The Mushroom at the End of the World* (2015), as well as the co-edited collection *Arts of Living on a Damaged Planet* (2017). She is currently developing a transdisciplinary program for exploring the Anthropocene.

Jessica Ullrich is Honorary Professor of art history and aesthetics at the Academy of Fine Arts Muenster and Lecturer of art education at the Berlin University of the Fine Arts. She studied art history, fine arts, and German literature in Frankfurt as well as Arts Administration in Berlin. She is editor of *Tierstudien*, the German journal on animal studies and representative of Minding Animals Germany.

Ben Valentine is a writer who works for Exhibit Columbus, an annual exploration of architecture, art, design, and community. For the last ten years Ben has written about, presented, and curated art around the world. Ben is deeply committed to sharing with a wide audience, and has worked as an art history teacher in Cambodia, helped run Sammaki Community Arts in Cambodia, and worked in Public Programming for SA SA BAS-SAC, in Phnom Penh. His work has appeared in such venues as *Salon*, *Hyperallergic*, *The New Inquiry*, *Motherboard*, *Arts Asia Pacific*, *Los Angeles Review of Books*, and many more.

Alexander Weheliye is professor of African American Studies at Northwestern University, where he teaches black literature and culture, critical theory, social technologies, and popular culture. He is the author of *Phonographies: Grooves in Sonic Afro-Modernity* (2005), which was awarded the Modern Language Association's William Sanders Scarborough Prize for Outstanding Scholarly Study of Black American Literature or Culture, and *Habeas Viscus: Racializing Assemblages, Biopolitics, and Black Feminist Theories of the Human* (2014). His current work includes a critical history of the intimate relationship between R&B music and technology since the late 1970s, as well as another project that establishes Blackness as an ontology of ungendering.

Eyal Weizman is a British Israeli intellectual and architect. He is Professor of Spatial and Visual Cultures at Goldsmiths, University of London, and a founding director there of the Centre for Research Architecture. He is the director of the research agency Forensic Architecture. In 2013 he designed a permanent folly in Gwangju, South Korea. which was documented in the book *The Roundabout Revolution* (2015). In addition to serving on the boards of several academic journals, Weizman is a board member of the Centre for Investigative Journalism and the Technology Advisory Board of the International Criminal Court in the Hague, and has been on the boards of the Israeli human rights organization B'Tselem in Jerusalem, amongst others.

Angela Willey is a feminist science studies scholar whose research addresses the naturalization of coupled forms of social belonging and the conditions of possibility for the emergence and sustainability of alternate forms. She joined the Five College faculty in 2011 and teaches feminist science studies, feminist epistemologies and research, and queer and sexuality studies in Women, Gender, Sexuality Studies at the University of Massachusetts Amherst, Gender Studies at Mount Holyoke College, and the School of Critical Social Inquiry at Hampshire College. Her training is in feminist theory and the history of race, gender, and sexuality in the biosciences in Women's Studies at Emory University and contemporary feminist theory at the Gender Institute at the London School of Economics.

Cary Wolfe's books and edited collections include *Animal Rites: American Culture, The Discourse of Species, and Posthumanist Theory* (2003), *What*

Is Posthumanism? (2010), and *Before the Law: Humans and Other Animals in a Biopolitical Frame* (2012). He is founding editor of the series *Posthumanities* at the University of Minnesota Press, which has published over fifty volumes to date. He currently holds the Bruce and Elizabeth Dunlevie Chair in English at Rice University, where he is Founding Director of 3CT: The Center for Critical and Cultural Theory. His most recent projects include *Ecological Poetics, or, Wallace Stevens's Birds* (2020) and *Ontogenesis beyond Complexity*, a special issue of the journal *Angelaki: Journal of the Theoretical Humanities* (2020).

Doo-Sung Yoo is a Korean new media artist who works in the United States and is Senior Lecturer of Art and Technology at The Ohio State University. He synthesizes scientific research within his artwork and interweaves interdisciplinary media between professional fields. He is currently focused on creating hybrid sculptural and interactive entities, in which disembodied animal organs are integrated with electronic devices within mechanical bodies and the human body. His hybrids have been featured in many exhibitions and art festivals throughout Asia, Europe, and North America, and have been focal points of academic conferences and publications in Poland, Canada, Russia, and the United States.

INDEX